A SYSTEM OF
SOCIAL SCIENCE
PAPERS RELATING TO
ADAM SMITH

By

ANDREW S. SKINNER

CLARENDON PRESS · OXFORD
1979

Oxford University Press, Walton Street, Oxford OX2 6DP

OXFORD LONDON GLASGOW
NEW YORK TORONTO MELBOURNE WELLINGTON
KUALA LUMPUR SINGAPORE JAKARTA HONG KONG TOKYO
DELHI BOMBAY CALCUTTA MADRAS KARACHI
NAIROBI DAR ES SALAAM CAPE TOWN

Published in the United States by Oxford University Press, New York

British Library Cataloguing in Publication Data

Skinner, Andrew Stewart
A system of social science.
1. Smith, Adam, b.1723
I. Title
300'.92'4 HB103.S6 79–40343
ISBN 0–19–828422–5

Set by Hope Services
Printed in Great Britain by offset lithography by
Billing & Sons Ltd, Guildford, London and Worcester

Preface

Most of the essays which make up this volume were written at different times and published in a variety of journals. In bringing them together it is intended to make them more accessible to the student, and at the same time to make it clear that the sections into which the book falls, while free-standing, are intended to make a single argument; a single commentary on Smith's system of social science. For the most part, the different chapters have been extensively rewritten in order to eliminate repetition, and to take account of changes of view. The exceptions are two papers of a relatively recent date (chapters 5 and 8) which are reprinted by kind permission of the *Scottish Journal of Political Economy* and the *Journal of the History of Ideas*. Chapter 6, on the Division of Labour, has been left virtually untouched, and was in fact written jointly with Ronald Meek. It is reproduced with the permission of Ronald Meek and the *Economic Journal*. Sections of chapter 2 are used by courtesy of Edinburgh University Press and of the University of Texas. Chapter 7 is a modified version of section 3 of my introduction to the Pelican edition of the *Wealth of Nations* and is reproduced, in part, with the permission of Penguin Books Ltd.

All references to Smith's works conform to the usages of the Glasgow edition, and the Table of Corresponding Passages of *The Wealth of Nations*, originally prepared by the present writer, is appended in order to facilitate use of the two main Cannan editions which are in general circulation.

Over the years I have incurred a number of debts, not all of which can be acknowledged here. I am however greatly indebted to A.L. Macfie, the Adam Smith Professor in my time as a student in Glasgow, and to the late Ronald Meek who lectured extensively on the history of economic thought at the same period. I am also indebted to my colleagues who worked on the Glasgow edition of Smith's *Works and Correspondence* and especially to D.D. Raphael, in addition to the two scholars just mentioned. I have also benefited greatly from

a long friendship with Donald Winch and from the writings of
Duncan Forbes — in my opinion the most perceptive of the
modern commentators on Smith's 'politics'.

Glasgow, 1978   A.S.S.

Contents

Abbreviations and References

WORKS OF ADAM SMITH

Corr.	*Correspondence*
Early Draft	'Early Draft' of *The Wealth of Nations*
EPS	*Essays on Philosophical Subjects*, included among which are:
Ancient Logics	'The History of the Ancient Logics and Metaphysics'
Ancient Physics	'The History of the Ancient Physics'
Astronomy	'The History of Astronomy'
English and Italian Verses	'Of the Affinity between certain English and Italian Verses'
External Senses	'Of the External Senses'
Imitative Arts	'Of the Nature of that Imitation which takes place in what are called the Imitative Arts'
Letter	'Letter to the Authors of the Edinburgh Review'
Stewart	Dugald Stewart, 'Account of the Life and Writings of Adam Smith'
Languages	*Considerations Concerning the First Formation of Languages*
LJ(A)	*Lectures on Jurisprudence*, Report of 1762-3
LJ(B)	*Lectures on Jurisprudence*, Report dated 1766
LRBL	*Lectures on Rhetoric and Belles Lettres*
TMS	*The Theory of Moral Sentiments*
WN	*The Wealth of Nations*

References to Corr. give the number of the letter (as listed in the volume of Smith's *Correspondence* in the Glasgow edition), the date, and the name of Smith's correspondent.

Reference to LJ and LRBL give the volume (where applicable) and the page number of the manuscript (shown in the printed texts of the Glasgow edition). References to LJ(B) add the page number in Edwin Cannan's edition of the *Lectures on Justice, Police, Revenue and Arms* (1896). References to LRBL give the page number in John M. Lothian's edition of the *Lectures on Rhetoric and Belles Lettres* (1963).

References to the other works listed above locate the relevant paragraph, not the page, in order that any edition may be consulted (in the Glasgow edition, the paragraph numbers are printed in the margin). Thus:

Astronomy, 11.4	'History of Astronomy', Sect. II, §4
Stewart, I.12	Dugald Stewart, 'Account of the Life and Writings of Adam Smith', Sect. I, §12
TMS I.i.5.5	*The Theory of Moral Sentiments*, Part I, Sect. i, Chap. 5, §5
WN V.i.f.26	*The Wealth of Nations*, Book V, Chap, i, sixth division, §26

OTHER WORKS

Essays on Adam Smith	*Essays on Adam Smith*, edited by Andrew Stewart Skinner and Thomas Wilson (1975)
HV	John Millar, *Historical View of the English Government* (1786, new edn. in 4 vols., 1803)
Rae, *Life*	John Rae, *Life of Adam Smith* (1895)
Scott, *ASSP*	William Robert Scott, *Adam Smith as Student and Professor* (1937)

I

Introduction

I

While we now familiarly refer to the 'Scottish Enlightenment',
it is an interesting fact that many writers much closer to the
'event' were aware of an 'efflorescence of genius' in the latter
half of the eighteenth century, and that they too recognized
it to be remarkable. Thus the fictional figure Matthew Bramble
in Tobias Smollett's *Humphry Clinker* described mid-century
Edinburgh as a 'hot-bed of genius' when referring to his
meetings with 'many authors of the first distinction; such as
the two Humes, Robertson, Smith, Wallace, Blair, Ferguson,
Wilkie, etc.'.[1] In the same vein, Walter Scott in *Guy Mannering*
refers to such men as a 'circle never closed against strangers
of sense and information, and which has perhaps at no period
been equalled, considering the depth and variety of talent
which it embraced and concentrated'.[2] David Hume recorded
no more than a matter of fact when he noted that 'really it is
admirable how many Men of Genius this Country produces at
present'. He went on:

Is it not strange that, at a time when we have lost our Princes, our
Parliaments, our independent Government, even the Presence of our
chief Nobility, are unhappy, in our Accent & Pronunciation, speak a
very corrupt Dialect of the Tongue which we make use of; is it not
strange, I say, that, in these Circumstances, we shou'd really be the
People most distinguish'd for Literature in Europe?[3]

There are many sides to the explanation of this phenomenon: the rapid rate of economic advance after the benefits
of Union began to be felt, the failure of the 1745 Rebellion
which drew attention to the Highlands and presented con-

---

[1] 'Letter to Dr. Lewis, Edr. August 8.'
[2] *Guy Mannering*, chapter 39.
[3] Letter 135, addressed to Gilbert Elliot of Minto, dated 2 July 1757, in *Letters
of David Hume*, ed. J.Y.T. Greig (1932), i. 255.

temporary philosophers with what Duncan Forbes aptly
described as a 'sociological museum at Edinburgh's back
door',[4] the increasing inflow of information about primitive
peoples — all contributed to a 'new spirit'.[5] As David Hume
noted in his essay 'Of the Refinement in the Arts'; 'The spirit
of the age affects all the arts, and the minds of men being
once roused from their lethargy, and put into a fermentation,
turn themselves on all sides, and carry improvements into
every art and science.'

There is no real counterpart to this movement, or level of
activity, in contemporary England, although as Trevor-Roper
has pointed out the 'enlightenment' as a whole 'owes much
to England. The Englishmen Bacon, Locke, and Newton were
its prophets; the English Revolution of 1688 was its political
starting point; the English deists were its midwives. But in
England itself, by 1750, these forces were spent.'[6] Smith
himself clearly recognized the point in his first publication, a
Letter to the Authors of the Edinburgh Review (1756). In
this in some ways remarkable document, Smith noted that
the *Encyclopédie* articles often explained the ideas of Bacon,
Boyle, and Newton with 'perspecuity and good judgement',
and there is certainly no tincture of insularity in his observation that 'As, since the Union, we are apt to regard ourselves
in some measure as the countrymen of those great men, it
flattered my vanity, as a Briton, to observe the superiority
of the English philosophy thus acknowledged by their rival
nation' (§5). Smith warned his readers against too close a
concentration on the productions of a country, namely
Scotland, 'which is but just beginning to attempt figuring
in the learned world', while reminding them that the 'original
and inventive genius of the English has not only discovered
itself in natural philosophy, but in morals, metaphysics, and
part of the abstract sciences. Whatever attempts have been
made in modern times towards improvement in this conten-

    [4] 'Scientific Whiggism: Adam Smith and John Millar', in *Cambridge Journal*, 7
(1953-4).
    [5] Hugh Trevor-Roper, 'The Scottish Enlightenment', in *Studies on Voltaire and
the Eighteenth Century*, 58 (1967).
    [6] 'The Idea of the Decline and Fall of the Roman Empire', in *The Age of
Enlightenment*, ed. W.H. Barber *et al.* (1967), 418.

tious and unprosperous philosophy, beyond what the ancients have left us, have been made in England' (§ 10).

Yet at the same time, Smith too was well aware of the current dominance of French philosophical work. In this connection he drew the attention of the editors to the contributions of Diderot, Alembert, Daubenton, Buffon, and Réaumur. Of especial significance is the fact that Smith emphasized the importance of Rousseau's essay on the 'origin of inequality' and the concern there shown with the 'first beginnings and gradual progress of society' (Letter, § 12). In the conclusion of the Letter, Smith also voiced his admiration for Voltaire, describing him as 'the most universal genius perhaps which France has ever produced'. In 1765 Smith visited Geneva, where he met Voltaire. For the moment however, it is of most importance to note Smith's awareness, at this relatively early stage, of the significance of the wider, European, contribution to science. As Dugald Stewart pointed out in commenting on the Letter, 'The observations on the state of learning in Europe are written with ingenuity and elegance; but are chiefly interesting, as they shew the attention which the Author had given to the philosophy and literature of the Continent, at a period when they were not much studied in this island' (Stewart, I. 25). Yet at the same time, it is now recognized that the Scottish contribution to the 'enlightenment' assumed a growing importance in the years after 1755 and that Smith's own reputation has come to rival that of Voltaire at least in some fields. The essays which follow constitute a modest commentary on Smith's range of interest in what are now known as the 'social' sciences, although before proceeding directly to them it may be useful to say something about the two periods of his life which seem to have shaped his career as a thinker.

II

When Smith first came to Glasgow in 1737 the city had a population of less than 17,000, and a small College consisting of only twelve professors. Eleven years previously, Glasgow had been visited by Daniel Defoe, who found the College to be 'very high and very august' while pronouncing the city as a whole to be 'the cleanest and beautifullest, and

best built city in Britain, London excepted'[7] — sentiments which were to be echoed later in the century by Dr. Johnson.[8]

Smith was fortunate in his choice of university and in the period of his attendance. There is little doubt that Smith acquired most benefit from teachers professing a single subject, such as Alexander Dunlop, the then Professor of Greek. But two men in particular are worth noting in view of Smith's later interests. The first of these was Robert Simson (1687–1768), whom Smith later described, together with his fellow-student Matthew Stewart (father of Dugald), as 'The two greatest mathematicians that I ever have had the honour to be known to, and, I believe, the two greatest that have lived in my time' (TMS III. 2.20). Smith could well have acquired from these men that early interest in mathematics to which Dugald Stewart referred in his memoir (Stewart, I.7):

Dr Maclaine of the Hague, who was a fellow-student of Mr Smith's at Glasgow, told me some years ago, that his favourite pursuits while at that University were mathematics and natural philosophy; and I remember to have heard my father remind him of a geometrical problem of considerable difficulty, about which he was occupied at the time when their acquaintance commenced, and which had been proposed to him as an exercise by the celebrated Dr Simson.

This general interest in mathematics and natural philosophy is an important one in view of Smith's early work on Astronomy, and of the fact that this essay was one of the very few which he did not order to be destroyed before his death.

But the most important influence was surely Francis Hutcheson (1694–1746); a former pupil of Gerschom Carmichael (who may have done much to stimulate his interest in economic questions).[9] Hutcheson had been appointed to the Moral Philosophy Chair in 1730. He lectured, in English rather than Latin, three days a week on classical sources, and five days on Natural Religion, Morals, Jurisprudence, and Government. His capacity as a lecturer[10] seems to have been remarkable and his influence considerable, especially through

---

[7] Daniel Defoe, *A Tour Through the Whole Island of Great Britain*, vol. 3, Letter XII.

[8] Rae, *Life*, 88. Smith's career as a student is reviewed in chapter 2.

[9] On Hutcheson, see W.R. Scott, *Francis Hutcheson* (1900).

[10] Hutcheson's influence as a teacher is reviewed in W. Leechman's preface to the posthumously published *System of Moral Philosophy* (1755).

the emphasis given to civil and religious liberty.[11] As Dugald Stewart was to observe, Hutcheson's academical lectures also 'appear to have contributed very powerfully to diffuse, in Scotland, that taste for analytical discussion, and that spirit of liberal inquiry, to which the world is indebted for some of the most valuable productions of the eighteenth century' (Stewart, Note B).

Smith entered Balliol as a Snell Exhibitioner in 1740 and to begin with found it an unhappy experience. His health was poor and if he found himself in a situation where political feeling was predominantly Jacobite, it was also one which was more than a little 'anti-Scotch'. But the sharpest contrast was between the two universities; between a situation which was dominated by the vigorous teaching of people like Simson and Hutcheson, and another where the 'greater part of the publick professors have, for these many years, given up altogether even the pretence of teaching' (WN V. i. f. 8). For Smith, contemporary Oxford was all too clearly one of those 'sanctuaries in which exploded systems and obsolete prejudices found shelter and protection' (V. i. f. 34).

Later he set himself to explain a phenomenon which had continued to interest him, and found part of that explanation in the size of Church benefices, which tended to draw off the best candidates from the colleges, in sharp contrast to small and poorer countries, such as Geneva, Holland, and Scotland (WN V. i. g. 39). But in practice, Smith placed most emphasis on the problem of incentive.

The effects which Smith isolated were many and various. For example, he suggested that large numbers of charitable foundations and exhibitions (such as the Snell) had the effect of obliging students to attend colleges irrespective of the quality of the service they received, while pointing also to the consequences of preventing free movement between colleges and even between different teachers in the same college. In the same vein he criticized the residence requirements for degrees, insisting that the latter were 'a mere piece

[11] Hutcheson's political views are considered by Caroline Robbins in *The Eighteenth Century Commonwealthman* (revised edn., 1968) and in the same author's '"When It Is That Colonies May Turn Independent": An Analysis of the Environment and Politics of Francis Hutcheson', *William and Mary Quarterly*, third series, 11 (1954).

of quackery', while describing the former as a device to ensure that the students would spend long enough in their institutions to permit a profit to be made from their stay.[12] Smith also pointed to the dangers involved in self-government, and concluded that 'The discipline of colleges and universities is in general contrived, not for the benefit of the students, but for the interest, or more properly speaking, for the ease of the masters' (WN V. i. f. 15). But undoubtedly Smith's main theme was designed to draw attention to the dangers of large academic salaries paid irrespective of competence or industry, believing as he did that 'In every profession, the exertion of the greater part of those who exercise it, is always in proportion to the necessity they are under of making that exertion' (V. i. f. 4).

There can be little doubt that Smith's experience of contemporary Glasgow and Oxford led him to think carefully about the organization of universities, nor that the conclusions which he reached were to have a profound effect on his treatment of public works when he came to complete this section of the *Wealth of Nations*.

Equally, there is no doubt that he was grateful for this experience taken as a whole. Writing to the Principal of Glasgow University in 1787, accepting the office of Rector, Smith recalled with evident pleasure the 'abilities and virtues of the never to be forgotten Dr. Hutcheson' and acknowledged his debt to the University both for educating him and for sending him to Oxford.[13] In the case of Oxford, this was more than a gilded memory in that Smith's six years' residence there allowed him to lay the foundations of an extensive knowledge of classical, as well as of French and Italian literature; a knowledge which was to stand him in good stead on returning to Scotland. At the same time, the study of belles-lettres proved a lasting interest, to such an extent, indeed, that as late as 1785 Smith still had two 'great works upon the anvil':

one is a sort of Philosophical History of all the different branches of Literature, of Philosophy, Poetry and Eloquence; the other is a sort of

[12] Letter 143, addressed to William Cullen, dated London, 20 September 1774. The views expressed in this letter were later elaborated in WN V.i.f, 'Of the Expence of the Institutions for the Education of Youth'.
[13] Letter 274, addressed to Dr. Archibald Davidson, dated Edinburgh, 16 November 1787.

theory and History of Law and Government. The materials of both are in a great measure collected, and some Part of both is put into tollerable good order. But the indolence of old age, tho' I struggle violently against it, I feel coming fast upon me, and whether I shall ever be able to finish either is extremely uncertain.[14]

III

Smith returned to Kirkcaldy in 1746 apparently without any real plans, although it was not long before his literary studies provided him with an opportunity for employment. In 1748 Henry Home (later Lord Kames), together with Robert Craigie and James Oswald (a childhood friend), sponsored a set of public lectures on rhetoric.[15] A.F. Tytler informs us that the lectures were delivered 'to a respectable auditory, chiefly composed of students in law and theology'.[16] The lectures were certainly successful at least to the extent that the course was carried on by Robert Watson and later by Hugh Blair after Smith left Edinburgh — Blair was in fact to become the first professor of Rhetoric in Edinburgh University. Smith himself gained 'above 100 Pound a Year' for his efforts — as Hume reminded him in 1758.[17] But Smith's growing reputation also brought further rewards. On 9 January 1751 he was elected by the Senate of Glasgow University to the Chair of Logic, following the death of Professor Loudon. On taking up this appointment, Smith seems to have continued the work he had begun in Edinburgh, by delivering what his pupil John Millar described as 'a system of Rhetoric and Belles-lettres' (Stewart, I.16).

Today this may seem an odd choice for a professor of Logic (although the Glasgow Chair is still in Logic and Rhetoric), but in the eighteenth century it was not considered strange. Indeed Professor Stevenson, Professor of Logic in Edinburgh from 1730 to 1775 and a distinguished precursor of Smith, objected to the foundation of Blair's chair as an encroachment

[14] Letter 248, addressed to La Rochefoucauld, dated Edinburgh, 1 November 1785.

[15] The circumstances are reviewed in J.M. Lothian's introduction to Smith's *Lectures on Rhetoric* (1963).

[16] A.F. Tytler, *Memoirs of the Life and Writings of Henry Home of Kames* (1807), i. 190.

[17] Letter 25, dated 8 June 1758.

on his proper province.[18] The reason for such an objection, and for the association of subjects, may be found in Millar's full description of Smith's course:

In the Professorship of Logic, to which Mr Smith was appointed on his first introduction into this University, he soon saw the necessity of departing widely from the plan that had been followed by his predecessors, and of directing the attention of his pupils to studies of a more interesting and useful nature than the logic and metaphysics of the schools. Accordingly, after exhibiting a general view of the powers of the mind, and explaining so much of the ancient logic as was requisite to gratify curiosity with respect to an artificial method of reasoning, which had once occupied the universal attention of the learned, he dedicated all the rest of his time to the delivery of a system of rhetoric and belles lettres. The best method of explaining and illustrating the various powers of the human mind, the most useful part of metaphysics, arises from an examination of the several ways of communicating our thoughts by speech, and from an attention to the principles of those literary compositions which contribute to persuasion or entertainment. By these arts, every thing that we perceive or feel, every operation of our minds, is expressed and delineated in such a manner, that it may be clearly distinguished and remembered. There is, at the same time, no branch of literature more suited to youth at their first entrance upon philosophy than this, which lays hold of their taste and their feelings (Stewart, I.16).

It proved impossible to evaluate this claim for almost two hundred years, until the discovery by J.M. Lothian of a set of Smith's lectures which were given during his last full session as a professor, in 1762-3. However, as W.S. Howell has pointed out, there can be no doubt that Smith's emphasis was on the communication of ideas and the different forms of discourse which men typically employ.[19] Smith isolated four kinds of communication (instruction, entertainment, conviction, and persuasion) to which there correspond four kinds of discourse (the historical, poetical, didactical, and oratorical). Howell has pointed out that Smith built on existing foundations, but that he may be described as the 'earliest and most independent' of the new thinkers in making rhetoric a general theory covering not only the persuasive, but all forms of literature

---

[18] On Stevenson's teaching, see Lothian, op. cit. xxv–xxix.

[19] 'Adam Smith's Lectures on Rhetoric: An Historical Assessment', *Speech Monographs*, 36 (1969), reprinted in *Eighteenth Century British Logic and Rhetoric* (1971) and in *Essays on Adam Smith*.

(*Essays on Adam Smith*, 42, 20). In practice, one of the most original aspects of Smith's system was also one of the most valuable from the standpoint of his treatment of the moral (or social) sciences, namely his inclusion of didactic (or scientific) discourse within his general theory of communication.

In a lecture (24) delivered 'sine libro' Smith argued that didactic discourse could have two aims: to prove a proposition to an audience which required to be convinced, or to 'deliver a system of any science'. In the latter case, he suggested that there are two possible methods of delivery:

Either, first, we lay down one or a very few principles by which we explain the several rules or phenomena, connecting one (with the?) other in a natural order; or else we begin with telling that we are to explain such and such things, and for each advance a principle either different or the same with those which went before (LRBL ii. 132, ed. Lothian, 139).

Smith continued to note that

In the same way, in Natural Philosophy, or any other science of that sort, we may either, like Aristotle, go over the different branches in the order they happen to [be] cast up to us, giving a principle, commonly a new one, for every phenomenon; or, in the manner of Sir Isaac Newton, we may lay down certain principles, primary [known?] or proved, in the beginning, from whence we account for the several phenomena, connecting all together by the same chain. This latter, which we may call the Newtonian method, is undoubtedly the most philosophical, and in every science, whether of Morals or Natural Philosophy, etc., is vastly more ingenious, and for that reason more engaging, than the other. It gives us a pleasure to see the phenomena which we reckoned the most unaccountable, all deduced from some principle (commonly, a well-known one) and all united in one chain, far superior to what we feel from the unconnected method (LRBL ii. 133–4, ed. Lothian, 139–40).

A number of points deserve some notice before going further. First it is worth observing that Smith here describes a method of argument (which he himself employed) in terms of the need to work with a small number of basic, well-known principles. Secondly, it will be seen that Smith associates philosophy with certain sources of pleasure and that he suggests that the choice of the Newtonian 'method' is linked with the fact that it is 'more ingenious' and therefore 'more engaging' than the other. Thirdly, it should be recalled that Smith in fact claimed that Descartes had been the first to use the

method here described as Newtonian, while going on to
indicate that Descartes's work 'does not perhaps contain a
word of truth' and that it was no more than 'one of the most
entertaining romances that have ever been wrote' (LRBL ii.
133-4, ed. Lothian, 139-40). These sentiments are echoed in
the *Edinburgh Review* article of 1756 where Smith explains
the attraction of the Cartesian system in terms of the method
used, while going on to describe it as 'fanciful', 'ingenious
and elegant, tho' fallacious' (Letter, § 5). In short, Smith had
apparently recognized that there may be a difference between
the method used in *expounding* a system and that employed
in *developing* it. Descartes and Newton may thus be seen to
share a method of *argument*, although Newton differed from
his distinguished predecessor in respect of the way in which
he claimed to have confirmed his results. To the eighteenth-
century mind, illusion and fantasy could only be avoided by
using in conjunction, and in the appropriate order, the
method of analysis (associated with Aristotle) and that of
synthesis (associated with Descartes).[20] It was in this way that
the experimental philosophy of Newton had been developed
— although Smith himself duly noted that he had been antici-
pated by Galileo (Astronomy, IV. 44).

Some of these subjects reappear in Smith's essay on Astronomy where he examined the 'principles which lead and direct
philosophical enquiries'. The method of Newton, however,
is common to all Smith's enterprises and especially to his
studies of man in society — studies on which he embarked
more formally when he moved to the Chair of Moral Philosophy in 1752. To quote once again from Millar:

His course of lectures on this subject was divided into four parts. The
first contained Natural Theology; in which he considered the proofs of
the being and attributes of God, and those principles of the human
mind upon which religion is founded. The second comprehended Ethics,
strictly so called, and consisted chiefly of the doctrines which he afterwards published in his Theory of Moral Sentiments. In the third part,
he treated at more length of that branch of morality which relates to
justice, and which, being susceptible of precise and accurate rules, is for
that reason capable of a full and particular explanation (Stewart, I. 18).

[20] Cf. Colin MacLaurin, *An Account of Sir Isaac Newton's Philosophical
Discoveries* (1748, 3rd ed. 1775), 9.

In the last part of his lectures, he examined those political regulations which are founded, not upon the principle of *justice*, but that of *expediency*, and which are calculated to increase the riches, the power, and the prosperity of a State. ... What he delivered on these subjects contained the substance of the work he afterwards published under the title of An Inquiry into the Nature and Causes of The Wealth of Nations (Stewart, I. 20).

While the lectures on theology have not been discovered as yet, it is at least possible that Smith's position would have shown agreement with that of Newton, who 'infers from the structure of the visible world, that it is governed by *One Almighty* and *All Wise Being*'.[21] Colin MacLaurin, one of Newton's most influential expositors, continued to state quite baldly that 'The plain argument for the existence of the Deity, obvious to all . . . is from the evident contrivance and fitness of things for one another . . . There is no need for nice and subtle reasonings in this matter: a manifest contrivance immediately suggests a contriver'.[22]

While Smith seems unlikely to have agreed with all of this statement, there is no doubt that he did make use of a number of Newtonian analogies whose implications are at least not inconsistent with the view of God as the Divine Architect or Great Superintendent of the Universe. For example Smith made wide use of mechanistic analogies, seeing in the universe a 'great machine' wherein we may observe 'means adjusted with the nicest artifice to the ends which they are intended to produce' (TMS II. ii. 3. 5). In the same way he noted that 'Human society when we contemplate it in a certain abstract and philosophical light, appears like a great, an immense machine' (TMS VII. iii. 1. 2) — a position which leads quite naturally to a functionalist thesis and to Smith's distinction between efficient and final causes (TMS II. ii. 3. 5). In fact, as we shall see, Smith argues that over almost the whole range of human activity man is led 'by an invisible hand to promote an end which was no part of his intention' — a common enough thesis at the time of writing.[23]

The remaining parts of Smith's lectures, that is, the ethics,

[21] MacLaurin, op. cit. 396.
[22] Op. cit. 400.

[23] WN IV.ii.9; cf. TMS IV.i.10.

jurisprudence, and economics, may all be seen not only to share a common methodology but also to employ analogies of the kind we have just been considering. Moreover, each area of interest may be regarded, like the rhetoric, as a *system* of thought — a concept which, interestingly enough, Smith also illustrated in terms of a mechanistic analogy in remarking that

Systems in many respects resemble machines. A machine is a little system, created to perform, as well as to connect together, in reality, those different movements and effects which the artist has occasion for. A system is an imaginary machine invented to connect together in the fancy those different movements and effects which are already in reality performed (Astronomy, IV. 19).

But the ethics, jurisprudence, and economics were also seen by Smith as the parts, separate but interconnected, of an even wider system of social science: a point which emerges clearly from the advertisement to the sixth edition of the *Theory of Moral Sentiments*, published in the year of Smith's death. In this advertisement, Smith observed:

In the last paragraph of the first Edition of the present work, I said, that I should in another discourse endeavour to give an account of the general principles of law and government, and of the different revolutions which they had undergone in the different ages and periods of society; not only in what concerns justice, but in what concerns police, revenue, and arms, and whatever else is the object of law. In the *Enquiry concerning the Nature and Causes of the Wealth of Nations*, I have partly executed this promise; at least so far as concerns police, revenue, and arms. What remains, the theory of jurisprudence, which I have long projected, I have hitherto been hindered from executing, by the same occupations which had till now prevented me from revising the present work. Though my very advanced age leaves me, I acknowledge, very little expectation of ever being able to execute this great work to my own satisfaction; yet, as I have not altogether abandoned the design, and as I wish still to continue under the obligation of doing what I can, I have allowed the paragraph to remain as it was published more than thirty years ago, when I entertained no doubt of being able to execute every thing which it announced (§ 2).

The 'occupations' to which Smith referred were connected with his duties as a Commissioner of Customs and of the Salt Duties in Scotland; offices to which he was preferred in 1778 and which caused him to take up residence in Edinburgh. In fact the theory of jurisprudence was never completed,

although generous traces of the historical perspective to which Smith referred appear in Books III and V of the *Wealth of Nations*, and in the two sets of lectures on jurisprudence which have so far been discovered.

The links between the parts of this great plan are many and various. The TMS for example may be regarded as an exercise in social philosophy, which was basically designed to show the way in which so self-regarding a creature as man erects (by natural as distinct from artificial means) barriers against his own passions, thus explaining the observed fact that he is always found in 'troops and companies'. The argument places a good deal of emphasis on the importance of general rules of behaviour which are related to experience and may thus vary in content, together with the need for some system of government or magistracy as a precondition of social order. The historical analysis, with its four socio-economic stages, complements this argument by formally considering the origin of government and by explaining to some extent the forces which cause variations in accepted standards of behaviour over time. Both are related in turn to the economics, at least in so far as the historical argument explains the origins and nature of the particular type of socio-economic structure with which the analysis of the *Wealth of Nations* is concerned, while the *Theory of Moral Sentiments* provides an account of the psychological assumptions upon which both these analyses depend. It is this view of the interconnections which exist between the parts of Smith's system which in the main explains the focus of the following papers, and the order in which they are placed.

2

Science and the Role of the Imagination*

I

In a lecture entitled 'The Biographical Approach' Ernest Mossner once remarked on the difficulties which face the biographer of Smith.[1] Smith was a poor correspondent who found the act of writing painful, and it is well known that he took great pains, before his death, to destroy a great quantity of papers which might have given us much more information with regard to the *man*.[2] But in another sense the quarry is a peculiarly rich one since Smith did leave, directly or indirectly, a great deal of material in the form of books or lecture notes which tell us much as to the qualities of his *mind*.

Of the many influences at work on Smith, Hume was arguably the most important, at least in so far as he adopted three characteristic positions which also inform Smith's works. First, Hume insisted that the study of human nature is a necessary precondition for the study of all forms of human activity, and that this principle even extended to the field of science:

It is evident, that all the sciences have a relation, greater or less, to human nature; and that, however wide any of them may seem to run from it, they still return back by one passage or another. Even *Mathematics, Natural Philosophy, and Natural Religion*, are in some measure dependent on the Science of MAN; since they lie under the cognizance of men, and are judged of by their powers and faculties (*Treatise*, intro., § 4).

Secondly, Hume argued that the science of man must be

---

* This chapter is a modified version of two previous attempts to deal with the Astronomy: 'Adam Smith: Philosophy and Science', *Scottish Journal of Political Economy*, 19 (1972) and 'Adam Smith: Science and the Role of the Imagination', in W.B. Todd (ed.), *Hume and the Enlightenment: Essays presented to Ernest Campbell Mossner* (1974).

[1] *Adam Smith: The Biographical Approach* (1969).

[2] The familiar details are recorded in John Rae's *Life*, chapter 32.

developed by the use of the 'experimental' method, or as he put it, 'as the science of man is the only solid foundation for the other sciences, so, the only solid foundation we can give to this science itself must be laid on experience and observation' (*Treatise*, intro., § 7).

Thirdly, Hume suggested that the study of man, thus constituted, would yield the conclusion that 'there is a great uniformity among the actions of men, in all nations and ages, and that human nature remains still the same, in its principles and operations' (*Inquiry Concerning Human Understanding*, VIII. 7). In fact Smith had surprisingly little to say on the subject of method (in the sense of considering the techniques of analysis and synthesis), but there can be no doubt that he too followed Hume's lead. It is also quite clear that he made use of Hume's hypothesis with regard to the constant principles of human nature, especially in those of his works which deal with the activities of man in society. For example, in his economic analysis Smith makes use of the hypothesis that man is motivated by a desire to seek pleasure and to avoid pain; that he is self-regarding, possessed of certain propensities (for example, to 'truck and barter') and objectives (for example, to 'better his condition'). These judgements are used throughout Smith's economics and lie at the basis of his explanation of the way in which resources come to be allocated between alternative uses. The pursuit of some level of satisfaction always sought, but never in fact attained, is also essential to Smith's explanation of the development of productive forces over time, and, ultimately, to his theory of historical change with its four distinct socio-economic stages.[3]

However, Smith's use of the basic Humean hypothesis is also evident in his other works — significantly those which are in one way or another concerned with the study, or exercise, of human *understanding*: works such as the *Lectures on Rhetoric*, the *Theory of Moral Sentiments*, and the *Essays on Philosophical Subjects*.[4] For example, the lectures make it

[3] The 'four stages of society are hunting, pasturage, farming and commerce'. LJ(B), 149, ed. Cannan, 107.

[4] The essays were published in 1795, edited by Joseph Black and James Hutton. Medical doctors by training, both men became firm friends of Smith's in his later years, and with him founded the Oyster Club, which met once a week in Edinburgh's Grassmarket.

plain that Smith regarded the study of 'literary composition' as an important source of information with regard to the powers of the human mind, while in addition Smith's theory of rhetoric was designed to show that the manner in which we organize discourse of various kinds often reflects our own psychology, together with an intuitive knowledge of the mental characteristics of those whom we seek to persuade, teach, or otherwise influence. If in this sense we can say that the *Rhetoric* was concerned with the qualities of the human mind and their uses, then it will also be apparent that the *Theory of Moral Sentiments* may, from one point of view, fall within the same category. It is quite obvious of course that in this work Smith was concerned with problems of morals as such; a point which is usefully illustrated by his concern with the question, 'wherein does virtue consist? Or what is the tone of temper, and tenour of conduct, which constitutes the excellent and praise-worthy character . . . ?' (VII. i. 2) The question asked reflects Smith's concern with a specific subject, but also with an area of human experience which involves some act of judgement on the part of the individuals concerned. This aspect of Smith's work is clearly disclosed in the title of his book, and his statement of the second main question facing the moral philosopher, namely, '*by what means* does it come to pass, that the *mind* prefers one tenour of conduct to another . . . ?' (VII. i. 2. Italics supplied.)

The same general feature is to be found in the *Essays on Philosophical Subjects*, at least to the extent that Smith was concerned with the stimulus given to the exercise of the understanding by *sentiments* such as *surprise, wonder,* or *admiration*. Smith's objectives were quite clearly stated at the outset of the essay on astronomy where he remarked that 'It is the design of this Essay to consider particularly the nature and causes of each of these sentiments, whose influence is of far wider extent than we should be apt upon a careless view to imagine' (Intro., § 7). It is surely interesting to observe that these three works are all concerned (albeit in different ways) with the exercise of the human mind or the stimuli to which it may be subject; that they were all worked out in the 1750s, thus placing them among Smith's earliest areas of

interest; and that they may show Hume's influence to a striking degree. Indeed, as Professor Raphael has remarked:

Adam Smith was one of the few people of his time who took the measure of Hume's positive achievements in philosophy; Smith's emphasis on the constructive role of the imagination in his theory of scientific method, and the function which he assigned to nature in his ethical theory, must both have come from an appreciation of Hume.[5]

In what follows we shall be mainly concerned with Smith's essay on astronomy with a view to showing the role which Smith ascribed to the imagination in scientific discourse.[6] At the same time it is hoped that this discussion may have a certain 'biographical' value, by throwing some light on Smith's own predispositions as a thinker. To this end, the chapter will be divided into two main parts: the first will be concerned with the psychological assumptions of the model, and the second with their application to the history of astronomy.

II

The Assumptions

The psychological assumptions which Smith employed in the essays under discussion are fundamentally simple: he assumes that man is endowed with certain faculties and propensities such as reason, reflection, and imagination, and that he is motivated by a desire to acquire (or avoid) the sources of pleasure (or pain).[7] In this context pleasure relates to a state

---

[5] D.D. Raphael, 'The Impartial Spectator', *Proceedings of the British Academy*, 58 (1972), reprinted in *Essays on Adam Smith*. Apart from Hume, Smith may have been influenced by a series of articles published in the *Spectator* (411-21), 'On the Pleasures of the Imagination'. These wide-ranging essays gave a good deal of emphasis to the 'pleasure of the understanding'.

[6] For comment see S. Moscovici, 'A propos de quelque travaux d'Adam Smith sur l'histoire et la philosophie des sciences', in *Revue d'Histoire des Sciences et de leur Applications*, 9 (1956); J.F. Becker, 'Adam Smith's Theory of Social Science', *Southern Economic Journal*, 28 (1961-2); H.F. Thomson, 'Adam Smith's Philosophy of Science', *Quarterly Journal of Economics*, 79 (1965); J.R. Lindgren, 'Adam Smith's Theory of Enquiry', *Journal of Political Economy*, 77 (1969); T.D. Campbell, *Adam Smith's Science of Morals* (1971), Part I; J.R. Lindgren, *The Social Philosophy of Adam Smith* (1973), chapter 1; W.P.D. Wightman, 'Adam Smith and the History of Ideas' in *Essays on Adam Smith*; and Vernard Foley, *The Social Physics of Adam Smith* (1977), chapter 2.

[7] Cf. Hume: 'There is implanted in the human mind a perception of pain and pleasure as the chief spring and moving principle of all its actions.' *Treatise*, I. iii. 10. 2.

of the imagination,'or 'What may be called the natural state of
the mind, the state in which we are neither elated nor de-
jected, the state of sedateness, tranquillity, and composure ...'
(Imitative Arts, II. 20). In this case such a state may be attained
where the mind contemplates objects which satisfy certain
conditions; conditions which are quite well expressed in a
passage from the *Theory of Moral Sentiments* where it is
pointed out that 'Connected variety, in which each new appearance seems to be introduced by what went before it, and
in which all the adjoining parts seem to have some natural
relation to one another, is more agreeable than a disjointed
and disorderly assemblage of unconnected objects' (V. 1. 9).
We derive a feeling of pleasure, Smith argues, from the contemplation of relation, similarity, or order; from a certain
association of ideas. As Smith remarked in a passage which
clearly shows the influence of Hume:

> When two objects, however unlike, have often been observed to follow
> each other, and have constantly presented themselves to the senses in
> that order, they come to be so connected together in the fancy, that
> the idea of the one seems, of its own accord, to call up and introduce
> that of the other. If the objects are still observed to succeed each other
> as before, this connection, or, as it has been called, this association of
> their ideas, becomes stricter and stricter, and the habit of the imagin-
> ation to pass from the conception of the one to that of the other, grows
> more and more rivetted and confirmed (Astronomy, II. 7).[8]

He added that under such circumstances 'There is no break,
no stop, no gap, no interval. The ideas excited by so coherent
a chain of things seem, as it were, to float through the mind
of their own accord, without obliging it to exert itself, or to
make any effort in order to pass from one of them to another'
(II. 7).[9] While emphasizing that the imagination *is* indolent and

---

[8] Cf. Hume, 'Of the Connection and Association of Ideas', *Treatise*, I. i. 4. For
comment on the relationship between Smith and Hume, see D.D. Raphael, 'The
true old Humean Philosophy and its influence on Adam Smith', in *David Hume:
Bicentenary Papers*, ed. S.P. Morice (1977).

[9] A similar passage occurs in TMS V. 1. 2, where it is stated that 'When two
objects have frequently been seen together, the imagination acquires a habit
of passing easily from the one to the other'. Smith emphasizes that it is 'the
unusualness alone of the succession' which occasions some stop or interruption
in the 'progress of the imagination' (Astronomy, II. 11). J.R. Lindgren in particular has emphasized that Smith's interest in conventional knowledge has often been
underestimated (*Social Philosophy*, 6).

that it finds no stimulus to thought under such conditions,[10] Smith struck a more original note in going on to argue that this would not be the case where the 'appearances' were in any way irregular or unexpected:

But if this customary connection be interrupted, if one or more objects appear in an order quite different from that to which the imagination has been accustomed, and for which it is prepared, the contrary of all this happens. We are at first surprised by the unexpectedness of the new appearance, and when that momentary emotion is over, we still wonder how it came to occur in that place (II. 8).[11]

In other words we feel surprise when some object (or number of objects) is drawn to our attention which does not fall into an expected pattern; a sentiment quickly followed by that of *wonder*, where the latter is defined in these terms: 'The stop which is thereby given to the career of the imagination, the difficulty which it finds in passing along such disjointed objects, and the feeling of something like a gap or interval betwixt them, constitute the whole essence of this emotion' (II. 9). Wonder, in short, involves a source of pain (or disutility); a feeling of discomfort which gives rise to 'uncertainty and anxious curiosity', to 'giddiness and confusion', which can in extreme cases lead to mental derangement. Smith made much of this point, to the extent of illustrating his case by reference to the rational individual 'all at once transported alive to some other planet, where nature was governed by laws quite different from those which take place here' (II. 10).

The response to this situation then involves the pursuit of some explanation, with a view to relieving the mind from a state of disequilibrium; a natural reaction designed to eliminate the sense of wonder by providing some appropriate ordering of the phenomena in question. As he put it, the imagination 'endeavours to find out something which may fill

[10] This point may be reflected in Smith's concern that the modern labourer, whose functions are restricted in scope and number, may suffer, as a result, from a certain numbness of the understanding: 'The man whose whole life is spent in performing a few simple operations, of which the effects too are, perhaps, always the same, or very nearly the same, has no occasion to exert his understanding . . . He naturally loses, therefore, the habit of such exertion, and generally becomes as stupid and ignorant as it is possible for a human creature to become.' WN V. i. f. 50.
[11] Cf. Hume: 'There is commonly an astonishment attending everything extraordinary.' *Treatise*, I. iii. 14. 24.

up the gap, which, like a bridge, may so far at least unite those seemingly distant objects, as to render the passage of the thought betwixt them smooth, and natural, and easy' (II. 8).[12]

Before going further, it may be useful to elaborate on Smith's argument by reviewing the two types or species which he used to illustrate the processes above described. In the first case, Smith considered objects where the link was provided by *similarity* (rather than *relation*), suggesting in this instance that we would naturally tend to place such objects in certain 'sorts' or 'categories'.[13] 'It is evident that the mind takes pleasure in observing the resemblances that are discoverable betwixt different objects. It is by means of such observations that it endeavours to arrange and methodise all its ideas, and to reduce them into proper classes and assortments' (II. 1). He also added that we take pleasure in referring a particular object

to some species or class of things, with all of which it has a nearly exact resemblance; and though we often know no more about them than about it, yet we are apt to fancy that by being able to do so, we show ourselves to be better acquainted with it, and to have a more thorough insight into its nature (II. 3).

Now so long as the individual objects which are presented to us fall within some existing classification, the mind can retain a position of equilibrium: 'But when something quite new and singular is presented, we feel ourselves incapable of doing this. The memory cannot, from all its stores, cast up any

---

[12] Smith makes a related point in the *Lectures on Rhetoric*, LRBL ii. 36, ed. Lothian, 95, in remarking that: 'We should never leave any chasm or gap in the thread of the narration, even though there are no remarkable events to fill up that space. The very notion of a gap makes us uneasy . . .' Similar points are made at ii. 196, 205–6; ed. Lothian, 167, 172.

[13] Smith makes much of this point in his work on language, where it is pointed out that 'The different mental operations, of arrangement or classing, of comparison, and of abstraction, must all have been employed, before even the names of the different colours, the least metaphysical of all nouns adjective, could be instituted' (Languages, §7). Smith also refers to 'that love of analogy and similarity of sound, which is the foundation of by far the greater part of the rules of grammar' (§§16, 25). Similar arguments appear in the *Lectures on Rhetoric*, LRBL i. 17–31, ed. Lothian, 7–11. It is interesting to observe that Smith's main objection to Johnson's *Dictionary* related to a plan which struck him as insufficiently 'grammatical'. 'The different significations of a word are indeed collected; but they are seldom digested into general classes.' Quoted in Lindgren, *The Early Writings of Adam Smith* (1967), 6.

image that nearly resembles this strange appearance' (II. 3). Hence the feeling of surprise and wonder, together with the response to it, as the individual struggles to connect the object in question to some class of objects. The observer 'must find out some resemblance or other, before he can get rid of that Wonder, that uncertainty and anxious curiosity excited by its singular appearance, and by its dissimilitude with all the objects he had hitherto observed' (II. 4). Smith also made the interesting point that new appearances would often lead to *new* classifications, and that 'The further we advance in knowledge and experience, the greater number of divisions and subdivisions of those Genera and Species we are both inclined and obliged to make' (II. 2). In the second case, Smith argued that when some *relation* of things strikes the *observer* as unusual he will also be subject to the emotions above mentioned. For example:

The motion of a small piece of iron along a plain table is in itself no extraordinary object, yet the person who first saw it begin, without any visible impulse, in consequence of the motion of a loadstone at some little distance from it, could not behold it without the most extreme Surprise; and when that momentary emotion was over, he would still wonder how it came to be conjoined to an event with which, according to the ordinary train of things, he could have so little suspected it to have any connection (II. 6).

Once again the mind suffers a disturbance, and once again responds by endeavouring to find some train of intermediate events which will satisfy the need for explanation:

Thus, when we observe the motion of the iron, in consequence of that of the loadstone, we gaze and hesitate, and feel a want of connection betwixt two events which follow one another in so unusual a train. But when, with Des Cartes, we imagine certain invisible effluvia to circulate round one of them, and by their repeated impulses to impel the other, both to move towards it, and to follow its motion, we fill up the interval betwixt them, we join them together by a sort of bridge, and thus take off that hesitation and difficulty which the imagination felt in passing from the one to the other (II. 8).

The argument thus proceeds along exactly similar lines to the previous case, although it may be useful to take this opportunity of emphasizing two aspects of it. First, it will be noted that man is impelled to seek an explanation for observed appearances as a result of some subjective feeling

of discomfort, and that the resulting explanation is therefore designed to meet some *psychological* need. Secondly, Smith argues that the explanation offered can only satisfy the mind if it is coherent, capable of accounting for observed appearances, and stated in terms of 'familiar' or plausible principles — requirements satisfied by the Cartesian argument above mentioned, since 'Motion after impulse is an order of succession with which of all things we are the most familiar' (II. 8).

Although the examples so far used are drawn from the reactions of the casual observer to the phenomena he contemplates, the main point of Smith's argument is to show that the philosopher (or scientist) is also subject to the same basic (universal) principles of human nature.[14] Indeed, from one point of view the main difference between the philosopher and the non-philosopher is to be found in the type and range of problems with which the two parties are concerned. For nature as a whole, Smith suggested, 'seems to abound with events which appear solitary and incoherent' and which therefore 'disturb the easy movement of the imagination' (II. 12). Under these circumstances the philosopher feels the disutility involved in the sentiments of surprise and wonder, and reacts to them by endeavouring to find some explanation. As Smith puts it: 'Wonder, therefore, and not any expectation of advantage from its discoveries, is the first principle which prompts mankind to the study of Philosophy, of that science which pretends to lay open the concealed connections that unite the various appearances of nature' (III. 3). Philosophy in all its forms, natural as well as moral, thus emerges as 'the science of the connecting principles of nature' (II. 12), with, as its ultimate end, 'the repose and tranquillity of the imagination' (IV. 13). Although these motives are of universal application, the purposes of philosophy are made especially clear in Smith's discussion of astronomy, where he argues that the task of theory is to introduce 'order into this chaos of jarring and discordant appearances, to allay this tumult of the imagination, and to restore it, when it surveys the great revolutions of the universe, to that tone of tranquillity and

[14] As Campbell points out, the words 'philosophy' and 'science' were at this time used almost interchangeably (op.cit., p.25).

composure, which is both most agreeable in itself, and most suitable to its nature' (II. 12).

The similarities between the philosopher and the non-philosopher are therefore emphasized, although Smith did take considerable pains to bring out a number of important differences between them. For example, he pointed out that in any developed society philosophy would tend to emerge as a distinct trade like any other, and its practitioners as 'men of speculation, whose trade it is, not to do any thing, but to observe every thing; and who, upon that account, are often capable of combining together the powers of the most distant and dissimilar objects' (WN I. i. 9). As a result certain differences emerge between the two groups, which 'arise not so much from nature, as from habit, custom, and education' (WN I. ii. 4). These differences involve things like knowledge, and powers of observation, and are important in that they permit the philosopher to perceive problems of connection to which the non-philosopher may be insensible. For example, Smith cites the case of artisans such as dyers, brewers, and distillers, who handle processes which strike the skilled observer as complex, but which do not seem so to the artisan himself 'who has been for many years familiar with the consequences of all the operations of his art'. In a passage which may reflect his own experience, Smith records the amusement which such questions often excite, since the artisan 'cannot conceive what occasion there is for any connecting events to unite those appearances, which seem to him to succeed each other very naturally. It is their nature, he tells us, to follow one another in this order, and that accordingly they always do so' (Astronomy, II. 11). In the same way Smith points out that men are so familiar with the conversion of food into flesh and bone that they do not (typically) think about the processes involved; that ordinary men 'have seldom had the curiosity to inquire by what process of intermediate events this change is brought about. Because the passage of the thought from the one object to the other is by custom become quite smooth and easy' (II. 11). Similarly, Smith remarked that 'After a little use and experience . . . looking-glasses cease to be wonders altogether; and even the ignorant become so familiar with them, as not to think that

their effects require any explication' (Imitative Arts, I. 17). But just as the botanist differs from the casual gardener, or the musician from his auditor, so the philosopher

who has spent his whole life in the study of the connecting principles of nature, will often feel an interval betwixt two objects, which, to more careless observers, seem very strictly conjoined. By long attention to all the connections which have ever been presented to his observation, by having often compared them with one another, he has, like the musician, acquired, if one may say so, a nicer ear . . . (Astronomy, II. 11).

This is an important point because it also means that the philosopher is less likely to be completely reassured by the 'explanations' offered (by himself or others) for jarring and discordant appearances and, therefore, that speculation need not cease after a generally acceptable solution has been found for a particular problem. Or, as Smith remarked in referring to the simpler problem of explaining the movement of scenery on a stage: 'In the Wonders of nature . . . it rarely happens that we can discover so clearly this connecting chain' (II. 9).

A second major difference between the philosopher and the non-philosopher is to be found in the pleasure to be derived, directly or indirectly, from the exercise of the intellectual faculties. In fact Smith devoted a good deal of attention to the 'pleasing satisfaction of science', while indicating that it had many sources. Thus he pointed out that once we have succeeded in providing an acceptable and coherent account of some observed phenomena, the very existence of that explanation may heighten our appreciation of the 'appearances' themselves, thus representing a source of satisfaction in addition to that acquired from the explanation itself. In this way, for example, we may learn to understand, but also to admire a complex social structure once its 'hidden springs' have been exposed; we understand and thus admire the animal body once we know something of its structure; the theory of astronomy helps us to admire the heavens through presenting the 'theatre of nature' as a 'coherent, and therefore a more magnificent spectacle' (II. 12). In a rather similar vein Smith adverted to the pleasure to be derived from effort of a philosophical kind, in suggesting that men 'pursue this study for its own sake, as an original pleasure

or good in itself, without regarding its tendency to procure them the means of many other pleasures' (III. 3).[15]

We may therefore conclude that while the principles of human nature are to be regarded as constant, the philosopher emerges as a very different creature from the unskillful spectator. Yet at the same time Smith evidently believed that the popular reception of scientific work could have an important influence on its future course, in arguing: 'we observe, in general, that no system, how well soever in other respects supported, has ever been able to gain any general credit on the world, whose connecting principles were not such as were familiar to all mankind' (Astronomy, II. 12).[16]

III

The Astronomy

Most of these points find further illustration in the History of Astronomy, where Smith reviewed four main systems of thought, not with a view to judging their 'absurdity or probability, their agreement or inconsistency with truth and reality', but rather with a view to considering how far each of them was fitted to 'sooth(e) the imagination' — 'that particular point of view which belongs to our subject' (II. 12). Looked at in this way, the analysis has a 'static' aspect at least in so far as it is designed to show the extent to which each of the four systems reviewed actually does succeed in 'soothing' the imagination. But Smith goes further than his stated object in noting that the theories which he reviews followed each other in a certain sequence, and in exposing the causal links which, he felt, might explain that sequence.

[15] Cf. Hume: 'the pleasure of study consists chiefly in the action of the mind, and the exercise of the genius and understanding in the discovery or comprehension of any truth.' *Treatise*, II. iii. 10. 6, 'Of Curiosity, or the Love of Truth'. Smith's old teacher, Francis Hutcheson, had also emphasized that we 'have delight in exercising our own rational, inventive and active powers; we are pleased to behold the like exercises in others, and the artful effects of them'. *System of Moral Philosophy* (1755), II. 2. James Hutton also gave prominence to the theme: 'The proper object of science is truth, and the motive of it is pleasure', in his *Investigations of the Principles of Knowledge* (1794), II. i. 4.

[16] Smith uses this point to explain why the 'chemical philosophy' had in all ages 'crept along in obscurity, and been so disregarded by the generality of mankind' (Astronomy, II. 12).

The essence of Smith's argument would seem to be that each system at the time of its original statement satisfied the needs of the imagination, but that each was subject to a process of modification as new problems came to light; a process of modification which resulted in a degree of complexity which ultimately became unacceptable to the imagination. This in turn paves the way for a new kind of response — the production not just of *an* account, but of an *alternative* account (in this case of the heavens); a new thought-system designed to explain the same problems as the first, at least in its most complex form, but in a different way.

From one point of view this is the classic pattern of cultural history — human activity released within a given environment ultimately causing a qualitative change in that environment — as illustrated, say, by the development of language or the transition from feudalism to the commercial stage (WN III). But there is a difference, partly because 'environment' here refers to a state of knowledge, and partly because the reactions of individuals are now described as self-conscious — that is designed deliberately to modify an existing thought-system or to replace it with a more acceptable alternative.

We may usefully illustrate the burden of Smith's argument by commenting on the rise, progress, and decline of the first great astronomical system, that of Concentric Spheres.

As Smith presents the case, the first astronomers were faced with the need to explain the movements of three different types of object: Sun, Moon, and Stars. This was effected, he suggests, in terms of a theory of Solid Spheres, each one of which was given a circular but regular motion, for two reasons. First, he suggested that 'A circle, as the degree of its curvature is every where the same, is of all curve lines the simplest and the most easily conceived' (IV. 51). Secondly, Smith considered that 'The equality of their motions was another fundamental idea, which, in the same manner, and for the same reason, was supposed by all the founders of astronomical systems. For an equal motion can be more easily attended to, than one that is continually either accelerated or retarded' (IV. 52). In the first system, the sky was regarded as the roof of the universe, while the stars, being apparently static in respect of their relative positions, 'were naturally

thought to have all the marks of being fixed, like so many gems, in the concave side of the firmament, and of being carried round by the diurnal revolutions of that solid body' (IV. 1). Given this explanation, Smith argued, it was equally natural to explain the movements of the Sun and Moon in terms of a hypothesis of the same kind, thus rendering the 'theory of the heavens more uniform' than could otherwise have been the case. In this instance, since the Sun and Moon change their relative positions, each was given a sphere of its own, one inside the other (in order to account for the eclipse) and supposed 'to be attached to the concave side of a solid and transparent body, by whose revolutions they were carried round the earth' (IV. 2). Additional spheres were subsequently added in order to account for the movement of the five planets or 'wandering stars' until a system emerged which represented the earth as 'self-balanced and suspended in the centre of the universe, surrounded by the elements of Air and Ether, and covered by eight polished and cristalline Spheres, each of which was distinguished by one or more beautiful and luminous bodies, and all of which revolved round their common centre, by varied, but by equable and proportionable motions' (IV. 5). As Smith pointed out, such a system of thought appealed to the imagination by apparently providing a coherent explanation of the 'different movements and effects already in reality performed', and connected, by simple and familiar processes, the 'grandest and most seemingly disjointed appearances in the heavens'. He added: 'If it gained the belief of mankind by its plausibility, it attracted their wonder and admiration; sentiments that still more confirmed their belief, by the novelty and beauty of that view of nature which it presented to the imagination' (IV. 5).[17] Indeed, even if some contemporaries recognized that such a system did not account for *all* appearances, the degree of completeness was such that the generality of men would be tempted to 'slur over' (IV. 6) such problems. In fact, Smith went on to suggest that this beautiful and appealing construction *of the intellect* might 'have stood the examination of all ages, and have gone

---

[17] It is remarked in TMS I. i. 4. 3 that 'approbation heightened by wonder and surprise, constitutes the sentiment which is properly called admiration'.

down triumphant to the remotest posterity' had there been 'no other bodies discoverable in the heavens' (IV. 4). But of course such bodies were discovered, and this together with the fact that Eudoxus was not one of the 'generality of men' led to the need to modify the existing system, and the addition of more spheres, as a means of accounting for changes in the relative positions of the planets. As a result Eudoxus raised the total number of spheres to 27, Callippus to 34, Aristotle 'upon a yet more attentive observation' to 56, until Francostorio, 'smit with the eloquence of Plato and Aristotle', felt it necessary to raise the number of spheres to 72. In short, the existing, relatively simple system of Eudoxus was gradually modified in order to meet the needs of the imagination when faced with new problems to be explained, until a situation was reached where the explanation offered actually violated the basic prerequisite of simplicity. As Smith put it: 'This system had now become as intricate and complex as those appearances themselves, which it had been invented to render uniform and coherent. The imagination, therefore, found itself but little relieved from that embarrassment, into which those appearances had thrown it, by so perplexed an account of things' (IV. 8). In consequence, another system was developed by Apollonius (subsequently refined by Hipparchus and Ptolemy) which distinguished between the 'real and apparent motion of the heavenly bodies' and solved the problem of changes in relative position by supposing that 'the Sun and the other Planets revolved in circles, whose centres were very distant from the centre of the Earth'. At the same time, the adherents of this system attempted to account for the irregular movements of the planets:

By supposing, that in the solidity of the Sphere of each of the Five Planets there was formed another little Sphere, called an Epicycle, which revolved round its own centre, at the same time that it was carried round the centre of the Earth by the revolution of the great Sphere, betwixt whose concave and convex sides it was inclosed (IV. 10).

Once again, we face a system which was designed to 'introduce harmony and order into the mind's conception of the movements of those bodies', and which once again succeeded to a degree. However, the same argument is advanced: namely, that a gradual (and inevitable) process of modification to the

system involved a progressive increase in its degree of compli-
cation, until a situation was reached where 'this imaginary
machine, though, perhaps, more simple, and certainly better
adapted to the phænomena than the Fifty-six Planetary
Spheres of Aristotle, was still too intricate and complex for
the imagination to rest in it with complete tranquillity and
satisfaction' (IV. 19). Indeed, Smith argued that the situation
became even more complex with the work done by the
Schoolmen, and especially Purbach, who laboured to rec-
oncile the Aristotelian doctrine of Solid Spheres with the
later system of Eccentric Spheres and Epicycles in the form
given it by Ptolemy. As Smith suggested, Purbach 'as well as
all those who had worked upon the same plan before him, by
rendering this account of things more complex, rendered it
still more embarrassing than it had been before' (IV. 25).

It will be observed that this illustration introduces a new
element into Smith's discussion, namely, the attempt made
not merely to explain observed events, but to find consistency
between conflicting accounts of those events. Thus, the
(modified) system of Eccentric Spheres was to suffer the
same fate as its predecessor, and for the same reason, being
ultimately replaced by the Copernican. Indeed Copernicus
provides a good example of Smith's reliance on the role of
the imagination, in that 'The confusion, in which the old
hypothesis represented the motions of the heavenly bodies,
was, he tells us, what first suggested to him the design of
forming a new system, that these, the noblest works of
nature, might no longer appear devoid of that harmony and
proportion which discover themselves in her meanest productions' (IV. 28). Like the system which it was to replace,
the Copernican managed to account for observed appearances;
in the manner of a 'more simple machine' requiring 'fewer
movements', it represented 'the Sun, the great enlightener of
the universe, whose body was alone larger than all the Planets
taken together, as established immoveable in the center,
shedding light and heat on all the worlds that circulated
around him in one uniform direction, but in longer or shorter
periods, according to their different distances' (IV. 32). It
was to prove an attractive hypothesis to some, not merely
because of the beauty and simplicity of the system, but also

because the novelty of the view of nature thus provided excited a certain feeling of wonder and surprise:

For, though it is the end of Philosophy, to allay that wonder, which either the unusual or seemingly disjointed appearances of nature excite, yet she never triumphs so much, as when, in order to connect together a few, in themselves, perhaps, inconsiderable objects, she has, if I may say so, created another constitution of things, more natural indeed, and such as the imagination can more easily attend to, but more new, more contrary to common opinion and expectation, than any of those appearances themselves (IV. 33).

This was emphatically the case with a system which 'moved the earth from its Foundations, stopt the revolution of the Firmament, made the sun stand still'.

Yet at the same time, Smith argued that the system was by no means acceptable to all, or even to those who confined their attention to astronomical matters, the difficulty being that Copernicus had invested the earth with a velocity which was 'unfamiliar', that is, which ran counter to normal experience. The imagination, Smith suggested, tended to think of the earth as ponderous 'and even averse to motion' (IV. 38) and it was this difficulty which led to the formulation of the alternative system of Tycho Brahe — a system partly prompted by jealousy of Copernicus, but none the less a system to some extent compounded of that of the latter and of Ptolemy. In this system, 'the Earth continued to be, as in the old account, the immoveable center of the universe' (IV. 42). Smith added that Brahe's account was 'more complex and more incoherent than that of Copernicus. Such, however, was the difficulty that mankind felt in conceiving the motion of the Earth, that it long balanced the reputation of that otherwise more beautiful system' (IV. 43).

In other words, the coherence and simplicity of the Copernican system was qualified by the unfamiliarity of one of its central principles; a problem which was so important as to render a more complex account more acceptable to some than it could otherwise have been. Interestingly enough, Smith represents subsequent developments as involving an attempt to make the more elegant system (of Copernicus) acceptable to the imagination by removing the basic difficulty — that is, by providing a plausible explanation for the move-

ment of the earth. In this connection Smith argued that the astronomical work done by Kepler contributed to the completion of the system, while research on the problem of motion by Galileo had helped to remove some of the more telling objections to the idea of a moving earth. But in terms of the general acceptance of the idea of the earth spinning at high velocity Smith gave most emphasis to the work of Descartes, who had represented the planets as floating in an immense ocean of ether containing 'at all times, an infinite number of greater and smaller vortices, or circular streams' (IV. 62). Once the imagination accepted a hypothesis based on the familiar principle of motion after impulse, it was a short step to the elimination of the central difficulty, since 'it was quite agreeable to its usual habits to conceive' that the planets 'should follow the stream of this ocean, how rapid soever' (IV. 65). He added, in a significant passage, that under such circumstances 'the imaginations of mankind could no longer refuse themselves the pleasure of going along with so harmonious an account of things. The system of Tycho Brahe was every day less and less talked of, till at last it was forgotten altogether' (ibid.).

Yet, as Smith went on to note, the modifications introduced by Descartes were not prompted by *astronomical* knowledge so much as by a desire to produce a plausible explanation for the Copernican thesis. Moreover, he noted that further observations, especially those of Cassini, supported the authority of laws first discovered by Kepler for which the Cartesian 'theory' could provide no explanation. Under such circumstances, the latter system, while it 'might continue to amuse the learned in other sciences . . . could no longer satisfy those that were skilled in Astronomy' (IV. 67).

But at the same time, the Copernican system, if complete, was still cumbersome, and destined in due time to give way to yet another, capable of accounting more completely for observed appearances, in terms of a smaller *number* of basic principles, and of successfully predicting their future movement. This was the system of Newton: 'a system whose parts are all more strictly connected together, than those of any other philosophical hypothesis. Allow his principle, the universality of gravity, and that it decreases as the squares of the

distance increase, and all the appearances, which he joins together by it, necessarily follow' (IV. 76). Moreover, the basic principles involved could be regarded as familiar, since

The gravity of matter is, of all its qualities, after its inertness, that which is most familiar to us. . . . The law too, by which it is supposed to diminish as it recedes from its centre, is the same which takes place in all other qualities which are propagated in rays from a centre, in light, and in every thing else of the same kind (IV. 76).

While Smith wrote with real enthusiasm about Newton's contribution and its current reception in France, he added a characteristic warning in stating that

even we, while we have been endeavouring to represent all philosophical systems as mere inventions of the imagination, to connect together the otherwise disjointed and discordant phænomena of nature, have insensibly been drawn in, to make use of language expressing the connecting principles of this one, as if they were the real chains which Nature makes use of to bind together her several operations. Can we wonder then, that it should have gained the general and complete approbation of mankind, and that it should now be considered, not as an attempt to connect in the imagination the phænomena of the Heavens, but as the greatest discovery that ever was made by man, the discovery of an immense chain of the most important and sublime truths, all closely connected together, by one capital fact, of the reality of which we have daily experience (IV. 76).

IV

The remarkable essay whose content we have just reviewed was one of Smith's earliest works, and perhaps the product of his youthful interest in mathematics and natural philosophy. While we know that it was written before 1758, the Astronomy seems to have attracted Smith's interest throughout his life. In 1773 for example he took steps to preserve the manuscript in the event of his death, writing to Hume on 16 April (Letter 137) in these terms:

As I have left the care of all my literary papers to you, I must tell you that except those which I carry along with me there are none worth the publishing, but a fragment of a great work which contains a history of the Astronomical Systems that were successively in fashion down to the time of Des Cartes. Whether that might not be published as a fragment of an intended juvenile work, I leave entirely to your judgement; tho I begin to suspect myself that there is more refinement than solidity in some parts of it. This little work you will find in a thin folio paper book in my writing desk in my bedroom.

In 1790 Lord Loughborough wrote to David Douglas indicating that he understood Smith had been engaged in 'correcting' the essay,[18] and Smith himself, true to his earlier decision, allowed his executors, Black and Hutton, to publish it as part of 'a plan which he had once formed, for giving a connected history of the liberal sciences and elegant arts'.

The essay itself may well have owed much to Smith's early and wide-ranging interest in the sciences. It will be recalled in this connection that Smith had drawn attention, in the *Edinburgh Review* article of 1756, to the contributions of Buffon, Daubenton, and Réaumur, and that his own library contained copies of the works of D'Alembert, Diderot, Buffon, and Maupertuis. The work done in the field of biology by men such as these was of profound importance, associated as it is with the introduction of the 'great chain' thesis and of those theories of 'transformism' which were being developed in the late 1740s and early 1750s. Such theories may well have affected the way in which research was conducted in other fields, and it has in fact been suggested that they were 'intimately related to the entrance of historicism into the European intellectual outlook'.[19] It is distinctly possible that the climate of opinion thus engendered may have been an important influence on the development of that historical perspective which is so clearly illustrated by the Astronomy.

Moreover, Smith's idea of a historical sketch of intellectual history cannot be said to have been an isolated attempt, since

[18] Scott, *ASSP* 313.

[19] By mid-century, work in biology had produced two main theses: the first, that of the 'great chain of being', the second a theory of evolution which was associated with Diderot and Maupertuis. The latter had been influenced by Réaumur, and was one of the first avowed disciples of Newton in France. See A.O. Lovejoy, *The Great Chain of Being* (1936) and B. Glass, 'Maupertuis, Pioneer of Genetics and Evolution', together with L.G. Crocker, 'Diderot and Eighteenth Century Transformism', both in *Forerunners of Darwin*, ed. Glass, Temkin, and Strauss (1959). In the same volume ('Buffon and the Problem of Species'), Lovejoy suggested that the 'Leibnitian calculus' which brought the 'notion of the continuum into fashion' was one of the forces which prepared men's minds for the concept of evolution. In the *Great Chain*, Lovejoy pointed out that evolutionary theses were 'becoming familiar in very widely recognised writings before the middle of the eighteenth Century' and cited as examples Young's poem *Night Thoughts* (1742-4) and Mark Akenside's *The Pleasures of Imagination* (1744). Lovejoy also drew attention to the importance of Epicurean-inspired accounts of evolution in the third of his *Essays in the History of Ideas* (1948).

there were others in the field such as Turgot,[20] D'Alembert, and Jean-Etienne Montucla. Indeed, as Dugald Stewart pointed out:

The mathematical sciences, both pure and mixed, afford, in many of their branches, very favourable subjects for theoretical history; and a very competent judge, the late M. d'Alembert, has recommended this arrangement of their elementary principles, which is founded on the natural succession of inventions and discoveries, as the best adapted for interesting the curiosity and exercising the genius of students. The same author points out as a model a passage in Montucla's History of Mathematics, where an attempt is made to exhibit the gradual progress of philosophical speculation, from the first conclusions suggested by a general survey of the heavens, to the doctrines of Copernicus. It is somewhat remarkable, that a theoretical history of this very science (in which we have, perhaps, a better opportunity than in any other instance whatever, of comparing the natural advances of the mind with the actual succession of hypothetical systems) was one of Mr Smith's earliest compositions, and is one of the very small number of his manuscripts which he did not destroy before his death. (Stewart, II. 49.)

While Smith could not have read Turgot's unpublished thesis, and Montucla's work appeared too late (1758) to be of influence, he had read D'Alembert's *Preliminary Discourse*, the first part of which is relevant for the student of Smith's essay.

The differences between the two men are obvious. Unlike Smith, D'Alembert argued that men would first seek useful knowledge and then, having developed techniques such as the mathematical, proceed to subjects such as astronomy, 'the study of which, next to the study of ourselves, is most worthy of our application because of the magnificent spectacle which it presents to us'. Yet at the same time there are interesting parallels, especially in respect of D'Alembert's emphasis on the imagination, which he defined as 'the talent of creating by imitating' and as a 'creative faculty'. He also adverted to the fact that the principles used in any form of explanation will be the more fertile the fewer they are in number, and added: 'in the hierarchy of our needs and of the objects of

[20] The argument is developed in Turgot's *Discourse at the Sorbonne*, delivered in December 1750. The work, entitled 'A Philosophical Review of the Successive Advances of the Human Mind', appears in translation in R.L. Meek, *Turgot on Progress, Sociology and Economics* (1973) and was previously noticed by W. Walker Stephens, *The Life and Writings of Turgot* (1895), 164.

our passions, pleasure holds one of the highest places, and curiosity is a need for anyone who knows how to think, especially when this restless desire is enlivened with a sort of vexation at not being able to satisfy itself entirely'.[21]

Yet at the same time it must be recognized that despite parallels and anticipations Smith's knowledge of astronomy was almost as remarkable as the uses to which it was put. It is surely noteworthy that Smith managed to present the pattern of historical development as involving a process of transition which could be expounded in terms of the rise, decline and replacement of a number of systems, culminating in the work of Newton. This is a notable and original achievement which would appear, at least on the surface, to anticipate in a striking way the basic theses contained in Thomas Kuhn's *Structure of Scientific Revolutions* (1962). Like Kuhn, Smith works in terms of systems (paradigms), within which development takes place (Kuhn's route to normal science) until finally overtaken first by the crisis state and then by revolution (i.e. the substitution of one paradigm for another). It is a remarkable coincidence that Kuhn and Smith should have produced arguments which have such a degree of similarity; that they should both have done so after working on the study of astronomy; and that they should both have isolated Copernicus' famous preface as 'one of the classic descriptions of a crisis state'.

Yet it is not so much the form of the argument as its basic principles which are most striking. In fact, Smith's discussion of the principles which lead and direct philosophical enquiries concentrates, as we have seen, on the needs of the imagination — on broadly psychological needs — so that as Richard Olson has recently pointed out:

The great significance of Smith's doctrine is that since it measures the value of philosophical systems solely in relation to their satisfaction of the human craving for order, it sets up a human rather than an absolute or natural standard for science, and it leaves all science essentially hypothetical. Furthermore, Smith implied that unceasing change rather than permanence must be the characteristic of philosophy.[22]

[21] *The Preliminary Discourse to the Encyclopedia of Diderot*, translated by R.N. Schwab (1963), 16.

[22] *Scottish Philosophy and British Physics, 1750–1880* (1975), 123. The hypothetical element in Smith's thought was also emphasized by Moscovici, op. cit. For an interesting comparison, see Kuhn, op.cit. 169.

It was exactly this perspective which led Smith to utter the warning which was quoted in the conclusion of the preceding section and which led him to take the bold and novel step, in an age dominated by Newton, of reminding his readers that the content of that system was not necessarily 'true'.

While this position does seem accurately to express the burden of Smith's argument, three points might be suggested by way of qualification. First, the argument of the Astronomy could be taken to suggest that once the nature of intellectual activity is understood it may become possible to control its subjective elements.[23] Secondly, it should be recalled that Smith did not claim an *exclusive* role for the sentiments of suprise, wonder, and admiration, but rather asserted that the role fulfilled by them was 'of far wider extent than we should be apt upon a careless view to imagine'. Third, it is worth remarking that while Smith regarded all intellectual constructions as products of the imagination and designed to meet its needs, he also indicated that there were differences between the natural and moral sciences arising from the contrasting problems of verification. As he put the point in the *Theory of Moral Sentiments* (VII. ii. 4. 14):

A system of natural philosophy may appear very plausible, and be for a long time very generally received in the world, and yet have no foundation in nature, nor any sort of resemblance to the truth. The vortices of Des Cartes were regarded by a very ingenious nation, for near a century together, as a most satisfactory account of the revolutions of the heavenly bodies. Yet it has been demonstrated, to the conviction of all mankind, that these pretended causes of those wonderful effects, not only do not actually exist, but are utterly impossible, and if they did exist, could produce no such effects as are ascribed to them. But it is otherwise with systems of moral philosophy, and an author who pretends to account for the origin of our moral sentiments, cannot deceive us so grossly, nor depart so very far from all resemblance to the truth.[24]

[23] Given the importance of such elements it is interesting to note that C. West Churchman should have unwittingly suggested a new role for the 'impartial spectator' as expounded in the *Theory of Moral Sentiments* in observing that 'no observation can become objective unless the observer is also observed objectively'. *The Design of Enquiring Systems* (1971), 150, and see generally, chapter 7.

[24] Cf. D'Alembert: 'If one judges impartially those vortices which today seem almost ridiculous, it will be agreed, I daresay, that at that time nothing better could be imagined' (*Preliminary Discourse*, 79).

Yet Smith had earlier remarked that some philosophers, notably mathematicians, 'are frequently very indifferent' about the reception which they may meet with from the public, enjoying as they do the 'most perfect assurance, both of the truth and of the importance of their discoveries'. He added:

The great work of Sir Isaac Newton, his *Mathematical Principles of Natural Philosophy*, I have been told, was for several years neglected by the public. The tranquillity of that great man, it is probable, never suffered, upon that account, the interruption of a single quarter of an hour. Natural philosophers, in their independency upon the public opinion, approach nearly to mathematicians, and, in their judgments concerning the merit of their own discoveries and observations, enjoy some degree of the same security and tranquillity (TMS III. 2. 20).

But there can be no doubt that Smith did as a matter of fact draw attention to the importance of the 'subjective side of science',[25] both in emphasizing the role of the imagination when reviewing his basic principles and in illustrating the working of these principles by reference to the history of astronomy. Thus, for example, when speaking of the introduction of the ingenious 'equalizing circle' in the system of eccentric spheres, he noted that 'Nothing can more evidently show, how much the repose and tranquillity of the imagination is the ultimate end of philosophy' (Astronomy, IV. 13) than this device, and later commented on the ease with which 'the learned give up the evidence of their senses to preserve the coherence of the ideas of their imagination' (IV. 35). In the same way, he emphasized the pleasure to be derived from simplicity, order, coherence, and indicated that because men find beauty to be a source of pleasure, then they may unwittingly give the products of the intellect a form which satisfies purely aesthetic criteria.[26] Hence the Newtonian

[25] *The Subjective Side of Science*, by I.I. Mitroff (1974), see especially chapter 7, 'Objectivity in Science'.

[26] In the Imitative Arts, II. 30, Smith likened the pleasure to be derived from the contemplation of a great system of thought to that acquired from listening to a 'well composed concerto of instrumental music' and remarked that: 'In the contemplation of that immense variety of agreeable and melodious sounds, arranged and digested, both in their coincidence and in their succession, into so complete and regular a system, the mind in reality enjoys not only a very great sensual, but a very high intellectual, pleasure, not unlike that which it derives from the contemplation of a great system in any other science.'

'method' as described in the *Lectures on Rhetoric and Belles Lettres* may be used *because* it is 'more ingenious and for that reason more engaging' than any other. In the same vein it is interesting to note that Smith should have referred to a *propensity*, natural to all men, 'to account for all appearances from as few principles as possible' (TMS VII. ii. 2. 14).

It was also in this connection that he recognized the importance of analogy in suggesting that philosophers, in attempting to explain unusual 'appearances', often did so in terms of knowledge gained in unrelated fields.[27] In this way Smith suggested that reasoning by analogy might affect the nature of the work done, in the manner of the Pythagoreans who first studied arithmetic and then explained 'all things by the properties of numbers' — or the modern physician who 'lately gave a system of moral philosophy upon the principles of his own art' (Astronomy, II. 12). 'In the same manner also, others have written parallels of painting and poetry, of poetry and music, of music and architecture, of beauty and virtue, of all the fine arts; systems which have universally owed their origin to the lucubrations of those who were acquainted with the one art, but ignorant of the other.' Indeed, Smith went further in noting that in some cases the analogy chosen could become not just a source of 'ingenious similitudes' but even 'the great hinge upon which every thing turned' (ibid.).

This in turn leads on to the discussion of another side of the problem, again illustrated by the Astronomy, namely that different types of philosopher may produce conflicting accounts of the same thing, without any real possibility of communication. Thus Smith noted that at a certain stage of development the Cartesian system 'might continue to amuse the learned in other sciences, but could no longer satisfy those that were skilled in Astronomy' (IV. 67); that the Copernican system had been adopted by astronomers even though inconsistent with the laws of physics as then known (IV. 35); that

---

[27] Cf. *Turgot*, ed. Meek, 46: 'The senses constitute the unique source of our ideas: the whole power of our mental faculties is restricted to combining the ideas which they have received from the senses: hardly even can they form combinations of ideas of which the senses do not provide them with a model. Hence that almost irresistible tendency to judge of what one does not know by what one knows; hence those delusive analogies to which the first men in their immaturity abandoned themselves with such little thought. . . .'

the system of eccentric spheres had been accepted by astronomers and mathematicians, but not by philosophers in general:
'Each party of them too, had . . . completed their peculiar
system or theory of the universe, and no human consideration
could then have induced them to give up any part of it'
(IV. 18). As this implies, there may be a certain unwillingness
to accept ideas formulated in a particular way, and even
resistance to the reception of new ones as a result of certain
'prejudices'. Some of these are obvious: for example, the
'natural prejudices of the imagination' (IV. 52) which partly
explained the original resistance to the idea of a moving earth.
Others are more complex, especially those which Smith
described as prejudices of education.[28] For example, Smith
pointed out that resistance to the acceptance of Copernican
ideas was partly explained by the 'Peripatetic Philosophy, the
only philosophy then known in the world' (IV. 38), and
added, with reference to the system as a whole, that 'When it
appeared in the world, it was almost universally disapproved
of, by the learned as well as by the ignorant. The natural
prejudices of sense, confirmed by education, prevailed too
much with both, to allow them to give it a fair examination
(IV. 35). In the same way, the immediate followers of
Copernicus were held to have faced objections which were
'necessarily connected with that way of conceiving things,
which then prevailed universally in the learned world' (IV. 39).

Smith also noted the constraint on the development of new
knowledge represented by reverence for the past (IV. 20),
and made a good deal of national prejudice in the *Letter to
the Authors of the Edinburgh Review*, observing that the
attachment of French philosophers to the system of Descartes
had for a time 'retarded and incumbered the real advance-
ment of the science of nature' (§ 5).

All of these points relate to the role of the subjective in
science and suggest difficulties with regard to both the formulation and the communication of ideas. It is therefore particularly interesting to observe, as a matter of fact, that points

---

[28] Cf. Hume, *Treatise*, I. iii. x. 1: 'But though education be disclaimed by philosophy, as a fallacious ground of assent to any opinion, it prevails nevertheless in
the world, and is the cause why all systems are apt to be rejected at first as new
and unusual.'

such as those made by Smith have often been 'confirmed' by those whose business it has been to examine the *behaviour* of philosophers (in Smith's sense of the term).[29] To go no further than the recent past, it is a striking fact that one evaluation of the scientific contribution of the Apollo Moon Missions should have reached the conclusion that 'Science is not the totally rational enterprise that we have believed it to be' — a reference not to the investment involved but to the variety of ways in which a group of scientists interpreted a common body of evidence and the conflicts that developed in consequence.[30] It is equally striking that T.S. Kuhn's work on scientific revolutions should also have emphasized the problems of communication which exist (Smith's 'prejudices of education'), and that he should have explained the development of ideas in terms of systems of thought whose ultimate fate was self-destruction. It is also noteworthy that another writer interested in a branch of applied mathematics (such 'favourable subjects for theoretical history') should have reached conclusions on the basis of developments in the 1930s which are, in appearance, even closer to Smith's than those of Kuhn. In his *Years of High Theory*, G.L.S. Shackle drew attention to the thinker's search for 'consistency, coherence, order', and while noting that 'Theoretical advance can spring only from theoretical crises' also confirmed that the 'scientist's ultimate aim is to see everything as an illustration of a very few basic principles incapable of further unification'. There is an even more dramatic parallel in the following statement, which could well serve as a summary of Smith's whole thesis:

The chief service rendered by a theory is the setting of minds at rest. So long as we have a satisfying conceptual structure, a model or a taxonomy which provides for the filing of all facts in a scheme of order, we are absolved from the tiresome labour of thought, and the uneasy consciousness of mystery and a threatening unknown ... Theory serves deep needs of the human spirit: it subordinates nature to man, imposes a beautiful simplicity on the unbearable multiplicity of fact, gives comfort

[29] It is for example one of the themes of Israel Scheffler's study, *Science and Subjectivity*, that the orthodox or 'standard view' of science is 'coming increasingly under fundamental attack' (p.7).

[30] 'On Evaluating the Scientific Contribution of the Apollo Moon Missions via Information Theory: A Study of the Scientist–Scientist Relationship', I.I. Mitroff and R.O. Mason, *Management Science* 20, (1974).

in the face of the unknown and the unexperienced, stops the teasing of mystery and doubt which, though salutary and life-preserving, is uncomfortable, so that we seek by theory to sort out the justified from the unjustified fear. Theories by their nature and purpose, their role of administering to 'a good state of mind', are things to be held and cherished. Theories are altered or discarded only when they fail us.[31]

But perhaps the most striking parallel is with Karl Popper's *Logic of Scientific Discovery* (1959, 2nd edn. 1972), in so far as he emphasized the importance of psychological elements and rejected the role commonly ascribed to the 'legendary method' of science; the 'myth of a scientific method that starts from observation and experiment and then proceeds to theories' (p.279). Smith's emphasis on the principles which lead and direct philosophical enquiries may also seem to imply that the Newtonian method as described by MacLaurin cannot explain the *origin* of theories, even if Smith does not suggest that the techniques of the experimental method are inconsistent with their subsequent development.[32]

Points such as these may lend some support to Smith's assessment of the principles of human nature and to his belief that these principles were constant through time. It was of course, this belief that made it possible to conceive of the moral sciences as being on a par with the natural, thus matching the achievements of Newton in this field. For Dugald Stewart, the application of this 'fundamental and leading idea' to the various branches of theoretical history was to become 'the peculiar glory of the latter half of the eighteenth century, and forms a characteristic feature in its philosophy'.[33] What Smith does is to leave the reader of these essays in some doubt as to wherein exactly that glory is to be found: in a contribution to knowledge or to the composure of the imagination, or both.

In the same vein, it should be observed that in reviewing the principles which lead and direct philosophical enquiries Smith may have revealed a great deal as to his own drives as a thinker. In this respect his marked predilection for systematic argument may be particularly significant in that this feature may be found in all his major works — ethics, jurisprudence, and economics, not to mention the Astronomy itself.

---

[31] *The Years of High Theory* (1967), 288–9.
[32] See above, chapter 1, 10.   [33] *Works*, ed. Hamilton (1854), i. 70.

3

Moral Philosophy and Civil Society*

Smith's work on moral philosophy has a great deal in common with that of other members of the Scottish School[1] and especially with Hutcheson and Hume, both men for whom he had a profound and genuine admiration. We have already noticed Smith's description of his teacher as the 'never to be forgotten' Hutcheson and it is well known that he regarded Hume as 'by far the most illustrious philosopher and historian of the present age' (WN V.i.g.3). The three have much in common, in respect of methodology, their interest in human nature, and in the attempt which each made to elucidate the features of those bonds which make life in society possible. In what follows some attempt will be made to comment on the latter question, beginning with a brief discussion of Smith's relationships with his predecessors.

I

In Part VII of the *Theory of Moral Sentiments* Smith commented at length on the work of other thinkers who had addressed themselves to the two main questions which he

---

* This section comprises a wholly reworked version of a shorter argument which made section 2 of the introduction to Books I–III of the *Wealth of Nations* (Pelican Classics, Harmondsworth 1970, 2nd edn. 1974).

[1] Commentaries which the present writer has found most helpful include: Glen Morrow, *The Ethical and Economic Theories of Adam Smith* (Cornell Studies in Philosophy, No. 13) and the same author's 'Adam Smith: Moralist and Philosopher', in *Adam Smith, 1776–1926* (1928); A.L. Macfie, *The Individual in Society* (1967); Dugald Stewart's Biographical Memoir, section 2, and T.D. Campbell, *Adam Smith's Science of Morals* (1971). There is now also J.R. Lindgren, *The Social Philosophy of Adam Smith* (1973) and Vernard Foley, *The Social Physics of Adam Smith* (1977). James McCosh's *Scottish Philosophy* (1875) remains a helpful commentary on the School as a whole. The introduction to the Glasgow edition of the *Theory of Moral Sentiments*, ed. D.D. Raphael and A.L. Macfie (1976), has valuable sections on the influence of Stoic philosophy and on Smith's relation to contemporary thinkers.

considered to fall within the proper province of the moral philosopher:

First, wherein does virtue consist? Or what is the tone of temper, and tenour of conduct, which constitutes the excellent and praise-worthy character, the character which is the natural object of esteem, honour, and approbation? And, secondly, by what power or faculty in the mind is it, that this character, whatever it be, is recommended to us? Or in other words, how and by what means does it come to pass, that the mind prefers one tenour of conduct to another, denominates the one right and the other wrong; considers the one as the object of approbation, honour, and reward, and the other of blame, censure, and punishment? (TMS VII. i. 2).

In each case, Smith showed that a number of authors had attained some part of the truth, while rejecting other features of their work — a characteristic of his commentary which suggests that he set out to resolve the 'jarring and discordant' appearances which the different philosphical traditions seemed to present, and that his own work had a synthetic character at least to some extent. We may take the two questions in turn.

In dealing with the first question, Smith suggested that all previous systems of moral philosophy could be placed within three broad categories (itself an interesting example of his capacity for classification) according as they found virtue to consist in *propriety, prudence*, or *benevolence*: 'Besides these three, it is scarce possible to imagine that any other account can be given of the nature of virtue' (VII. ii. 4).

By *propriety* Smith means something very like a kind of balance, and groups under this head all those systems which found virtue to consist not in the exercise of any particular 'affection' or disposition 'but in the proper government and direction of all our affections, which may be either virtuous or vicious according to the objects which they pursue, and the degree of vehemence with which they pursue them' (VII. ii. 1).

Plato, Aristotle, and Zeno are cited as the main classical examples; Clarke, Woollaston, and particularly Shaftesbury[2] as the most important modern authors.

[2] Samuel Clarke, *Discourse of Natural Religion* (7th edn., 1728); William Wollaston, *Religion of Nature Delineated* (1724); Anthony Ashley Cooper, 3rd Earl of Shaftesbury, *Inquiry Concerning Virtue*, in *Characteristics of Men, Manners, Opinions, Times*, ii (1711).

However, although Smith did agree that propriety is an essential ingredient in every virtuous action, he also felt that it is not always the sole ingredient (VII. ii. 1. 50). Moreover, the existing systems were rejected on the ground that they did not provide 'any precise or distinct measure by which this fitness or propriety of affection can be ascertained or judged of' (VII. ii. 1. 49), and because in emphasizing the importance of a balance of expression, they gave undue weight to the 'awful' and respectable virtues, such as self-command, at the expense of milder, but no less important virtues, such as benevolence.

The chief representative of the second system, that which found virtue in *prudence*, is Epicurus, who, Smith suggests, rested his case on two main propositions: first, that in 'ease of body . . . and in security or tranquillity of mind, consisted . . . the most perfect state of human nature' (VII. ii. 2. 7) and, second, that bodily pleasure and pain were the sole ultimate objects of natural desire or aversion. In this system temperance can be seen as prudence with regard to pleasure, and justice as prudence with regard to tranquillity — a state of mind which is attainable only in so far as our actions do not cause others to regard us with indignation. Smith accepted that 'Our success or disappointment in our undertakings must very much depend upon the good or bad opinion which is commonly entertained of us, and upon the general disposition of those we live with, either to assist or to oppose us' (VII. ii. 2. 13). But at the same time he rejected the general tenor of the approach partly on the ground that it too gave too little emphasis to the 'soft and amiable' virtues, in celebrating the importance of 'the habits of caution, vigilance and sobriety'. Smith also rejected an argument which seemed to suggest that an action could only be regarded as virtuous in so far as it contributes to some end, thus echoing the earlier criticism (TMS IV) of Hume's alleged reliance on utility as the basis of approbation.

The third system was that which found virtue in *benevolence*. Here the main classical examples were the Eclectics; the more important modern authorities being Ralph Cudworth, and especially Francis Hutcheson, who, 'of all the patrons of this system, ancient or modern . . . was undoubtedly, beyond

all comparison, the most acute, the most distinct, the most philosophical, and what is of the greatest consequence of all, the soberest and most judicious' (VII. ii. 3. 3).[3] Smith clearly recognized that benevolence was a virtue, while pointing out that the defect of Hutcheson's account lay in its emphasis on the amiable virtues and in the corresponding neglect of the awful and respectable virtue of self-command (featured by the proponents of propriety) and of the inferior virtues of prudence, and temperance (as noted by Epicurus and his followers). But Smith's main objection was to Hutcheson's assertion that self-love 'was a principle which could never be virtuous in any degree or in any direction' (VII. ii. 3. 12). Against this, Smith argued that a regard 'to our own private happiness and interest . . . appear upon many occasions very laudable principles of action' (VII. ii. 3. 16), adding:

whatever may be the case with the Deity, so imperfect a creature as man, the support of whose existence requires so many things external to him, must often act from many other motives. The condition of human nature were peculiarly hard, if those affections, which, by the very nature of our being, ought frequently to influence our conduct, could upon no occasion appear virtuous, or deserve esteem and commendation from any body (VII. ii. 3. 18).[4]

In dealing with the second major question, Smith once again concentrated on three main groups: namely, those who approached the study of the 'means by which' judgements are formed by emphasizing the importance of self-love, reason, or sentiment. As in the previous case, a threefold classification is used, although here there is one important difference: in dealing with the initial problem Smith considered three distinct approaches to the definition of virtue, whereas in the second he deals with different theories which follow each other in sequence; a sequence which has something of a dialectical character reminiscent of the analysis of the Astronomy.

[3] Ralph Cudworth, *A Treatise Concerning Eternal and Immutable Morality* (1731); Francis Hutcheson, *Inquiry Concerning Moral Good and Evil*, III. i, ed. D.D. Raphael, *British Moralists 1650–1800* (1969), 328.

[4] It should be noted however that Hutcheson only argued that self-interested activities did not command *moral* approbation as distinct from approval — a theme which is developed at some length in his *System of Moral Philosophy* (1755), Book I, chapter 8. See below, 110n.

To begin with, Hobbes is described as representative of the first 'school' and alleged to have adopted the position that 'The very ideas of laudable and blamable, ought to be the same with those of obedience and disobedience' (VII. iii. 2. 1). Cudworth is cited as representative of the second school, that is, as one of those who found the origin of judgement in *reason*, and as the critic of writers, such as Hobbes, who 'affirm justice and injustice to be only by law and not by nature'. Smith accepted Cudworth's contention that law could not be the source of the distinction between right and wrong, while rejecting the view that our *first* perceptions can be attributed to reason. As Smith noted: 'If virtue . . . in every particular instance, necessarily pleases for its own sake, and if vice as certainly displeases the mind, it cannot be reason, but immediate sense and feeling, which . . . reconciles us to the one, and alienates us from the other' (VII. iii. 2. 7).

In this Smith followed the lead of Hutcheson, who had the merit, as he was quick to admit, 'of being the first who distinguished with any degree of precision in what respect all moral distinctions may be said to arise from reason, and in what respect they are founded upon immediate sense and feeling' (VII. iii. 2. 9). In fact Hutcheson placed most stress on the latter, ascribing our capacity to distinguish between right and wrong to a special (internal) sense, the moral sense, which was held to be analogous to (external) senses such as sight, sound, or taste. To this Hutcheson added a sense of honour and of shame, a public sense, and a sympathetic sense, 'by which, when we apprehend the state of others, our hearts naturally have a fellow feeling with them'.[5] Smith thoroughly approved of Hutcheson's emphasis on immediate sense and feeling in regard to moral judgement, to the extent of stating that

In his illustrations upon the moral sense he has explained this so fully, and, in my opinion, so unanswerably, that, if any controversy is still kept up about this subject, I can impute it to nothing, but either to inattention to what that gentleman has written, or to a superstitious attachment to certain forms of expression, a weakness not very uncommon among the learned (ibid.).

[5] *System of Moral Philosophy*, vol. i, p.19. See Generally Book I, chapters 2 and 3.

Yet at the same time Smith rejected the basis of Hutcheson's explanation of the moral sentiments:

Against every account of the principle of approbation, which makes it depend upon a peculiar sentiment, distinct from every other, I would object; that it is strange that this sentiment, which Providence undoubtedly intended to be the governing principle of human nature, should hitherto have been so little taken notice of, as not to have got a name in any language. The word moral sense is of very late formation, and cannot yet be considered as making part of the English tongue (VII. iii. 3. 15).

Hume (whose doctrines are reviewed in TMS IV) was in broad agreement with Hutcheson at least to the extent of agreeing with the latter that 'Morality, according to your Opinion as well as mine, is determin'd merely by Sentiment.[6] At the same time Hume comes even closer to the position later adopted by Smith in suggesting that we must begin with 'the nature and force of sympathy';[7] a force which allows the observer to approve or disapprove, for example, of situations which contribute to feelings of pleasure or pain as expressed by another party. We may derive some satisfaction from the pleasure manifested by the possessor of an object: 'Here the object . . . pleases only by its tendency to produce a certain effect. That effect is the pleasure or advantage of some other person. Now, the pleasure of a stranger for whom we have no friendship, pleases us only by sympathy.'[8] Hume went on to argue that the same principle (utility) explains our feelings with regard to beauty, as well as morals, enabling Smith to conclude that 'No qualities of the mind, he observes, are approved of as virtuous, but such as are useful or agreeable either to the person himself or to others; and no qualities are disapproved of as vicious but such as have a contrary tendency' (IV. 2. 3).

In fact, there was a good deal in Hume's position which Smith could accept, such as his emphasis on sentiment rather than reason and (again in the manner of Hutcheson) the importance which he ascribed to sympathy and fellow-feeling.

[6] Quoted in Norman Kemp Smith, *The Philosophy of David Hume* (1966), 20. There is an interesting account of the influence of Hutcheson on Hume at pp. 12–20 and in chapter 2 of this work.
[7] *A Treatise of Human Nature*, III. i. 7.
[8] Ibid. III. i. 8.

Smith also agreed that perception of the 'utility' of an action added a 'new beauty' to it, and accepted Hume's argument that moral judgement was typically disinterested.

But Smith rejected Hume's reliance on utility as the *initial* ground of approval, partly on the ground that 'the sentiment of approbation always involves in it a sense of propriety quite distinct from the perception of utility' (IV. 2. 5).

In fact, Smith's achievement was to produce a system of thought which answered both of the major questions with which moral philosophy was concerned, by taking a route which differed from that chosen by his contemporaries, even if it did follow the same general direction. In handling the question as to the means by which the mind forms judgements concerning what is fit to be done or to be avoided, Smith greatly developed mechanisms, already mentioned by Hutcheson and Hume, which involved the use of sympathy, reason, imagination, and the concept of the observer or spectator. At the same time, he succeeded in producing an argument which gave due weight to the amiable virtues, such as benevolence, to the 'awful' virtues such as self-command, and to the 'inferior' virtues such as prudence — thus including certain elements from each of the three traditions which he had initially isolated. It may be of more importance to note that Smith did so in the context of a discussion which was designed to explain the manner in which men erect effective barriers against their own passions, by natural, as distinct from artificial, means — thus bringing us to the main theme of this chapter.[9]

II

Smith's own theory might well be regarded as an extensive commentary on the text: 'There is no virtue without propriety, and wherever there is propriety some degree of approbation is due. But ... though propriety is an essential ingredient in every virtuous action, it is not always the sole ingredient' (TMS VII. ii. 1. 50). In expounding on this text, Smith first explains what is meant by the concept of propriety before going on to draw a distinction between propriety and virtue,

---

[9] Cf. M.A. Goldberg, *Smollett and the Scottish School* (1959), 11–13.

and propriety and merit. In fulfilling these tasks he first considers actions or expressions of feeling which do not have consequences for others, before going on to examine the more complex case where a judgement has to be formed with regard both to the actions of the agent and the reactions of the subject. We may take these in turn.

On Smith's argument, the process by which we distinguish between objects of approval or disapproval involves a complex of abilities and propensities which include sympathy, imagination, reason, and reflection. To begin with, he stated that man is possessed of a certain 'fellow-feeling': 'How selfish soever man may be supposed, there are evidently some principles in his nature, which interest him in the fortune of others, and render their happiness necessary to him, though he derives nothing from it except the pleasure of seeing it' (TMS I. i. 1. 1). This fellow-feeling, or interest in the fortune of others, permits us to feel joy or sorrow as it were on their behalf, and to form a judgement as to whether or not the circumstances faced by an individual contribute to a state of pleasure or of pain. An expression of sympathy (broadly defined) for another person thus involves an act of reflection and imagination on the part of the observer or spectator, in the sense that we can only form a judgement with respect to the situation faced by another person 'by changing places in the fancy' with him.

The question of *propriety* becomes relevant when we go beyond the consideration of the *circumstances* facing the subject, to examine the extent to which his actions or 'affections' (i.e. expressions of feeling) are appropriate to the conditions prevailing or to the objects which they seek to attain. Smith thus defined propriety or impropriety as consisting in 'the suitableness or unsuitableness, in the proportion or disproportion which the affection seems to bear to the cause or object which excites it' (I. i. 3. 6).

Given the principles so far established, it follows that where the spectator of another man's conduct seeks to form an opinion as to its propriety, he must 'bring home to himself' both the circumstances *and* the 'affections' of the person judged. As before, Smith argued that such a judgement on the part of the spectator must involve an effort of the imagin-

ation, since 'When we judge in this manner of any affection, as proportioned or disproportioned to the cause which excites it, it is scarce possible that we should make use of any other rule or canon but the correspondent affection in ourselves' (I. i. 3. 9). The same basic principles also apply when we seek to form an opinion with regard to the propriety of our *own* conduct, in that we do so by attempting to visualize the way in which the real or supposed spectator might react to it:

We can never survey our own sentiments and motives, we can never form any judgment concerning them; unless we remove ourselves, as it were, from our own natural station, and endeavour to view them as at a certain distance from us. But we can do this in no other way than by endeavouring to view them with the eyes of other people, or as other people are likely to view them (III. i. 2).

Now this argument means that the actions of all men are judged by either the real or the supposed spectator of their conduct, and that 'When the original passions of the person principally concerned are in perfect concord with the sympathetic emotions of the spectator, they necessarily appear to this last just and proper' (I. i. 3. 1).

The argument in fact raises two distinct but connected problems, affecting the person judged and the person who judges. In the first place, it is evident that the spectator can only 'enter into' the situation of another to a limited degree; the problem being that we have 'no immediate experience of what other men feel'. As Smith pointed out: 'Mankind, though naturally sympathetic, never conceive, for what has befallen another, that degree of passion which naturally animates the person principally concerned' (I. i. 4. 7). It was in recognition of this point that Smith went on to argue that the *degree* to which the spectator can 'enter into' the feelings of the subject can involve a virtue — the 'soft and amiable' virtue of sensibility or humanity.

Secondly, it is evident that if the reactions of the spectator provide the means by which the conduct of others is judged, and if the spectator has no immediate experience of what other men feel, then it follows that an action which is considered to be 'proper' by the spectator must involve an element of restraint on the part of the agent. In other words, the person judged of can only attain the agreement, and thus the ap-

proval, of the spectator 'by lowering his passion to that pitch, in which the spectators are capable of going along with him. He must flatten, if I may be allowed to say so, the sharpness of its natural tone, in order to reduce it to harmony and concord with the emotions of those who are about him' (I. i. 4. 7).

It thus follows that before actions or expressions of feeling can be approved of by the spectator an element of restraint *must* be present; a certain mediocrity of expression with which Smith associated the 'awful and respectable' virtue of self-command.[10] In this way Smith made due allowance for both sets of virtues and in so doing illustrated what he meant by saying that propriety was an essential, but not the sole, ingredient of virtue. As he noted 'the virtues of sensibility and self-command are not apprehended to consist in the ordinary, but in the uncommon degrees of those qualities' (I. i. 5. 6). There is, in short, a considerable difference between 'those qualities and actions which deserve to be admired and celebrated, and those which simply deserve to be approved of' (I. i. 5. 7).

In cases of this kind, when we are determining the degree of blame or applause which seems due to any action, we very frequently make use of two different standards. The first is the idea of complete propriety and perfection ... The second is the idea of that degree of proximity or distance from this complete perfection, which the actions of the greater part of men commonly arrive at. Whatever goes beyond this degree, how far soever it may be removed from absolute perfection, seems to deserve applause; and whatever falls short of it, to deserve blame (I. i. 5. 9).

Smith went on to observe that the *point of propriety*, that is, 'the degree of any passion which the impartial spectator approves of, is differently situated in different passions'; and that the point of propriety stands high in the case of those passions where

the immediate feeling or sensation is more or less agreeable to the person principally concerned: and that, on the contrary, the passions which the spectator is least disposed to sympathize with, and in which,

[10] Ralph Anspach has recently emphasized the pleasure to be derived from 'role-switching' as described above and from the process of attaining a concordance of view between subject and observer. 'The Implications of the *Theory of Moral Sentiments* for Adam Smith's Economic Thought', *History of Political Economy*, 4 (1972).

upon that account, the point of propriety may be said to stand low, are those of which the immediate feeling or sensation is more or less disagreeable, or even painful, to the person principally concerned. This general rule, so far as I have been able to observe, admits not of a single exception (VI. iii. 14).

Thus, for example, the disposition 'to the affections which tend to unite men in society — to humanity, kindness, natural affections are more apt to offend by their defect than their excess', while 'The disposition to the affections which drive men from one another, and which tend, as it were, to break the bands of human society; the disposition to anger, hatred, envy, malice, revenge; is, on the contrary, much more apt to offend by its excess than by its defect' (VI. iii. 16).

The latter points serve to introduce the second side of Smith's account, namely, his interest not merely in the judgement of an action in relation to the 'cause or object which excites it' but also in relation to the end proposed or the effects produced. In this connection, Smith argued that the *merit* or *demerit* of an action would depend on the beneficial or hurtful effects which it tended to produce and that judgement in such cases would involve framing an opinion as to the propriety of the action of the agent and of the reaction of the subject. More specifically, Smith argued that our sense of the *merit* of an action 'seems to be a compounded sentiment, and to be made up of two distinct emotions; a direct sympathy with the sentiments of the agent, and an indirect sympathy with the gratitude of those who receive the benefit of his actions' (II. i. 5. 2). It then follows that 'In the same manner as our sense of the impropriety of conduct arises from a want of sympathy, or from a direct antipathy to the affections and motives of the agent, so our sense of its demerit arises from what I shall here . . . call an indirect sympathy with the resentment of the sufferer' (II. i. 5. 4). Smith emphasizes four points which derive from this argument.

First, that our estimate of the merit or demerit of an action must be linked to our understanding of the *motives* of the agent and not merely of its consequences. ('We do not . . . thoroughly and heartily sympathize with the gratitude of one man towards another, merely because this other has been the cause of his good fortune, unless he has been the cause of it

from motives which we entirely go along with.' II. i. 4. 1.) Nor, he points out, can we sympathize entirely with the resentment which one man feels for another 'unless he has been the cause of it from motives which we cannot enter into'.

Secondly, Smith argued that actions which are judged to have the quality of 'merit' dispose us to *reward*, by virtue of our fellow-feeling with both the agent and the subject.

But when to the hurtfulness of the action is joined the impropriety of the affection from whence it proceeds, when our heart rejects with abhorrence all fellow-feeling with the motives of the agent, we then heartily and entirely sympathize with the resentment of the sufferer. Such actions seem then to deserve, and, if I may say so, to call aloud for, a proportionable punishment; and we entirely enter into, and thereby approve of, that resentment which prompts to inflict it (II. i. 4. 4).

Thirdly, it is argued that 'the greater and more irreparable the evil that is done, the resentment of the sufferer runs naturally the higher; so does likewise the sympathetic indignation of the spectator' (II. ii. 2. 2). Hence loss of life arouses the highest degree of resentment, in those most immediately connected with the slain, followed by loss of liberty or property, which are followed in turn by breach of contract — on the ground that to 'be deprived of that which we are possessed of, is a greater evil than to be disappointed of what we have only the expectation' (ibid.).

Finally, Smith reminds us that resentment is 'one of the most ungovernable passions' of man's nature and that it is only approved of when 'properly humbled, and entirely brought down to the level of the sympathetic indignation of the spectator'. He added:

When indeed the animosity of the sufferer exceeds, as it almost always does, what we can go along with, as we cannot enter into it, we necessarily disapprove of it. We even disapprove of it more than we should of an equal excess of almost any other passion derived from the imagination. And this too violent resentment, instead of carrying us along with it, becomes itself the object of our resentment and indignation. We enter into the opposite resentment of the person who is the object of this unjust emotion, and who is in danger of suffering from it. Revenge, therefore, the excess of resentment, appears to be the most detestable of all the passions, and is the object of the horror and indignation of every body (II. i. 5. 8).

While the defect of this passion may be complained of, Smith seems to have believed that excess was the more likely, thus explaining the admiration extended to those who are capable of controlling such a 'rude' and frequently 'undisciplined' impulse.

III

It will be evident that Smith's argument is in large measure designed to explain the manner in which we form judgements as to the propriety or merit of actions taken by ourselves or others, and that such judgements always have a 'social' reference. Or, as Smith put it:

Were it possible that a human creature could grow up to manhood in some solitary place, without any communication with his own species, he could no more think of his own character, of the propriety or demerit of his own sentiments and conduct, of the beauty or deformity of his own mind, than of the beauty or deformity of his own face. . . . Bring him into society, and he is immediately provided with the mirror which he wanted before (TMS III. 1. 3).

The basic point is that men react to the images thus presented in a way which suggests that they are important to them: it is for this reason that we seek a certain mediocrity of expression in our affections and to conform to the different 'points of propriety' which are associated with the 'social' and 'unsocial' passions. As Smith said, 'Without the restraint which this principle imposes, every passion would, upon most occasions, rush headlong, if I may say so, to its own gratification' (VI. concl. 2). The suggestion then is that men regard the opinion of their fellows as important; a point which Smith made explicit in remarking that

Nature, when she formed man for society, endowed him with an original desire to please, and an original aversion to offend his brethren. She taught him to feel pleasure in their favourable, and pain in their unfavourable regard. She rendered their approbation most flattering and most agreeable to him for its own sake; and their disapprobation most mortifying and most offensive (III. 2. 6).

Yet at the same time, Smith observed that this general disposition may be insufficient of itself to secure adequate levels of control over our passions or expressions of feeling, for reasons which are connected with the basic mechanisms

by virtue of which judgements are formed, namely, the actual or supposed spectators of our conduct, who are required to be at once impartial and well informed.[11]

In the case of the actual spectator it is evident that the accuracy of judgement must be a function of the information available, and that information with respect to the feelings of a person external to him can never be complete. Smith's point is of course that we can generally acquire a level of information which is at least sufficient to permit us to arrive at an informed judgement, when contemplating the observed circumstances of an individual or his reaction to them, and that this is all that is necessary. But at the same time there is evidently one area where it is particularly difficult to get access to the necessary information, namely, that which relates to the *motives* which prompt a person to act in a particular way. This is obviously an important problem, given Smith's contention that knowledge of motive is essential to the decision as to whether or not an action partakes of any degree of merit or demerit. Smith formally recognized the point in the discussion of justice when noting that men typically judge 'by the event and not by the design', observing that in this lay some advantage: 'That necessary rule of justice ... that men in this life are liable to punishment for their actions only, not for their designs and intentions, is founded upon this salutary and useful irregularity in human sentiments concerning merit or demerit, which at first sight appears so absurd and unaccountable' (II. iii. 3. 2). Yet at the same time it is evident that while this 'irregularity' may be useful in one sense, in another it may have a contrary tendency in that it constitutes a 'great discouragement' to virtue. The problem thus raised was in fact solved in Smith's model by the use of an additional hypothesis, namely, that men desire not only the approval of their fellows but also to be worthy of that approval, or, as Smith expressed it:

this desire of the approbation, and this aversion to the disapprobation of his brethren, would not alone have rendered him fit for that society for which he was made. Nature, accordingly, has endowed him, not only with a desire of being approved of, but with a desire of being what

---

[11] For specialized comment on the 'spectator' concept, see especially the articles by T.D. Campbell and D.D. Raphael in *Essays on Adam Smith*.

ought to be approved of; or of being what he himself approves of in other men. The first desire could only have made him wish to appear to be fit for society. The second was necessary in order to render him anxious to be really fit (III. 2. 7).

Hence the importance in Smith's theory of the 'supposed' or 'ideal' spectator of our own conduct (that is, that spectator who is always well-informed with regard to our own motives), and his argument that we are really subject to two sources of judgement — that of the 'man without' and that of 'the man within'. 'The jurisdiction of the man without, is founded altogether in the desire of actual praise, and in the aversion to actual blame. The jurisdiction of the man within, is founded altogether in the desire of praise-worthiness, and in the aversion to blame-worthiness' (III. 2. 32). It is not then the 'soft power of humanity' which ensures that we impose some control over our own passions or activities, but 'reason, principle, conscience, the inhabitant of the breast, the man within, the great judge and arbiter of our conduct' (III. 3.4). It is moreover the expected judgement of the ideal spectator which supports us in the path of virtue when our just rewards are denied us, or our title to them unknown. Thus:

The man who is conscious to himself that he has exactly observed those measures of conduct which experience informs him are generally agreeable, reflects with satisfaction on the propriety of his own behaviour. . . . He looks back upon every part of it with pleasure and approbation, and though mankind should never be acquainted with what he has done, he regards himself, not so much according to the light in which they actually regard him, as according to that in which they would regard him if they were better informed (III. 2. 5).

While this argument seems to suggest that the judgement of the man within is independent of the man without, Smith took notice of two qualifications to the argument. First, he observed that the judgements of the man within could be 'so much shaken' in their steadiness and firmness 'that their natural effect, in securing the tranquillity of the mind, is frequently in a great measure destroyed' (III. 2. 32). Secondly, he noted that the judgement of the man within, 'the abstract and ideal spectator of our sentiments and conduct, requires often to be awakened and put in mind of his duty, by the presence of the real spectator' (III. 3. 38).

The second side of Smith's problem arises from the fact that man is presented as an active, self-regarding being. Interestingly enough, Smith often develops this theme within the context of broadly 'economic' aspirations,[12] while reminding the reader that self-interested activities often have a 'social' reference. As he noted, the 'advantages ... we propose by that great purpose of human life which we call bettering our condition' are to be 'observed, to be attended to, to be taken notice of with sympathy, complacency, and approbation' (I. iii. 2. 1). Earlier he had observed that 'it is chiefly from this regard to the sentiments of mankind, that we pursue riches and avoid poverty. For to what purpose is all the toil and bustle of this world? what is the end of avarice and ambition, of the pursuit of wealth, of power, and preheminence?' (ibid.) Perhaps with Hutcheson in mind, Smith positively warmed to his subject in remarking that a person appears 'mean-spirited' who does not pursue 'the more extraordinary and important objects of self-interest' with 'some degree of earnestness', in referring to those great objects of which the loss or acquisition 'quite changes the rank of the person', and to ambition as a 'passion, which when it keeps within the bounds of prudence and justice, is always admired in the world, and has even sometimes a certain irregular greatness, which dazzles the imagination' (III. 6. 7).

In fact Smith traced all this to a further 'irregularity' in our moral sentiments as illustrated by the fact that we are more disposed to sympathize with joy than with sorrow, thus explaining the observed tendency 'to make parade of our riches, and conceal our poverty' (I. iii. 2. 1). At the same time, Smith noted that this 'irregularity' brought with it certain advantages to society at large, if not necessarily to the individual 'whom heaven in its anger has visited with ambition' (IV. i. 8). First, he noted that the development of riches, together with man's disposition to admire those who possess the imagined conveniences which possession brings, contributes to social order and to the stability of authority: 'Upon this disposition of mankind, to go along with all the passions

---

[12] There is a useful treatment of this subject in Anspach, op. cit. 188–202.

of the rich and the powerful, is founded the distinction of ranks, and the order of society' (I. iii. 2. 3). Secondly, it is suggested that the pursuit of riches, even if it does not generate the happiness expected, necessarily involves the development of productive forces. Smith went on:

it is well that nature imposes upon us in this manner. It is this deception which rouses and keeps in continual motion the industry of mankind. It is this which first prompted them to cultivate the ground, to build houses, to found cities and commonwealths, and to invent and improve all the sciences and arts, which ennoble and embellish human life; which have entirely changed the whole face of the globe (IV. i. 10).

Thirdly, Smith observed that the pursuit of fortune provides the rich with the means of gratification, while at the same time giving employment to the poor and hence an opportunity to better their condition.

though they mean only their own conveniency, though the sole end which they propose from the labours of all the thousands whom they employ, be the gratification of their own vain and insatiable desires, they divide with the poor the produce of all their improvements. They are led by an invisible hand to make nearly the same distribution of the necessaries of life, which would have been made, had the earth been divided into equal portions among all its inhabitants, and thus without intending it, without knowing it, advance the interest of the society, and afford means to the multiplication of the species (ibid.).

Yet at the same time, Smith recognized that the pursuit and acquisition of riches could bring with them important sources of dispute between men. As he drily remarked, 'place, that great object which divides the wives of aldermen, is the end of half the labours of human life; and is the cause of all the tumult and bustle, all the rapine and injustice, which avarice and ambition have introduced into this world' (I. iii. 2. 8).

The basic problem which arises is that we may upon particular occasions fail to judge our own actions with the required degree of impartiality, even where we have the necessary information. As Smith put it:

There are two different occasions upon which we examine our own conduct, and endeavour to view it in the light in which the impartial spectator would view it: first, when we are about to act; and secondly, after we have acted. Our views are apt to be very partial in both cases; but they are apt to be most partial when it is of most importance that they should be otherwise (III. 4. 2).

First, 'When we are about to act, the eagerness of passion will seldom allow us to consider what we are doing, with the candour of an indifferent person' (III. 4. 3). Secondly, Smith noted that while we are likely to be able to judge our own actions in a clearer light after the event, this is of little benefit to those who may suffer from them, and that even here 'It is so disagreeable to think ill of ourselves, that we often purposely turn away our view from those circumstances which might render that judgment unfavourable' (III. 4. 4). This argument would thus seem to suggest that there will be many occasions on which men are unlikely to be able to form accurate judgements with respect to their own activities, and that they would therefore be unlikely to be able to impose on themselves the kind of restraint which the 'inhabitant within the breast' would normally recommend. As Smith remarked, in a passage which is likely to have attracted the attention of Robert Burns:

This self-deceit, this fatal weakness of mankind, is the source of half the disorders of human life. If we saw ourselves in the light in which others see us, or in which they would see us if they knew all, a reformation would generally be unavoidable. We could not otherwise endure the sight (III. 4. 6).[13]

In fact, Smith's solution to the logical problem thus raised involves no principle in addition to those already considered:

Nature . . . has not left this weakness, which is of so much importance, altogether without a remedy; nor has she abandoned us entirely to the delusions of self-love. Our continual observations upon the conduct of others, insensibly lead us to form to ourselves certain general rules concerning what is fit and proper either to be done or to be avoided (III. 4. 7).

In short, Smith suggests that our capacity to form judgements in particular cases permits us to frame general rules by the process of induction — thus formally admitting *reason* to the discussion of morality:

[13] O wad some Power the giftie gie us
To see oursels as ithers see us!
It wad frae mony a blunder free us,
 An' foolish notion;
What airs in dress an' gait wad lea'e us,
An' ev'n devotion! ('To a Louse.')

It is thus that the general rules of morality are formed. They are ultimately founded upon experience of what, in particular instances, our moral faculties, our natural sense of merit and propriety, approve, or disapprove of. We do not originally approve or condemn particular actions; because, upon examination, they appear to be agreeable or inconsistent with a certain general rule. The general rule, on the contrary, is formed, by finding from experience, that all actions of a certain kind, or circumstanced in a certain manner, are approved or disapproved of (III. 4. 8).

Reason, it will be observed, is not the original source of the distinction between what is fit and proper to be done or to be avoided but merely the means of elucidating general principles from a number of particular judgements, each one of which initially depends on the exercise of our moral sentiments.

These general principles or rules become, in turn, yardsticks against which we can judge our own conduct under all circumstances and are thus of 'great use in correcting the misrepresentations of self-love concerning what is fit and proper to be done in our particular situation' (III. 4. 12). Indeed, Smith went to far as to argue that without a regard to general rules of behaviour, 'there is no man whose conduct can be much depended upon' (III. 5. 2).

Given that general rules may be formulated in the way described, Smith went on to argue that men would be disposed to obey them for two reasons. First, men will typically obey the general rules of conduct because they wish to be praiseworthy. The voice which commands obedience is that of conscience or duty: 'a principle of the greatest consequence in human life, and the only principle by which the bulk of mankind are capable of directing their actions' (III. 5. 1).

Secondly, it is suggested that our disposition to obey is 'still further enhanced by an opinion which is first impressed by nature, and afterwards confirmed by reasoning and philosophy, that those important rules of morality are the commands and laws of the Deity, who will finally reward the obedient, and punish the transgressors of their duty' (III. 5. 3). Smith added that

The sense of propriety too is here well supported by the strongest motives of self-interest. The idea that, however we may escape the observation of man, or be placed above the reach of human punishment, yet we are always acting under the eye, and exposed to the punishment

of God ... is a motive capable of restraining the most headstrong passions (III. 5. 12).

It is in this way and for these reasons that men impose on themselves some degree of control over their passions. The general rules or accepted standards of behaviour represent a constant reminder of what we imagine the impartial spectator would approve or disapprove of on particular occasions. Once again the result is benefit to society at large; a benefit which also exposes at least one part of the Divine (?) Plan in that 'by acting according to the dictates of our moral faculties, we necessarily pursue the most effectual means for promoting the happiness of mankind, and may therefore be said, in some sense, to co-operate with the Deity, and to advance as far as in our power the plan of Providence' (III. 5. 7).

In terms of the problem of social order and stability the most important of the rules of behaviour are those which relate to justice, especially given that man is an active being whose activities may well involve him in situations which may have hurtful consequences for others. It is thus that the individual

In the race for wealth, and honours, and preferments ... may run as hard as he can, and strain every nerve and every muscle, in order to outstrip all his competitors. But if he should justle, or throw down any of them, the indulgence of the spectators is entirely at an end. It is a violation of fair play, which they cannot admit of (II. ii. 2. 1).

The indulgence of the spectators fails of course as a result of their fellow-feeling for those who suffer the consequences of the action taken by a third party, leading, as we have seen, to the approval of punishment and to the support of those rules of conduct which involve condemnation of acts of injustice:

Men, though naturally sympathetic, feel so little for another, with whom they have no particular connexion, in comparison of what they feel for themselves; the misery of one, who is merely their fellow creature, is of so little importance to them in comparison even of a small conveniency of their own; they have it so much in their power to hurt him, and may have so many temptations to do so, that if this principle did not stand up within them in his defence, and overawe them into a respect for his innocence, they would, like wild beasts, be at all times ready to fly upon him; and a man would enter an assembly of men as he enters a den of lions (II. ii. 3. 4).

While it is suggested that in this way 'man, who can subsist only in society, was fitted by nature to that situation for which he was made' (II. ii. 3. 1), Smith added that the final condition required for social stability was a system of positive law, embodying our conception of the rules of justice, and administered by some system of government or magistracy:

As the violation of justice is what men will never submit to from one another, the public magistrate is under a necessity of employing the power of the commonwealth to enforce the practice of this virtue. Without this precaution, civil society would become a scene of bloodshed and disorder, every man revenging himself at his own hand whenever he fancied he was injured (VII. iv. 36).

IV

There are a number of points arising from the previous argument which are worth noting:

(1) There is undoubtedly a certain elegance and ingenuity about the argument of the *Theory of Moral Sentiments* which is nowhere more obvious than in the way in which Smith made allowance for certain features of the three main types of theory which he reviewed (that is, those which emphasized prudence, benevolence, and self-command). The same feature is evident in the way in which he developed concepts, often found in Hutcheson and Hume, when addressing himself to the question as to the way in which moral judgements are formed. But, undoubtedly, the best example is to be found in the structure of Smith's own argument. As we have seen, Smith initially considered the concepts of propriety and merit, leading to the development of the spectator thesis and to the proposition that men will typically conform to the judgement of the spectator because the opinions of their fellows are thought to be important. The problems which then emerge are that the judgement of the spectator must be well informed and impartial, with the first resolved by the introduction of the *ideal* spectator and the second by reference to general rules or standards of behaviour. The rules themselves emerge as the result of man's capacity to frame judgements in particular cases; they are obeyed because men are held to seek to be worthy of approval, while those which

relate to justice are buttressed by the approval of punishment. In this way Smith represents social order as a balance of opposed forces, where that balance, in the shape of general rules of conduct, is attained by natural as distinct from artificial means. Whatever may be thought of its content, and the argument is often very plausible, there can be little doubt that the model developed in the *Theory of Moral Sentiments* possesses a certain elegance and economy of expression.

(2) It will be observed that Smith frequently considers the problem of judgement at a 'micro' level; that is, he concerns himself with the way in which individual men behave and with their capacity as individuals to frame general rules of conduct. The problem is handled within the context of a social structure which Smith knew to be complex, as evidenced by his concern with the 'constitution' of a state, made up of a mass of smaller associations (including the family) each generating their own loyalties. This kind of situation is not inconsistent with certain variations in accepted standards of behaviour; a point which Smith in fact made in the *Wealth of Nations* when describing the behaviour of different income groups. As he noted:

In every civilized society, in every society where the distinction of ranks has once been completely established, there have been always two different schemes or systems of morality current at the same time; of which the one may be called the strict or austere; the other the liberal, or, if you will, the loose system. The former is generally admired and revered by the common people: The latter is commonly more esteemed and adopted by what are called people of fashion (WN V. i. g. 10).

There is in fact no discussion in the *Theory of Moral Sentiments* as to how the conflicts of opinion which may result can be resolved, nor does Smith effectively discuss the way in which judgements made by individuals at the micro level are transformed into rules of behaviour which are perceived and obeyed by society at large. What he seems to have believed is that such general rules will naturally emerge from the normal patterns of social intercourse; that such rules will express what might be described as the 'conventional' morality and that their status will be reinforced by habit and education.

(3) The rules of behaviour above described are general to the

individual *and* to the society of which he is a member. They also emerge as being *useful* in the sense that without them there would be 'no man whose behaviour could be much depended upon', while in the absence of justice there would be no restraint on injury. However, Smith was careful to argue that these rules do not come into being *because* men grasp their utility; on the contrary, he insisted that they tend to emerge as the result of a natural response to experience. Thus, for example, Smith pointed out that the rules of justice (including equity) basically reflect man's fellow-feeling, while observing that

When by natural principles we are led to advance those ends, which a refined and enlightened reason would recommend to us, we are very apt to impute to that reason, as to their efficient cause, the sentiments and actions by which we advance those ends, and to imagine that to be the wisdom of man, which in reality is the wisdom of God (TMS II. ii. 3. 5).

The rules themselves, it should also be noted, vary in character. Those which relate to justice may often hinder us 'from hurting our neighbour'; they only involve restraint from injury and may thus be fulfilled by 'sitting still and doing nothing', while other rules may embody a more comprehensive and positive guide. The essential difference which emerges is that between the negative and positive virtues of justice and beneficence. As Smith put it:

The rules of justice may be compared to the rules of grammar; the rules of the other virtues, to the rules which critics lay down for the attainment of what is sublime and elegant in composition. The one, are precise, accurate, and indispensable. The other, are loose, vague, and indeterminate, and present us rather with a general idea of the perfection we ought to aim at, than afford us any certain and infallible directions for acquiring it (III. 6. 11).

It thus appears that while both sets of rules are useful to society, they must each, taken separately, be compatible with different levels of social experience. Smith noted that where men act with an eye to the positive rules of moral conduct, where their behaviour is characterized by beneficence rather than justice only, then that society 'flourishes and is happy'. If on the other hand justice alone is the rule, then life in society may be characterized by nothing more than 'a mercenary exchange of good offices according to an agreed valuation

(II. ii. 3. 2). Smith plainly regarded the first situation as the more typical and as involving a higher level of achievement than the second, although he was in no doubt as to which set of rules was the most important from the standpoint of social order:

Though Nature, therefore, exhorts mankind to acts of beneficence, by the pleasing consciousness of deserved reward, she has not thought it necessary to guard and enforce the practice of it by the terrors of merited punishment in case it should be neglected. It is the ornament which embellishes, not the foundation which supports the building, and which it was, therefore, sufficient to recommend, but by no means necessary to impose. Justice, on the contrary, is the main pillar that upholds the whole edifice. If it is removed, the great, the immense fabric of human society, that fabric which to raise and support seems in this world, if I may say so, to have been the peculiar and darling care of Nature, must in a moment crumble into atoms (II. ii. 3. 4).

(4) The rules of behaviour (depending as they do upon our capacity to form judgements in particular cases) must therefore be regarded as based upon experience. The rules of morality (including justice) embody a record of what we and others consider to be fit or proper to be done or to be avoided and may thus vary, as Smith recognized, between different societies at the same point in time and in the same society at different points in time. In this way Smith managed to remain within the framework of Montesquieu's emphasis on the variability of human experience, and drew from Edmund Burke the perceptive comment that 'A theory like yours founded on the Nature of man, which is always the same, will last, when those that are founded on his opinions, which are always changing, will and must be forgotten'.[14] Yet at the same time it is important to observe that while variations in standards or patterns of behaviour were recognized by Smith to be important, what he chose to emphasize was the presence of certain common elements. Thus in commenting on the role of custom and fashion, he observed that their effects 'upon the moral sentiments of mankind, are inconsiderable, in comparison of those which they give occasion to in some other cases; and it is not concerning the general style of character and behaviour, that those principles produce the

[14] Letter 38 from Edmund Burke, addressed to Smith, dated Westminster, 10 September 1759.

greatest perversion of judgment, but concerning the propriety or impropriety of particular usages' (V. 2. 12). And yet particular usages, he continued, could be of great significance, in that custom 'is capable of establishing, as lawful and blameless, particular actions, which shock the plainest principles of right and wrong' (V. 2. 14). In this connection Smith cited as an extreme example the classical practice of exposing children — a practice once based on necessity but which was still in force long after the circumstances which had first given occasion to it were no more.

In fact Smith gave a good deal of attention to one particular set of rules, namely those relating to justice, and noted that 'Every system of positive law may be regarded as a more or less imperfect attempt towards a system of natural jurisprudence, or towards an enumeration of the particular rules of justice' (VII. iv. 36). At the same time he observed that 'the interest of the government; sometimes the interest of particular orders of men who tyrannize the government, warp the positive laws of the country from what natural justice would prescribe', thus ensuring that 'Systems of positive law . . . though they deserve the greatest authority, as the records of the sentiments of mankind in different ages and nations . . . can never be regarded as accurate systems of the rules of natural justice' (VII. iv. 36). Yet Smith clearly believed that enquiries, like that of Grotius, into 'what were the natural rules of justice independent of all positive institution' (VII. iv. 37) could and should be undertaken, and announced his own intention to write such a book in the conclusion to the *Theory of Moral Sentiments*. While this aspect of Smith's promise was never fulfilled, he did, however, take up themes in the historical sections of the *Wealth of Nations* which complement some of the arguments of the *Theory of Moral Sentiments*, in formally examining the origin of government and in tracing the different revolutions which it had undergone 'in the different ages and periods of society'. In the bygoing Smith also managed to throw a good deal of light on those forces which 'warp the positive laws of the country from what natural justice would prescribe', and which also help to explain the causes of variation in accepted standards of behaviour over time. The theme of relativity which was so

marked a feature of the Astronomy is thus continued in the *Theory of Moral Sentiments* and is of course wholly consistent with Smith's interest in the theory of social history, which forms the subject of the next chapter.

4

Historical Theory*

While an interest in the past informs all Smith's works, there can be no doubt that he regarded the study of history as a separate subject in its own right. However, the kind of history in which Smith was most interested was that represented by the Astronomy — a style which Dugald Stewart described as 'theroretical or conjectural' in order to distinguish it from the 'orthodox' or 'vulgar'. While the term 'philosophical history' is probably to be preferred, Stewart was undoubtedly correct in stating that this type of study 'seems, in a peculiar degree, to have interested Mr. Smith's curiosity' and that 'Something very similar to it may be traced in all his different works, whether moral, political, or literary' (II. 44).

Smith's work on the history of civil society is particularly noteworthy, and among the first subjects to which he appears to have addressed himself. Even if we exclude the Edinburgh Lectures, it is now well known, from the account supplied by John Millar, that the third part of Smith's lectures delivered from the Moral Philosophy Chair had been concerned with 'that branch of morality which relates to justice', and that

Upon this subject he followed the plan that seems to be suggested by Montesquieu; endeavouring to trace the gradual progress of jurisprudence, both public and private, from the rudest to the most refined ages, and to point out the effect of those arts which contribute to subsistence, and to the accumulation of property, in producing correspondent improvements or alterations in law and government (Stewart, 1. 19).[1]

---

* This chapter is a modified version of a paper entitled 'An Economic Interpretation of History' which originally appeared in *Essays on Adam Smith*. Parts of it are reprinted by kind permission of the Clarendon Press.

[1] The most complete account of the whole argument is to be found in LJ(A) iv, which corresponds to the briefer treatment 'Of Public Jurisprudence' offered in LJ(B), Part 1. It is interesting to note that while LJ(A) deals with Private, Domestic, and Public Law in that order, LJ(B) reverses the sequence.

The reference to 'arts which contribute to subsistence' is particularly striking when we reflect that Smith managed to isolate four distinct modes of subsistence to which there correspond four types of socio-political structure — the stages of 'hunting, pasturage, farming, and commerce' (LJ(B) 149 ed. Cannan, 107).[2]

In fact, there are two dimensions to Smith's argument: first, the statement of certain 'sociological' propositions which are related to the 'four stages', and secondly, the application of these propositions to the interpretation of specific areas of historical experience. The main propositions are of continuing interest because of the relationships which were established between economic forces and other areas of activity; the historical aspect because it is here that these relationships are lent a dimension of greater complexity than their formal statement might imply.

II

The Propositions

(a) *Sources of Authority and the Origin of Government*

Perhaps the easiest way to approach the first side of the problem is to consider Smith's treatment of 'political' obligation. As we have seen, the *Theory of Moral Sentiments* only postulated the need for some kind of government or system of magistracy, without explaining how such systems originated or why men obey them.

In addressing himself to the latter problem Smith stated that the basis of obedience was to be found in the principles of *utility* and *authority*. In practice, he placed most emphasis on the latter and identified four main sources: personal qualifications, age, fortune, and birth. Taking these four sources in turn, he argued that personal qualities such as wisdom, strength, or beauty, while important as sources of individual distinction, were yet of rather limited political value, since they are all qualities which are open to dispute. As a result, he suggests that age, provided there is no 'suspicion of dotage', represents a more important source of

---

[2] The same division of stages appears in LJ(A) i. 27.

authority and of respect, since it is 'a plain and palpable quality' about which there can be no doubt (WN V. i. b. 6). Smith also observed that as a matter of fact age regulates rank among those who are in every other respect equal in both primitive and civilized societies, although its relative importance in the two cases is likely to vary.

The third source of authority, wealth, of all the sources of power is perhaps the most emphasized by Smith, and here again he cites two elements. First, he noted that through an 'irregularity' of our moral sentiments, men tend to admire and respect the rich (rather than the poor, who *may* be morally more worthy) as the possessors of all the imagined conveniences of wealth. Secondly, he argued that the possession of riches may also be associated with a degree of power which arises from the dependence of the poor for their subsistence. For example, the great chief who has no way of spending his surpluses other than in the maintenance of men acquires retainers and dependants who 'depending entirely on him for their subsistence, must both obey his orders in war, and submit to his jurisdiction in peace. He is necessarily both their general and their judge, and his chieftainship is the necessary effect of the superiority of his fortune' (WN V. i. b. 7). Finally, Smith argues that the observed fact of our tendency to venerate antiquity of family, rather than the upstart or newly rich, also constitutes an important source of authority which may reinforce that of riches. He concluded that 'Birth and fortune are evidently the two circumstances which principally set one man above another. They are the two great sources of personal distinction, and are therefore the principal causes which naturally establish authority and subordination among men' (V. i. b. 11).

Having made these points, Smith then went on to argue that just as wealth (and the subsequent distinction of birth) represents an important source of authority, so in turn it opens up an important source of dispute. In this connection we find him arguing that where people are prompted by malice or resentment to hurt one another, and where they can only be harmed in respect of person or reputation, then men may live together with *some* degree of harmony; the point being that 'the greater part of men are not very fre-

quently under the influence of those passions; and the very worst men are so only occasionally'. He went on to note that

As their gratification too, how agreeable soever it may be to certain characters, is not attended with any real or permanent advantage, it is in the greater part of men commonly restrained by prudential considerations. Men may live together in society with some tolerable degree of security, though there is no civil magistrate to protect them from the injustice of those passions (V. i. b. 2).

But in a situation where property can be acquired, Smith argued there could be an advantage to be gained by committing acts of injustice, in that here we find a situation which tends to give full rein to avarice and ambition. 'The acquisition of valuable and extensive property, therefore, necessarily requires the establishment of civil government. Where there is no property, or at least none that exceeds the value of two or three days labour, civil government is not so necessary' (ibid.). Elsewhere he remarked that 'Civil government, so far as it is instituted for the security of property, is in reality instituted for the defence of the rich against the poor, or of those who have some property against those who have none at all' (V. i. b. 12). It is a government, on Smith's argument, which in some situations at least is supported by a perception of its utility, at least on the side of the 'rich', but which must have evolved naturally and independently of any consideration of its necessity. In Smith's own words, 'Civil government supposes a certain subordination. But as the necessity of civil government gradually grows up with the acquisition of valuable property, so the principal causes which naturally introduce subordination gradually grow up with the growth of that valuable property' (V. i. b. 3).

In this way Smith stated the basic principles behind the origin of government and illustrated the four main sources of authority. In a subsequent part of the argument he then tried to show the way in which the outlines of society and government could vary, by reference to the four broad socioeconomic types above mentioned.

(b) *The Stages of Society*

The first stage of society was represented as the 'lowest and rudest' state, such 'as we find it among the native tribes of

North America' (WN V. i. a. 2). In this case, life is maintained through gathering the spontaneous fruits of the soil, and the dominant activities are taken to be hunting and fishing — a mode of acquiring subsistence which is antecedent to any social organization in production. As a result, Smith suggested that such communities would be small in size and characterized by a high degree of personal liberty — due of course to the absence of any form of economic dependence. Smith also observed that in the absence of private property, which was also capable of accumulation, disputes between different members of the community would be minor, 'so there is seldom any established magistrate or any regular administration of justice' in such states. He added that 'Universal poverty establishes there universal equality, and the superiority, either of age, or of personal qualities, are the feeble, but the sole foundations of authority and subordination. There is therefore little or no authority or subordination in this period of society' (V. i. b. 7).

The second social stage is that of pasture, which Smith represented as a 'more advanced state of society, such as we find it among the Tartars and Arabs' (V. i. a. 3). Here the use of cattle is the dominant economic activity, and the mode of subsistence meant, as Smith duly noted, that life would tend to be nomadic and the communities larger in size than had been possible in the preceding stage. More dramatically, Smith observed that the appropriation of herds and flocks, which introduced an inequality of fortune, was that which first gave rise to regular government. We also find here a form of property which can be accumulated and transmitted from one generation to another, thus explaining a change in the main sources of authority as compared to the previous period. As Smith put it:

The second period of society, that of shepherds, admits of very great inequalities of fortune, and there is no period in which the superiority of fortune gives so great authority to those who possess it. There is no period accordingly in which authority and subordination are more perfectly established. The authority of an Arabian scherif is very great; that of a Tartar khan altogether despotical (V. i. b. 7).

At the same time it is evident that the mode of subsistence involved must ensure a high degree of dependence on those

who must acquire the means of subsistence through the exchange of personal service, and those who, owning the means of subsistence, have no other way of expending it save on the maintenance of dependants, who at the same time contribute to their military power. Smith added that while the distinction of birth, being subsequent to the inequality of fortune, can have no place in a nation of hunters, this distinction 'always does take place among nations of shepherds' (V. i. b. 10). Since the great families lack, in this context, the means of dissipating wealth, it follows that 'there are no nations among whom wealth is likely to continue longer in the same families' (ibid.).

The third and fourth stages in Smith's scheme are much more complex than the first two and for this reason a fuller treatment of them will be postponed until the next section of the argument. However, enough may be said at this point to confirm the basic principles which Smith sought to establish.

In the agrarian case, for example, there are many obvious differences as compared to the pasturage economy. The most important form of property is now land (rather than cattle), while in addition some form of tillage will be practised — all of which indicates that societies will no longer be nomadic and that they are likely to be larger in size. Yet in a sense Smith chose to emphasize *similarities* with the previous stage: for here too property is likely to be distributed in a markedly unequal way, and to be transmitted from one member of a family to another through a number of generations. Here too the economy is basically designed for subsistence rather than exchange so that those who lack the means of subsistence can only acquire it through the provision of personal service. In this way those who own property acquire power by virtue of that fact, while those who have 'no equivalent to give in return for their maintenance' become members of a group who must obey their superiors 'for the same reason that soldiers must obey the prince who pays them' (III. iv. 5).

In the case of the stage of 'commerce' many of the principles so far mentioned also apply: wealth and birth remain important sources of distinction, as a result of the basic 'irregularity' in our moral sentiments of which Smith made so much in the *Theory of Moral Sentiments*. Property too

remains an important source of power, and Smith was certainly aware of the 'oppressive inequality' which was to be found even in the most advanced states. But here he chose to emphasize two important *contrasts* with the previous stages, especially with those of pasture and agriculture; differences which reflect the fact that the fourth stage features the production of goods with a view to exchange. In the first place, he argued that property derived from 'commercial' activity was *likely* to be *more* equally distributed and *unlikely* to be kept within particular families over long periods of time. Secondly, Smith suggested that where goods and services generally command a price, the *direct* dependencies of the second and third stages could no longer apply. As he put it:

In a country where there is no foreign commerce, nor any of the finer manufactures, a man of ten thousand a year cannot well employ his revenue in any other way than in maintaining, perhaps, a thousand families, who are all of them necessarily at his command. In the present state of Europe, a man of ten thousand a year can spend his whole revenue, and he generally does so, without directly maintaining twenty people, or being able to command more than ten footmen not worth the commanding (III. iv. 11).

By purchasing the products of other men's labour, the 'rich' contribute to their maintenance, while 'Each tradesman or artificer derives his subsistence from the employment, not of one, but of a hundred or a thousand different customers. Though in some measure obliged to them all, therefore, he is not absolutely dependent upon any one of them' (III. iv. 12).

Perhaps enough has been said to indicate that for Smith the relations of authority and dependence were of striking importance, that the relationships involved will manifest themselves in different ways in different situations, and that the operation of the same basic principles will generate the sharpest contrasts when comparing the third and fourth stages. The point was neatly put by Smith's contemporary, Sir James Steuart, when he remarked:

I deduce the origin of the great subordination under the feudal government, from the necessary dependence of the lower classes for their subsistence. They consumed the produce of the land, as the price of their subordination, not as the reward of their industry in making it produce.

I deduce modern liberty from the independence of the same classes, by the introduction of industry, and circulation of an adequate equivalent for every service.[3]

III

A Historical Application

Although Smith does refer to a *sequence* of four stages he was very far from suggesting that transition between them was inevitable under all circumstances. In the *Wealth of Nations*, for example, he noted that 'All the inland parts of Africa, and all that part of Asia which lies any considerable way north of the Euxine and Caspian seas, the antient Scythia, the modern Tartary and Siberia, seem in all ages of the world to have been in the same barbarous and uncivilized state in which we find them at present' (I. iii. 8).

The reason for this was simply that such countries did not satisfy the basic conditions for economic growth and cultural survival — ease of defence, fertility of the soil, and access to good communications by land and water. Thus Smith concluded that the Tartars would always be a nation of shepherds 'from the nature of their country' (including climate), while in Arabia agriculture was 'debarred by the ruggedness and steepness of the country' (LJ(A), iv. 56).

This situation does not make such peoples any less interesting from the point of view of the philosophical historian — indeed the Tartars, Arabs, Hottentots, and American Indians of the time were thought to provide invaluable evidence with regard to the broad outlines of the two first stages of society. But it does mean that historical experience involving progress must be sought elsewhere — specifically 'in Greece', where 'all the necessary circumstances for the improvement of the arts concurred' (LJ(A), iv. 62): an argument which firmly links social and cultural change with a capacity for economic growth. If Greek experience does not necessarily mark the beginning of history or define its early boundaries, it does represent the beginning of the process which was to lead to the 'present establishments in Europe'.

[3] *Principles of Political Oeconomy* (1767, ed. A.S. Skinner, 1966), i. 208–9.

Smith begins what is only a rudimentary sketch of early history by assuming that the early inhabitants of Attica had passed through the stage of hunting to that of pasture: 'The first inhabitants of Greece, as we find by the accounts of the historians, were much of the same sort with the Tartars' (LJ(A), iv. 56). The relations of authority and dependence would be those appropriate to the second stage, while in addition the organization of the 'state' would reflect its component associations. As Smith argued, in drawing a parallel with the hunting state:

As the affairs of each family would be determined by the members of it, of a village by the members of it, so would the affairs of the community or association of villages by the members of the whole directed by their president, and the chief president receiving the lead in all these would appear a sort of sovereign (LJ(A), iv. 37).

The first source of change in this system may be represented as attributable to the advent of agriculture; the second, to the need for protection against external threat. In practice the latter was particularly important in that it led to the development of the city as a defensive rather than as a trading institution. As Smith represents the case, Theseus, the chief of chiefs, encouraged this policy in the case of Athens and by so doing helped to reduce the power of the village heads. This is essentially a move towards kingship; one which did not last due to the fact that the distribution of property in such a relatively small state was unlikely to 'give the king or lord of it very great superiority over the nobles or other great men' (LJ(A), iv. 66). But growth, both in terms of manufacture and trade, became possible in the context of a state thus equipped to survive, and to an extent which presented it with two choices: to be a defensive or a 'conquering republick' — a politico-military decision which, Smith believed, had confronted all republics at some point in time (LJ(A), iv. 75). It is a choice which is forced upon the state by the need to protect the fruits of its own expansion and one which once made inevitably leads to failure and decay. As Smith put it, the growth of wealth based on commerce not only alters the balance of power away from the 'aristocratic' groups of the older constitution, it also reduces the number of fighting men and even their martial spirit, 'So that the very duration of the

state and the improvements naturally going on at that time, every one applying himself to some useful art, and commerce, the attendant on all these, necessarily undo the strength and cause the power to vanish of such a state till it be swallowed up by some neighbouring state' (LJ(A), iv. 81). Exactly the same problem was to arise, Smith noted, in the case of Rome, making it a prey to those savage nations which the state had been obliged to use in its own defence.

Perhaps four points are worth emphasizing before going further. First, it should be noted that the stage of 'commerce' may be said to have been attained in both Greece and Rome even 'tho' not, as now, particularly studied and a theory laid down' (LJ(A), iv. 93). Secondly, we should note that commerce did not lead to the elimination of all forms of slavery or of direct dependence, since the institution was found in both Greece and Rome at all stages of their development. Thirdly, it is apparent that while the tools of the stadial thesis may be used as aids to the understanding of classical societies, those societies showed marked cultural differences even where the relations of authority and dependence were the same. Finally, it is evident that Smith presents the causes of decline in terms of military weakness which is itself a function of economic growth. This suggests that more advanced societies are likely to be overwhelmed by the more primitive, so that if change can be said to be constant, it cannot always be said to be either linear or always to involve progressive changes in socio-economic structures.

The nations which overran the Western Empire were represented by Smith as having been at exactly the state of development which had been attained by the early inhabitants of Greece. Primitive peoples whose military power was of the awesome proportions appropriate to the second stage are thus shown to have come in contact with a much more sophisticated society, but one whose power was already on the decline. The result, as Smith duly noted, was the destruction of civilization as then known; a step backwards.

When the German and Scythian nations over-ran the western provinces of the Roman empire, the confusions which followed so great a revolution lasted for several centuries. The rapine and violence which the barbarians exercised against the antient inhabitants, interrupted the

commerce between the towns and the country. The towns were deserted, and the country was left uncultivated, and the western provinces of Europe, which had enjoyed a considerable degree of opulence under the Roman empire, sunk into the lowest state of poverty and barbarism (WN III. ii. 1).

At the same time, however, Smith argued that the domination of the barbarian nations had generated not only a desert, but also an environment from which a higher form of European civilization was ultimately to emerge.[4]

Smith's explanation of this general trend begins with the fact that the primitive tribes which overran the empire had already attained a relatively sophisticated form of the pasturage economy, with some idea of agriculture and of property in land.[5] He argued therefore that they would naturally use existing institutions in their new situation and that in particular their first act would be a division of the conquered territories.

> the chiefs and principal leaders of those nations, acquired or usurped to themselves the greater part of the lands . . . A great part of them was uncultivated; but no part of them, whether cultivated or uncultivated, was left without a proprietor. All of them were engrossed, and the greater part by a few great proprietors (III. ii. 1).

In this way we move in effect from a developed version of one economic stage to a primitive version of another; from the state of pasture to that of 'agriculture'. Under the circumstances outlined, property in land became the great source of power and distinction, with each estate assuming the form of a separate principality. As a result of this situation, Smith argued, a gradual change took place in the laws governing property, featuring the introduction of primogeniture and entails, designed to protect estates against division and to preserve a 'certain lineal succession'. The basic point emphasized was that in such periods of disorder 'The security of a landed

---

[4] Almost exactly this point was made by Dugald Stewart, *Works*, x. 147.

[5] Smith commented briefly on the implied sequence of stages in stating that men would 'naturally turn themselves to the cultivation of land' once the growth of population had put pressure on supplies derived from pasturage. He added 'The only instance that has the appearance of an objection to this rule is the state of the North American Indians. They, tho they have no conception of flocks and herds, have nevertheless some notion of agriculture.' (LJ(A) i. 29. Similar points are made in LJ(B) 150, ed. Cannan, 108.)

estate ... the protection which its owner could afford to
those who dwelt on it, depended upon its greatness. To divide
it was to ruin it, and to expose every part of it to be oppressed
and swallowed up by the incursions of its neighbours' (III. ii. 3).

Such institutions as these quite obviously reflect a change
in the mode of subsistence and in the form of property, thus
presenting some important contrasts with the previous stage.
On the other hand the great proprietor has still nothing on
which to expend his surpluses other than the maintenance of
dependants — and at the same time has a positive incentive to
do so since they contribute to his military power and hence
security. While Smith carefully distinguished between *retainers*
and *cultivators* in this context, he took pains to emphasize
that the latter group were in every respect as dependent on
the proprietor as the first, and added that 'Even such of them
as were not in a state of villanage, were tenants at will, who
paid a rent in no respect equivalent to the subsistence which
the land afforded them' (III. iv. 6).[6]

In short, the period was marked by clear relations of power
and dependence — but above all by disorder and conflict, and
it was from this source that the first important changes in the
outlines of the system were to come. As Smith put it by way
of summary:

In those disorderly times, every great landlord was a sort of petty prince.
His tenants were his subjects. He was their judge, and in some respects
their legislator in peace, and their leader in war. He made war according
to his own discretion, frequently against his neighbours, and sometimes
against his sovereign (III. ii. 3).

It was this state of conflict, Smith suggests, which gave the
proprietors some incentive to alter the pattern of landholding,
in two quite different ways. First, Smith argued that the heavy
demands which were inevitably made on their immediate
tenants (as distinct from villeins etc.) for military service
would inevitably change the quit-rent system in terms of
which land was normally held. Smith argued in effect that
the great lords would naturally begin to grant leases for a

---

⁶ It is pointed out in LJ(A) i. 119 that those who used the land initially 'paid
a small rent to the possessor, rather as an acknowledgment of their dependence
than as the value of the land'. Cf. the remarks made by Steuart above, 74, and
see generally the *Principles*, 206–17 and lxiii–lxviii.

term of years, and then in a form which gave security to the tenant's family and ultimately to his posterity. In this way, land came to be held as *feuda* rather than *munera*, being designed to give both parties a benefit: the lord, in terms of the supply of military service, and the tenant, security in the use of the land. Smith also noted certain consequential developments which reflected the basic purpose of the arrangement, namely to improve and protect the power of the great proprietor, in describing what he called the feudal *casualities*.[7]

Secondly, Smith argued that the same need for protection which altered the relationship between the great lord and his tenants would also lead to patterns of alliance between members of the former group and, therefore, to arrangements which gave some guarantee of mutual service and protection. It was for these reasons, Smith argued, that the lesser landowners entered into feudal arrangements with those greater lords who could ensure their survival (thus enhancing their ability to do so), just as the great lords would be led to make similar arrangements amongst themselves and with the king. These changes took place about the ninth, tenth, and eleventh centuries, and by imposing some shackles on the free enterprise of the proprietors contributed thereby to the emergence of a more orderly form of government.

However, while Smith did describe the feudal as a higher form of the agrarian economy, he also took some pains to emphasize the limited possibilities for economic growth which it presented; limitations which were themselves the reflection of the political institutions now prevailing. For example, he pointed out that the laws of primogeniture and entail hindered the sale and division of lands, and therefore their acquisition by those who might have sought to improve them. He also argued that the quit-rent system, so far as it survived, gave no incentive to industry, and that the institution of slavery ensured that it was in the interest of the ordinary individual to 'eat as much, and to labour as little as possible' (III. ii. 9). In the same way he also cited the disincentive

---

[7] See LJ(A) iv. 127 ff.; LJ(B) 53–7, ed. Cannan, 36–40, and WN III. iv. 9, V. ii. h. 5, 6.

effects of the arbitrary services and feudal taxes which were imposed at this time. But, undoubtedly, Smith placed most emphasis on the continuing problem of political instability:

The authority of government still continued to be, as before, too weak in the head and too strong in the inferior members, and the excessive strength of the inferior members was the cause of the weakness of the head. After the institution of feudal subordination, the king was as incapable of restraining the violence of the great lords as before. They still continued to make war according to their own discretion, almost continually upon one another, and very frequently upon the king; and the open country still continued to be a scene of violence, rapine, and disorder (III. iv. 9).

Once again, a state of instability was to produce some change in the outlines of the social system, and once again the motive behind it was *political* rather than *economic* — this time with the kings rather than the great lords as the main actors in the drama.[8]

IV

Emergence of the Exchange Economy

The kind of economy which Smith described as appropriate to the agrarian state is fundamentally a simple one. It consists of the usual division between town and country, that is, between those who produce food and those who make the manufactured goods without which no large country could subsist — the critical point being however that such an economy was not wholly based on exchange. The cities which Smith described were small, and composed of those merchants, tradesmen, and mechanics who were not bound to a particular place and who might find it in their (economic) interest to congregate together. Smith had in fact relatively little to say about the historical origins of such groupings, but he did emphasize that the inhabitants of the towns were in the same servile condition as the inhabitants of the country, and that the wealth which they did manage to accumulate under such unfavourable conditions was subject to the arbitrary exactions

---

[8] Smith also stressed the importance of the Church as a source of instability in WN V. i. g. 17, 22.

of both the king and those lords on whose territories they
might happen to be based or through which they might pass
(WN III. iii. 2).

But evidently some development must have been possible,
for Smith examines the role of the city from that period in
time when three distinctive features of royal policy with
regard to it were already in evidence. First, Smith noted that
cities had often been allowed to farm the taxes to which they
were subject, the inhabitants thus becoming 'jointly and
severally answerable' for the whole sum due (III. iii. 3).
Second, he noted that in some cases these taxes, instead of
being farmed for a given number of years, had been 'let in
fee', that is 'for ever, reserving a rent certain never afterwards
to be augmented' (III. iii. 4). Third, Smith observed that the
cities

were generally at the same time erected into a commonality or corporation, with the privilege of having magistrates and a town-council of
their own, of making bye-laws for their own government, of building
walls for their own defence, and of reducing all their inhabitants under
a sort of military discipline, by obliging them to watch and ward . . .
(III. iii. 6).

It was as a result of following these policies that some kings
had achieved the apparently remarkable result of freezing the
very revenues which were most likely to increase over time,
at the same time effectively curtailing their own power by
erecting 'a sort of independent republicks in the heart of their
own dominions' (III. iii. 7). Smith advanced two main reasons
to explain the apparent paradox: first, that by encouraging
the cities the king made it possible for a group of his subjects
to defend themselves against the power of the great lords
where he personally was unable to do so, and, secondly, that
by imposing a limit on taxation 'he took away from those
whom he wished to have for his friends, and, if one may say
so, for his allies, all ground of jealousy and suspicion that he
was ever afterwards to oppress them, either by raising the
farm rent of their town, or by granting it to some other
farmer' (III. iii. 8). The encouragement given to the cities
represented in effect a tactical alliance which was beneficial
to both parties, and in speaking of the burghers, Smith
remarked that 'Mutual interest . . . disposed them to support

the king, and the king to support them against the lords. They were the enemies of his enemies, and it was his interest to render them as secure and independent of those enemies as he could' (ibid.).

Smith also noted that this development was directly related to the weakness of kings, so that it was likely to be more significant in some countries than in others, and that in general the policy had been successful where employed.[9] He also remarked that the granting of powers of self-government to the inhabitants of the cities had set in motion forces which were ultimately to weaken the authority of the kings through creating an environment within which the forces of economic development could, for the first time, be effectively released. In Smith's own words:

Order and good government, and along with them the liberty and security of individuals, were, in this manner, established in cities at a time when the occupiers of land . . . were exposed to every sort of violence. But men in this defenceless state naturally content themselves with their necessary subsistence; because to acquire more might only tempt the injustice of their oppressors. On the contrary, when they are secure of enjoying the fruits of their industry, they naturally exert it to better their condition, and to acquire not only the necessaries, but the conveniencies and elegancies of life (III. iii. 12).

The stimulus to economic growth and to further social change was thus seen to emanate from the cities; institutions which had themselves been developed and protected in an attempt to solve a political problem. From this point, Smith's attention shifted to the analysis of the process of economic growth in the manufacturing, before going on the examine its impact on the agrarian, sector.

Smith clearly recognized that growth was limited by the size of the market and, since the agrarian sector was relatively backward, that the main stimulus to economic growth would

[9] In LJ(A) iv. 154, Smith also associated this trend with the military ambition of certain kings such as Edward I and Henry IV, 'the two most warlike of the English Kings'. It is also pointed out in WN III. iii. 11 that while the cities in England did not become so powerful as to be virtually independent (as in Italy and Switzerland, where the physical size and nature of the country made this possible), yet 'They became, however, so considerable that the sovereign could impose no tax upon them, besides the stated farm-rent of the town, without their own consent. They were, therefore, called upon to send deputies to the general assembly of the states of the kingdom.'

have to come from foreign trade. He therefore concluded that cities such as Venice, Genoa, and Pisa, all of which enjoyed ready access to the sea, had provided the models for the process, while noting that their development had been further accelerated by particular accidents such as the Crusades. In general however Smith laid most emphasis on three sources of encouragement to the development of trade and manufactures. First, he argued that in many cases agrarian surpluses could be acquired by the merchants and used in exchange for foreign manufactures, and suggested as a matter of fact that the early trade of Europe had largely consisted in the exchange 'of their own rude, for the manufactured products of more civilized nations'. Secondly, he argued that over time the merchants would naturally seek to introduce manufactures at home (with a view to saving carriage). Such manufactures, it was suggested, would require the use of foreign materials, thus inducing an important change in the general pattern of trade. Thirdly, he argued that some manufactures would develop 'naturally', that is through the gradual refinement of the 'coarse and rude' products which were normally produced at home and which were, therefore, based on domestic materials. Smith suggested that such developments were normally found in those cities which were 'not indeed at a very great, but at a considerable distance from the sea coast, and sometimes even from all water carriage' (III. iii. 20). That is, he suggested that manufactures might well develop in areas to which artisans had been attracted by the cheapness of subsistence, thus allowing trade to develop within the locality. Once some progress had been made in this way foreign trade become possible:

The manufacturers first supply the neighbourhood, and afterwards, as their work improves and refines, more distant markets. For though neither the rude produce, nor even the coarse manufacture, could, without the greatest difficulty, support the expence of a considerable land carriage, the refined and improved manufacture easily may. In a small bulk it frequently contains the price of a great quantity of rude produce (III. iii. 20).

Smith cited the silk manufacture at Lyons and Spital-fields as examples of the first category of manufactures; those of Leeds, Halifax, Sheffield, Birmingham, and Wolverhampton

as examples of the second, the natural 'offspring of agriculture' (III. iii. 19, 20). He also added that manufactures of the latter kind were generally posterior to those 'which were the offspring of foreign commerce' and that the process of development just outlined made it perfectly possible for the city within which growth took place to 'grow up to great wealth and splendor, while not only the country in its neighbourhood, but all those to which it traded, were in poverty and wretchedness' (III. iii. 13).

In the next stage of the analysis however, it was argued that this situation as outlined was unlikely to continue indefinitely; that the development of manufactures and trade within the cities was bound to impinge on the agrarian sector and, ultimately, to destroy the service relationships which still subsisted within it.[10] As Smith put it:

commerce and manufactures gradually introduced order and good government, and with them, the liberty and security of individuals, among the inhabitants of the country, who had before lived almost in a continual state of war with their neighbours, and of servile dependency upon their superiors. This, though it has been the least observed, is by far the most important of all their effects (III. iv. 4).[11]

Essentially, this process may be seen to stem from the fact that the development of trade and manufactures had given the proprietors a means of expending their wealth, other than in the maintenance of dependants. The development of commerce and manufactures, in short, had

gradually furnished the great proprietors with something for which they could exchange the whole surplus produce of their lands, and which they could consume themselves without sharing it either with tenants

[10] It is interesting to note that P.M. Sweezy should have rejected Maurice Dobb's thesis that feudalism broke down as a result of *internal* pressures in emphasizing the importance of foreign trade (i.e. an *external* force) both with regard to induced changes in taste and as an explanation for the fact that the cities 'became generators of commodity production in their own right'. *The Transition from Feudalism to Capitalism*, ed. Rodney Hilton (1976), 42.

[11] Smith went on to add that 'Mr. Hume is the only writer who, so far as I know, has hitherto taken any notice of it'. See especially Hume's essay 'Of Refinement in the Arts' and Duncan Forbes's introduction to Hume's *History* (Pelican, 1970), 38–43. Smith's statement is interesting when we recall that Steuart, Ferguson, Millar, and Kames had all published prior to the appearance of the *Wealth of Nations*. Since Smith can hardly have been unaware of these facts, it seems likely that his citation of Hume alone simply provides further evidence as to the age of this section of the work.

or retainers. All for ourselves, and nothing for other people, seems, in every age of the world, to have been the vile maxim of the masters of mankind (III. iv. 10).

This situation generated two results. First, since the proprietor's object was now to increase his command over the means of exchange, it would be in his interest to reduce the number of retainers,

till they were at last dismissed altogether. The same cause gradually led them to dismiss the unnecessary part of their tenants. Farms were enlarged, and the occupiers of land, notwithstanding the complaints of depopulation, reduced to the number necessary for cultivating it, according to the imperfect state of cultivation and improvement in those times (III. iv. 13).

Secondly, since the object was now to maximize the disposable surplus, it was in the proprietor's interest to change the forms of leasehold in order to encourage output and increase his returns. In this way, Smith traced the gradual change from the use of slave labour on the land,[12] to the origin of the 'metayer' system where the tenant had limited property rights, until the whole process finally resulted in the appearance of farmers properly so called 'who cultivated the land with their own stock, paying a rent certain to the landlord' (III. ii. 14). Smith added that the same process would tend over time to lead to an improvement in the conditions of leases, until the tenants could be 'secured in their possession, for such a term of years as might give them time to recover with profit whatever they should lay out in the further improvement of the land. The expensive vanity of the landlord made him willing to accept of this condition . . .' (III. iv. 13).

As a result of these two general trends, the great proprietors gradually lost their powers, both judicial and military,[13] until a situation was reached where 'they became as insignificant

[12] Smith argued in effect that slavery was undermined because of economic forces and thus rejected the claims of the Church (WN III. ii. 12). See also LJ(A) iii. 121. He also pointed out that slavery still subsisted in large parts of Europe, especially 'Russia, Poland, Hungary, Bohemia, Moravia, and other parts of Germany. It is only in the western and south-western provinces of Europe, that it has gradually been abolished altogether' (WN III. ii. 8). See also LJ(A) iii. 122 and LJ(B) 134, ed. Cannan, 96.

[13] In WN V. i. g. 25 Smith ascribed the decline in the temporal powers of the clergy to the same basic forces. In this connection he pointed out that although the clergy as a group had exerted greater power than the lords, due to their

as any substantial burgher or tradesman in a city. A regular government was established in the country as well as in the city, nobody having sufficient power to disturb its operations in the one, any more than in the other' (III. iv. 15).

Smith thus associated the decline in the feudal powers of the great proprietors with three general trends, all of which followed on the introduction of commerce and manufactures: the dissipation of their fortunes,[14] the dismissal of their retainers, and the substitution of a cash relationship for the service relationships which had previously existed between the owner of land and those who cultivated it.

As a result, we face a system where the disincentives to 'industry' had been removed from the agrarian sector, and where both sectors were, for the first time, fully interdependent at the domestic level.

Smith thus argues in effect that the *quantitative* development of manufactures based on the cities eventually produced an important *qualitative* change in creating the institutions of the exchange economy, that is, of the fourth economic stage. It is in this situation that the drive to better our condition, allied to the insatiable wants of man (referred to in the *Theory of Moral Sentiments*), provides the maximum possible stimulus to economic growth, and ensures that the gains accruing to town and country are both mutual and reciprocal. Or, as Smith put it:

The great commerce of every civilized society, is that carried on between the inhabitants of the town and those of the country. It consists in the exchange of rude for manufactured produce, either immediately, or by the intervention of money, or of some sort of paper which represents money. . . . The gains of both are mutual and reciprocal, and the division of labour is in this, as in all other cases, advantageous to all the different persons employed in the various occupations into which it is subdivided (III. i. 1).

greater cohesion, none the less their authority declined rather sooner due to the fact that in general the benefices of the clergy were smaller than the fortunes of the barons.

[14] Smith did note however that this general trend had not been matched in Germany due to the size of the country and the extent of the estates which were held by individuals. As he pointed out in LJ(A) iv. 166, the German nobles 'could not possible by any personall luxury, consume all their revenues; they therefore contrived to have a great number of retainers and dependents, and have accordingly become absolute'. Similar points are made in LJ(B) 60-1, ed. Cannan, 43.

It is moreover, a situation which effectively eliminates the direct dependence of the previous period; where each productive service commands a price and therefore ensures that while the farmer, tradesman, or merchant must depend upon his customers, yet 'Though in some measure obliged to them all ... he is not absolutely dependent upon any one of them' (III. iv. 12).

It may now be apparent that Smith's argument is very largely concerned with the analysis of the nature of the agrarian economy and with the causes of transition from it to the fourth economic stage in its *modern*, as distinct from *classical*, form; that is, the stage with which the economic analysis of the *Wealth of Nations* was formally concerned. It would also appear that Smith's argument taken as a whole has three characteristic features which are worthy of note. First, he consistently argues that the whole process of change depends on the self-interest of individuals: for example, it is this motive which is seen to lie behind the alliances formed by the great proprietors, the protection given to cities by kings, and the activities of the merchant classes. Secondly, it is evident that the motivation behind many of the most important changes was in fact political rather than simply economic. For example, the alliances formed by the great proprietors had a political object, as did the royal encouragement given to the cities themselves. Thirdly, it is argued that the whole process of change, and especially that involved in the transition from the feudal to the commercial state, depends on the activities of individuals who are themselves unconscious of the ultimate ends towards which such activities contribute. Or as Smith put it in reviewing the actions of the proprietors and merchants during the latter stages of the historical process which we have outlined:

A revolution of the greatest importance to the publick happiness, was in this manner brought about by two different orders of people, who had not the least intention to serve the publick. To gratify the most childish vanity was the sole motive of the great proprietors. The merchants and artificers, much less ridiculous, acted merely from a view to their own interest, and in pursuit of their own pedlar principle of turning a penny wherever a penny was to be got. Neither of them had either knowledge or foresight of that great revolution which the folly of

the one, and the industry of the other, was gradually bringing about (III. iv. 17).[15]

It is principles such as these which Smith used in explaining the rise of the classical civilizations and which are probably employed to best effect in tracing the emergence of the present establishments in Europe. Smith in fact took a wide historical sweep in producing a theory, admittedly incomplete, which was designed to lend order and coherence to what would otherwise have appeared to be a chaos of unconnected events. To this extent the description once offered of John Millar's teaching would also seem to apply to that of his master. For Smith too taught that we should not gaze 'with stupid amazement on the singular and diversified appearance of human manners and institutions', but rather consider them 'as necessary links in the great chain which connects civilized with barbarous society' (*Edinburgh Review*, 1803, 157).

Yet at the same time there are two important differences to be observed when we compare modern society with the sophisticated forms already attained in ancient Greece and Rome. First, it should be remarked that while elements of the 'commercial' stage are found in both, the modern economy is more properly an exchange economy in that this characteristic pervades *all* markets for goods and services. Secondly, it is worth noting that while there are important parallels to be found in the discussion of military problems, there are equally significant contrasts. The parallels arise in that the commercial features of both classical and modern societies are held to lead to a decline in the proportion of the population which is available for war, as well as in martial spirit. As Smith noted in his lectures, a 'bad effect of commerce is that it sinks the courage of mankind' — a judgement which seemed to be confirmed by the experience of the 1745 Rebellion when 'four or 5 thousand naked unarmed Highlanders took possession of the improved parts of this country without any opposition from the unwarlike inhabitants' (LJ(B), 331, ed. Cannan, 257–8). In the modern case Smith noted that the state could take steps to 'render the trade of a soldier a particular trade separate and distinct from

---

[15] The first printing of the Glasgow edition of WN has 'out' for 'about' in l. 2.

all others', and that it would have to do so given the spirit of the people and the increasing complexity (and therefore cost) of the arts of war. In fact it was the developing technology of warfare which, Smith believed, would help to *preserve* modern society from the threat posed by more primitive peoples (in sharp contrast to Graeco-Roman experience), thus sustaining the institutions of the exchange economy. As he argued in a notable passage from the *Wealth of Nations*:

In modern war the great expence of fire-arms gives an evident advantage to the nation which can best afford that expence; and consequently, to an opulent and civilized, over a poor and barbarous nation. In antient times the opulent and civilized found it difficult to defend themselves against the poor and barbarous nations. In modern times the poor and barbarous find it difficult to defend themselves against the opulent and civilized. The invention of fire-arms, an invention which at first sight appears to be so pernicious, is certainly favourable both to the permanency and to the extension of civilization (WN V. i. a. 44).

V

Conclusions

While it is hoped that the brief account which we have offered of Smith's argument is sufficient to delineate its major features, it may be appropriate to add some words of comment with regard to its general character and content in terms of two broad areas.

I. *Methodological*

Perhaps the most striking feature of the analysis which we have considered is that it purports to place the study of history on the same level as other social sciences by applying to history the methodology of Newton. The point is important for a number of reasons. First, we are reminded that 'theoretical or conjectural' history is only conjectural in the sense that there are some occasions on which principles which are derived from *known* facts must be applied to situations where facts are lacking. Or, as Dugald Stewart put it in discussing the problems of prehistory:

In this want of direct evidence, we are under a necessity of supplying the place of fact by conjecture; and when we are unable to ascertain how men have actually conducted themselves upon particular occasions,

of considering in what manner they are likely to have proceeded, from the principles of their nature, and the circumstances of their external situation (Stewart, II. 46).

Secondly, we are reminded that the claim to scientific status often implied that philosophical history was in some respects superior to other forms of historical writing — and in particular to the orthodox or narrative type. The terms used often invite this conclusion, as for example when Dugald Stewart referred to the 'habits of scientific disquisition' which were required of the natural historian, while expressing regret that William Robertson, perhaps the leading orthodox historian of his own time and country, had not prepared himself more for his incursions into this field. A rather similar impression is left by John Millar's statement that he would seek to 'point out the chief incidents of a constitutional history, lying in a good measure beneath that common surface of events which occupies the details of the vulgar historian' (HV iv. 101).

But whatever points Stewart or Millar may have intended to convey in making such remarks, it should be noted that Smith himself was very careful in his comments — as befits one who broke new ground in lecturing on the history of historians.[16] While we cannot fully examine these lectures here, it should be noted that Smith at no time expressed contempt for those historians who worked in different fields. He pointed out for example that the first historians, the poets, who had concerned themselves with the 'marvellous', provide valuable evidence as to the times in which they lived, and went on to argue that if Herodotus had many defects as a historian, yet 'We can learn from him rather the customs of the different nations and the series of events . . . in this way, too, we may learn a great deal' (LRBL ii. 47–8, ed. Lothian, 101). In addition Smith observed that historians such as Thucydides and Tacitus were particularly informative not only because of the way in which they recorded facts but also because they tended to emphasize the psychological pressures to which the main figures involved were subjected. He added that 'though this perhaps will not tend so much to

[16] See LRBL, lectures 16 to 19 and especially the latter. Smith's classification of types of historical writing affords an interesting parallel with Hegel's introduction to the lectures on the philosophy of history.

instruct us in the knowledge of the causes of events yet it will be more interesting and lead us into a science no less useful, to wit, the knowledge of the motives by which men act' (LRBL ii. 66, Lothian, 109). Smith, in short, quite clearly recognized that the narrative historian often supplied the materials on which the work of the philosophical historian was based.

Thirdly, we should recall that Smith did not himself claim that philosophical history had an exclusive title to be described as scientific in character. For example Smith referred to the objectivity or 'impartiality' which the orthodox historian has to maintain, in remarking that he fulfils his duty only when he 'sets before us the more interesting and important events of human life, points out the causes by which these events were brought about, and by this means points out to us by what manner and method we may produce similar good effects or avoid similar bad ones' (LRBL ii. 17-18, ed. Lothian, 85). In short, the historian must bring to his study a critical awareness of facts; he must study these facts objectively, and he must seek to elucidate their causes, qualities which led Smith to give particular praise to Thucydides (who reported events of which he was the witness) and Tacitus (who recorded the history of a nation). Of the modern historians, Smith considered Machiavelli to be incomparably the best, in the sense that he was the only one 'who has contented himself with that which is the chief purpose of history, to relate events and connect them with their causes, without becoming a party on either side' (LRBL ii. 68, ed. Lothian, 110-11).

Machiavelli is an interesting choice in that his example also reminds us that use of the 'constant principles of human nature' in the interpretation of events was not of itself the distinguishing feature of 'philosophical history' as written by Smith. For Machiavelli too employed exactly this hypothesis in seeking to provide a science of history. As he put it in a characteristic passage: 'If the present be compared with the remote past, it is easily seen that in all cities and in all peoples, there are the same desires and the same passions as there always were.'[17] We may therefore conclude that philosophical

---

[17] *The Discourses of Niccolo Machiavelli*, ed. L.J. Walker (1950), i. 302. Cf. Montesquieu, *Considerations of the Causes of the Greatness of the Romans and their Decline*, ed. Lowenthal (1965), 26.

history has no special claim to be regarded as more *scientific* than any other form of historical investigation, and that it cannot be regarded as the first exercise in writing a *science* of history. The distinguishing features are rather to be found in the particular hypotheses used and in the *nature* of the question asked; a question which was stated very neatly and exactly by Dugald Stewart (surely the most perceptive of contemporary commentators) when he remarked:

When, in such a period of society as that in which we live, we compare our intellectual acquirements, our opinions, manners, and institutions, with those which prevail among rude tribes, it cannot fail to occur to us as an interesting question, by what gradual steps the transition has been made from the first simple efforts of uncultivated nature, to a state of things so wonderfully artificial and complicated. Whence has arisen that systematical beauty which we admire in the structure of a cultivated language ... Whence the origin of the different sciences and of the different arts ... Whence the astonishing fabric of the political union; the fundamental principles which are common to all governments ... ?. (Stewart, II. 45).

Finally, we should recall, as the last point implies, that philosophical history is in no sense confined to the particular area of enquiry which has been the main subject of this chapter. As we have seen, Smith himself referred to his interest in 'a sort of Philosophical History of all the different branches of Literature' (Corr., Letter 248), and his editors, Black and Hutton, to 'a plan he had once formed for giving a connected history of the liberal sciences and elegant arts' (Advertisement to *Essays on Philosophical Subjects*). In the same way Dugald Stewart mentioned Smith's essay on the *Origin of Languages* as a 'very beautiful specimen of theoretical history' (Stewart, II. 55) and took notice of the fact that the mathematical sciences 'afford very favourable subjects' for treatment of this kind (Stewart, II. 49). Indeed it is probably true that Smith's history of astronomy is one of the most perceptive and complete versions of the thesis which Smith left us, starting as it does from a statement of the principles of human nature as relevant for the work of scientific or speculative thought, before going on to trace the development of knowledge in terms of four major astronomical systems, which culminate in the work of Newton (above, 35).

II. *Analytical*

It is worth observing, firstly, that Smith's historical account of the rise and progress of government amounted to a denial that they could be the work of artifice, that is, the result of the kind of contract which is associated with John Locke. Smith made this point quite explicitly in the lectures (following Hume), in arguing that the doctrine seemed to be peculiar to Great Britain and that it was one of which the greater part of mankind were entirely ignorant. As he said, the 'foundation of a duty cannot be a principle with which mankind is entirely unacquainted' (LJ(B), 16, ed. Cannan, 12). The same point was also made in another way when Smith argued that government originated with the first division of property and the appearance of subordination; a situation which 'introduces some degree of that civil government which is indispensably necessary for its own preservation: and it seems to do this naturally, and even independent of the consideration of that necessity' (WN V. i. b. 12). In the same way Smith's social and historical argument led him to dismiss the Hobbesian state of nature as an irrelevance, since 'there is no such state existing' (LJ(B), 3, ed. Cannan, 2), and while agreeing with Locke that 'Men may live together in society with some tolerable degree of security, though there is no civil magistrate' (WN V. i. b. 2) he confined this judgement to the first and rudest state (the North American Indian), which he denied could be defined as a 'state of nature'. The reason is obvious, since if we define human experience as something which is subject to a process of continuous change, then every state can be regarded as natural. The point was neatly put by Adam Ferguson when he enquired, 'If we are asked, therefore, Where the state of nature is to be found? we may answer, It is here; and it matters not whether we are understood to speak in the island of Great Britain, at the Cape of Good Hope, or the Straits of Magellan.'[18]

Secondly, we should recall that Smith's specific interest in *social* history found a number of precedents and parallels on the Continent and that he can be said to have been well aware

---

[18] Adam Ferguson, *The History of Civil Society* (1767), ed. Duncan Forbes (1966), 8. See generally Part I, Section 1 where Ferguson deals at some length with 'the question relating to the State of Nature'.

of the fact. It is interesting to note in this connection that as Quaestor for the University Library his purchases included the works of Giannonne, Daniel, and Brosse, and that he owned copies of Fénelon, Fontenelle, Rollin, Raynal, Mably, Duclos, and Chastellux, to name but a few.[19]

In many cases such writers are associated with something of a revolution in historical writing; a revolution whose nature is aptly expressed in Voltaire's comment that 'My principal object is to know, as far as I can, the manners of peoples, and to study the human mind. I shall regard the order of succession of kings and chronology as my guides, but not as the objects of my work.'[20] Writing much earlier, the Italian Giannonne felt able to state that his *History of Naples*, 'wherein the Policy, Laws and Customs of so noble a Kingdom, shall be treated separately', could be regarded for this reason as being altogether new.[21] But of course it was Giannonne's pupil, Montesquieu, who 'first showed that laws were not the arbitrary fiat of their makers' and who now seems to stand at the beginning of a major change in historical writing.[22] As John Millar often said, it was Montesquieu who first pointed out the way, and the acknowledgement finds an echo in Dugald Stewart's generous assessment of his influence (Stewart, II. 50).

Thirdly, it is appropriate to observe that the interest which Smith showed in economic forces also featured largely at the time. For example, Harrington was widely recognized as a

[19] See for example Carl Becker, *The Heavenly City of the Eighteenth-Century Philosophers* (1932), lecture 3; H.R. Trevor-Roper, 'The Scottish Enlightenment', in *Studies on Voltaire and the Eighteenth Century* (1967), vol. 58, and 'The idea of the Decline and Fall of the Roman Empire', in *The Age of Enlightenment*, ed. W.H. Barber (1967).

[20] Quoted in J.B. Black, *The Art of History* (1926), 34. See also J.H. Brumfitt, *Voltaire: Historian* (1958).

[21] Pietro Giannonne, *The Civil History of the Kingdom of Naples: Where the Author Clearly Demonstrates, That the Temporal Dominion and Power exercis'd by the Popes, has been altogether owing to the Ignorance, and Connivance of, or Concessions extorted from Secular Princes during the Dark Ages.* (Translated by James Ogilvy, 1729.) The introduction is especially informative; for comment see Trevor-Roper, *Studies on Voltaire*, 1653.

[22] Kingsley Martin, *French Liberal Thought in the Eighteenth Century*, ed. J.P. Mayer (1954), 152. In Scottish circles at least, the emphasis given to physical factors was widely discounted. See for example, Hume's essay 'Of National Characters' and John Millar's introduction to his *Origin of the Distinction of Ranks* (1771, ed. W.C. Lehmann, 1960).

'profound political writer' and as one who showed a 'thorough acquaintance with the true principles of democracy'.[23] Montesquieu too had shown an interest in the role of time in his *Considérations* (1752),[24] and had given some attention to economic factors in the *Esprit*, especially in Book XX where he examined the problem of 'How commerce broke through the barbarism of Europe'. The same basic theme is featured in Rousseau's *Origin of Inequality*, in Hutcheson's *System*, and especially in Hume's *History*, where he relates the increasing significance of that middling rank of men 'who are the best and firmest basis of public liberty' to the growth of commerce and industry.[25] Another notable figure in this general area is Lord Kames, who as early as 1747 had quite unequivocally linked the decline of feudal institutions to the appearance of arts and industry, in remarking that 'after the arts of Peace began to be cultivated, Manufactures and trade to revive in Europe, and Riches to increase, this Institution began to turn extremely burdensome. It first tottered and then fell by its own Weight, as wanting a solid foundation.'[26]

While it is not so much our purpose here to assess the extent of Smith's intellectual debts as to report on the existence of a climate of opinion, it should also be noted that the idea of distinct socio-economic stages was also entering the literature on quite a wide front. It is found, for example, as early as 1750 in Turgot's (unpublished) notes for a *Universal History*, in the first two books of Sir James Steuart's *Principles*,[27] first published in 1767 but completed

[23] Kames, *Sketches* (1774), ii. 197; Millar, HV iii. 286. Harrington's *Oceana* (1656, 3rd edn. 1747) was also praised in Hume's essay on 'The idea of a Perfect Commonwealth' and was given considerable attention by Francis Hutcheson in his *System of Moral Philosophy* (1755), Book 3, chap. 6: 'The Several Forms of Polity, with their Principal Advantages and Disadvantages'.

[24] Perhaps the best example of a truly dynamic theory of historical change is provided by Vico's remarkable *New Science* (1725). This work does not, however, seem to have had much direct impact at least in this country.

[25] For comment, see Forbes, Introduction to Hume's *History*, 39.

[26] *Essays Upon Several Subjects concerning British Antiquities* (1747). For comment see I.S. Ross, *Lord Kames and the Scotland of his Day* (1972).

[27] These points are made in Steuart's *Principles* (ed. Skinner) at lxiii and note; R.L. Meek, 'Smith, Turgot, and the Four Stages Theory', in *History of Political Economy*, vol. 3 (1971) and his introduction to *Turgot on Progress, Sociology and Economics* (1973).

in outline by 1758, and also in Kames's *Historical Law Tracts*, printed in the same year.[28]

However, it would appear that Smith must be regarded as a particularly influential figure in the development of this general line of thought; one which appears to have been especially dominant among Scottish writers at this time. It was in recognition of this point that Dugald Stewart felt moved to remark, in the course of an address to the Royal Society of Edinburgh, that

It will not, I hope, be imputed to me as a blamable instance of national vanity, if I conclude this Section with remarking the rapid progress that has been made in our own country during the last fifty years, in tracing the origin and progress of the present establishments in Europe. Montesquieu undoubtedly led the way, but much has been done since the publication of his works, by authors whose names are enrolled among the members of this Society (*Works*, x. 147).

Fourthly, it may be noted that even if the work done by Smith and his contemporaries finds parallels and precedents, nevertheless it does appear to have been remarkable for the *weight* of emphasis which was placed on economic factors. As we have seen, there were really two applications of the general thesis: first, the argument that the development of productive forces ultimately depended on the 'natural wants' of man; the point being that man is first subject to certain basic needs which, once satisfied, allow him to pursue more complex goals (WN III. iii. 12). The same point was made by Adam Ferguson in remarking that 'refinement and plenty foster new desires, while they furnish the means, or practice the methods, to gratify them'.[29] John Millar also linked these natural and insatiable desires to the development of productive forces, and even went so far as to argue that the latter would emerge in a sequence which corresponded to the four socio-economic stages.[30]

[28] The stadial argument figures especially in Tract I, 'Criminal Law', and Tract II, 'Promises and Covenants'. Dugald Stewart considered that Kames's *Law Tracts* provided some 'excellent specimens' of philosophical history (Stewart, II. 51).

[29] *History of Civil Society*, ed. Forbes, 216–17. See also the same author's *Principles of Moral and Political Science* (1792), chap. 3, section ix. The thesis is a feature of Smith's *Lectures* (for example, LJ(B) 206–11, ed. Cannan, 157–61) and TMS IV. i. i, 'Of the Beauty which the Appearance of Utility bestows upon all the Productions of Art, and of the extensive Influence of this Species of Beauty'.

[30] *Origins*, ed. Lehmann, 176, cf. 224.

The second application of the thesis is of course to be found in the link which Smith established between economic organization and the social structure, particularly with regard to the classes involved and the relations of power and dependence likely to exist between them. As we have seen, the link which was established between the form of economy and the social structure was remarkably explicit, so much so indeed as to permit William Robertson to state the main propositions which were involved with great accuracy and economy. As he put it, 'In every enquiry concerning the operations of men when united together in society, the first object of attention should be their mode of subsistence. According as that varies, their laws and policy must be different.'[31]

No doubt some of the writers who employed these propositions in the interpretation of the history of civil society could be accused of vulgar 'Marxism' in the sense that they were occasionally guilty of employing the arguments in an unqualified form.[32] But Smith did not commit any such 'error'. His carefully qualified view can be seen in many ways and is nowhere more obvious than in Smith's use of the economic stages, which are offered as general categories in terms of which the experience of different peoples can be interpreted rather than as templates to which that experience must be made to conform.

[31] *Works* v. 111 and 128. For comment on the work of what is in effect a Scottish Historical School, see especially the pioneering article of Roy Pascal, 'Property and Society: The Scottish Historical School of the Eighteenth Century', *Modern Quarterly* (1938); Gladys Bryson, *Man and Society: The Scottish Inquiry of the Eighteenth Century* (1945). Three notable contributions which followed are: R.L. Meek, 'The Scottish Contribution to Marxist Sociology' (1954), reprinted in *Economics and Ideology and Other Essays* (1967); Duncan Forbes, 'Scientific Whiggism: Adam Smith and John Millar', *Cambridge Journal*, 7 (1953–4); and W.C. Lehmann, *John Millar of Glasgow* (1960). For more recent comment on related subjects see L. Schneider, *The Scottish Moralists on Human Nature and Society* (1967), J.R. Lindgren, *The Social Philosophy of Adam Smith* (1973), and D.A. Reisman, *Adam Smith's Sociological Economics* (1976).

[32] Even the Marxist view is a qualified one: in a letter to J. Bloch, dated September 1890, Engels wrote that 'According to the materialist conception of history, the *ultimately* determining element in history is the production and reproduction of real life. More than this neither Marx nor I have ever asserted. Hence if somebody twists this into saying that the economic element is the *only* determining one, he transforms that proposition into a meaningless, abstract, senseless phrase.' *Marx–Engels, Selected Works* (1958), ii. 488.

Finally, we should note that while Smith did regard the processes of history as inherently complex, he did nonetheless associate these processes with certain definite trends. As we have seen, the growth of 'luxury and commerce' is represented as the inevitable outcome of normal human drives, and associated with the appearance of new sources of wealth together with a particular type of economy: an economy composed of interdependent sectors within and between which all goods and services command a price. These new forms of wealth allied to the high degree of personal liberty appropriate to the new patterns of dependence also brought with them a new social and political order — a form of 'constitution'[33] which was often cited as an explanation for, and in defence of, the English Revolution Settlement. In this way Whig principles could be put on a sound historical basis; a point which is neatly illustrated by Ramsay's comment on Lord Kames's abandonment of his early Jacobite leanings. Ramsay expressed no surprise that Kames should have finally concluded that the Revolution was 'absolutely necessary' after 'studying history and conversing with first rate people' — no doubt including Smith.[34] Rather similar sentiments were expressed by John Millar when he remarked that 'When we examine historically the extent of the tory, and of the whig principle, it seems evident, that from the progress of arts and commerce, the former has been continually diminishing, and the latter gaining ground in the same proportion' (HV iv. 304).[35] There is little doubt that Smith shared such opinions, or that he rejoiced in a situation where the personal liberty of the subject had been confirmed at the expense of the absolutist pretensions of kings. However, there are perhaps

---

[33] 'Upon the manner in which any state is divided into the different orders and societies which compose it, and upon the particular distribution which has been made of their respective powers, privileges, and immunities, depends, what is called, the constitution of that particular state' (TMS VI. ii. 2. 8).

[34] Ramsay, *Scotland and Scotsmen*, ed. Allardyce, from the Ochtertyre MS, i. 191 (1888).

[35] In LJ(A) v. 124, Smith associated the 'bustling, spirited, active folks' with the Whig interest, and the 'calm, contented folks of no great spirit and abundant fortunes' with the Tories. He also argues in this place that while the Tories favour the principle of authority, the Whig interest favoured that of utility in matters of government.

three points which should be made by way of qualification to this simple view.

First, while Smith did argue that the 'commercial' stage of socio-economic growth would have certain recognizable features, he did not suggest that it was incompatible with 'absolutist' government. For example both France and Spain could be regarded as 'developed' economies from a historical point of view, yet both were associated with monarchical systems which pretended to be absolutist.[36] Smith also made this point with respect to England, in arguing that the first effect of a developing manufacturing sector had been to *increase* the power of her kings (for example, the Tudors) at the expense of the lords;[37] the point being that the decline in the power of the lords had taken place before the same underlying causes elevated the Commons to a superior degree of influence.[38]

Secondly, Smith argued that England was really a special case, and that she alone had escaped from absolutism.[39] To a great extent this was the reflection of her own natural economic advantages (WN III. iv. 20), but Smith also emphasized other factors, many of which were of an extra-economic type. For example, he argued that the solution to the Scottish problem (brought about by union), allied to Britain's situation as an island, had obviated the need for a standing army,[40] and thus denied her kings an important instrument of oppression.

---

[36] Smith comments in WN I. xi. n. 1 that though 'the feudal system has been abolished in Spain and Portugal, it has not been succeded by a much better'.

[37] This point is made in LJ(A) iv. 159 and LJ(B) 59–60, ed. Cannan, 42, where it is stated that as a result of the growth of manufactures etc. 'the power of the nobility was diminished, and that too before the House of Commons had established its authority, and thus the king became arbitrary. Under the House of Tudor the government was quite arbitrary, the nobility were ruined, and the boroughs lost their power.'

[38] Smith considers the rise of the House of Commons in LJ(A) iv. 148 ff., LJ(B) 58–9, ed. Cannan, 40–1.

[39] Smith emphasized England's position as a special case at some length. See expecially LJ(A) iv. 168 where it is stated that 'In England alone a different government has been established from the naturall course of things. The situation and circumstances of England have been altogether different.' Cf. Millar, HV iv. 102–4 and Forbes's edition of Hume's *History*, 23.

[40] The same arguments are considered in the opening lecture of LJ(A) v where Smith also includes a review of the constitutional guarantees of English liberties. Similar arguments are stated in LJ(B) 61–4, ed. Cannan, 43–6, although at rather less length.

He added that Elizabeth I had also contributed to weaken the position of her successors by selling off Crown lands; a policy which was not unconnected with the fact that she had no direct heir. As Smith presents the case, it was the growing weakness of the Stuart kings (reflecting in part their own peculiarities of character), and the growing significance of the Commons, which had ultimately combined to produce that particular system of liberty which was now found in England. In England alone, he emphasized, liberty is secured by 'an assembly of the representatives of the people, who claim the sole right of imposing taxes' (WN IV. vii. b. 51).

Thirdly, it should be recalled that Smith rejoiced in the system of security which had been established in England and 'perfected by the revolution' (WN IV. v. b. 43) on moral, political, and economic grounds. Indeed he quite clearly believed that the natural effort of every man to better his condition, allied to the security given him under the law, had 'maintained the progress of England towards opulence and improvement in almost all former times, and . . . it is to be hoped, will do so in all future times' (II. iii. 36).

Yet Smith was very far from arguing that personal freedom, in the sense of security under the law, was incompatible with absolutism, and if he preferred the English model he was very far from suggesting that that experience represented the best of all possible worlds. In his *Early Draft* especially, Smith adverted to the 'oppressive inequality' of the modern economy,[41] and elsewhere drew attention to the fact that the House of Commons, whose power provided the foundation and protection of the liberty of the subject, could easily become a clearing-house for those sectional interests on which that power was collectively based (WN I. xi. p. 10). Smith was also well aware of the problem of corruption in politics and of the fact that the institutions of British Government were markedly unrepresentative.[42] 'It is in Britain alone

[41] The *Early Draft* opens chapter 2 with a long statement concerning the problem of inequality in the modern state.

[42] The distinction between personal and political freedom is a major feature of Duncan Forbes's article, 'Sceptical Whiggism, Commerce, and Liberty', in *Essays on Adam Smith*. See also Donald Winch, *Adam Smith's Politics: An Essay in Historiographic Revision* (1978), 40. One of the most interesting features of this valuable study is the attention given to Frances Hutcheson and to the contrast between his political views and those of Smith.

that any consent of the people is required, and God knows it is but a very figurative metaphoricall consent which is given here. And in Scotland still more than in England, as but very few have a vote for a Member of Parliament who give this metaphoricall consent' (LJ(A), v. 134).

Yet if Smith did notice many of the defects of modern society, and some of the problems which were to arise in the future, the general tenor of his argument must be said to be broadly optimistic with regard to the possibilities of economic and political development. In this respect his position is perhaps adequately summarized in the remarks of his pupil, Millar,[43] who wrote that when we contemplate the 'crowds of people . . . continually rising from the lower ranks . . . how habits of industry, have banished idleness . . . and have put it into the power of almost every individual by the exertion of his own talents, to earn a comfortable subsistence', then 'We cannot entertain a doubt of their powerful efficacy to propagate corresponding sentiments, of personal independence, and to instill higher notions of general liberty' (HV iv. 124–5). The point was not lost on the French revolutionary, Barnave, who, writing quite independently of Smith and his contemporaries, reached the conclusion that

As soon as the arts and commerce succeed in penetrating the life of the society, and of opening up a new source of wealth for the labouring class, a revolution is prepared in political laws; a new distribution of wealth produces a new distribution of power. Just as the possession of land created aristocracy, so industrial property gives rise to the power of the people. It acquires liberty; it grows in numbers, it begins to influence affairs.[44]

In so far as Smith's position can be adequately summarized in the manner suggested by this concluding section it is important to observe that his sociological and historical analyses suggest two points which are to be borne in mind. First, that the existence of the fourth economic stage *necessarily* implies a particular pattern of dependence in society and, secondly,

---

[43]   This view is contested, at least to some extent, in Winch, op. cit. 100–2.

[44]   Quoted in Laski, *The Rise of European Liberalism* (1936), 232. The socio-economic content of Steuart's *Principles* prompted the editor of the French translation (1789) to remark that of the advantages to be derived from reading the book: 'Le premier sera de convaincre, sans doute, que le révolution qui s'opere sous nos yeux était dans l'ordre des choses nécessaires.' Steuart, op. cit. 24n.

that the attainment of the fourth stage *may* generate the kind
of political and constitutional outcome which Smith found in
Great Britain. The first point is relevant for the understanding
of Smith's economics, to which we now turn, and the second
for the understanding of his treatment of the state, which is
the subject of the concluding chapter.

5

The Development of a System*

Smith's purely economic analysis attempted to explain the *modus operandi* of a type of economy which corresponds to the 'commercial' stage of the theory of history, so that the main features of this stage are implicit in the argument of the previous chapter. In addition it is noteworthy that Smith's economic analysis rests on a particular judgement regarding the nature of the social bond. The formal argument is developed in the *Theory of Moral Sentiments* but it should be stressed that only part of the argument there stated is relevant at this stage. That is to say, all that is necessary for the purposes of Smith's *economic* analysis is that men should be restrained from hurting one another both in respect of their persons and *property*.

I

It may be appropriate to consider certain aspects of the *Theory of Moral Sentiments* at the outset,[1] not least because it is now a familiar fact that Smith had intended to complete a wider system of social science of which this work and the *Wealth of Nations* were only parts.[2] The issue of consistency or inconsistency between the ethical and the economic work need not detain us here beyond noting that the contrast which was at one time drawn by commentators between sympathy on the one hand, and self-interest on the other, was often

---

* This article originally appeared in the *Scottish Journal of Political Economy*, 23 (1976).
    [1] References in this section are to the first edition of the *Theory of Moral Sentiments* printed for A. Miller and J. Bell in 1759. The particular edition used is a part of the David Murray Collection in Glasgow University Library and was presented by its author to Lord Kames. The first reference given is to the page numbers of this edition; the second indicates Part, Section, Chapter, and Paragraph number from the 6th edition (1790).
    [2] See above, 12.

based on a misunderstanding of the two terms. In fact the *Theory of Moral Sentiments* gave a good deal of attention to self-regarding propensities, although it must be said that the book was dominated by the concept of sympathy, in the sense of fellow-feeling. It is this capacity which, together with reason and imagination, permits us to judge the propriety of actions taken by others and to visualize how others would judge us when both impartial and well-informed. Since we have no immediate experience of what other men feel, Smith went on to associate the generous virtue of humanity with the degree to which the individual is capable of 'changing places in the fancy' with others, and linked the 'awful and respectable virtue' of self-command with the extent to which we are able to bring down our own expressions of feeling to a level that the spectator is capable of understanding. An essential premiss of the argument is that men typically regard the opinion of their fellows as important; that they seek to be approved of, and to be worthy of, that approval.

In practice Smith placed a great deal of emphasis on the latter assumptions, and in applying them to the economic sphere observed that actions of themselves self-regarding often have a social reference. For example, in section iii of Part I of the *Theory of Moral Sentiments*, having observed that 'mankind are disposed to sympathize more entirely with our joy than with our sorrow', he went on to note that

it is chiefly from this regard to the sentiments of mankind, that we pursue riches and avoid poverty. For to what purpose is all the toil and bustle of this world? what is the end of avarice and ambition, of the pursuit of wealth, of power, and preheminence? Is it to supply the necessities of nature? The wages of the meanest labourer can supply them . . . From whence, then, arises that emulation which runs through all the different ranks of men, and what are the advantages which we propose by that great purpose of human life which we call bettering our condition? To be observed, to be attended to, to be taken notice of with sympathy, complacency, and approbation, are all the advantages which we can propose to derive from it. It is the vanity, not the ease, or the pleasure, which interests us. But vanity is always founded upon the belief of our being the object of attention and approbation (108–10; I. iii. 2.1).

It is evident that Smith associated a degree of inequality with the drive to better our condition, going on from here to

make three interesting points all of which are associated with the argument thus far. First, he suggests that upon 'this disposition of mankind, to go along with all the passions of the rich and the powerful, is founded the distinction of ranks, and the order of society' (114; I. iii. 2. 3). Secondly, he noted that the rich have an important (almost physiocratic) function with regard to the distribution of the product. In a passage which contains a notable reference to the invisible hand, Smith remarks with regard to the rich man that

The homely and vulgar proverb, that the eye is larger than the belly, never was more fully verified than with regard to him. The capacity of his stomach bears no proportion to the immensity of his desires, and will receive no more than that of the meanest peasant. The rest he is obliged to distribute among those, who prepare, in the nicest manner, that little which he himself makes use of . . . They consume little more than the poor, and in spite of their natural selfishness and rapacity, tho' they mean only their own conveniency, tho' the sole end which they propose from the labours of all the thousands whom they employ, be the gratification of their own vain and insatiable desires, they divide with the poor the produce of all their improvements. They are led by an invisible hand to make nearly the same distribution of the necessaries of life, which would have been made, had the earth been divided into equal portions among all its inhabitants, and thus without intending it, without knowing it, advance the interest of the society, and afford means to the multiplication of the species (349–50; IV. i. 1. 10).

Thirdly, it is noteworthy that Smith should have stressed the importance of emulation on the part of the 'poor', that is those actively in pursuit of the status which wealth can bring and of its imagined conveniences. It was in this connection that he remarked on the deception involved in the pursuit of riches, meaning that, once attained, the realized satisfaction rarely equalled that which had been expected. He added that

it is well that nature imposes upon us in this manner. It is this deception which rouses and keeps in continual motion the industry of mankind. It is this which first prompted them to cultivate the ground, to build houses, to found cities and commonwealths, and to invent and improve all the sciences and arts, which ennoble and embellish human life; which have entirely changed the whole face of the globe, have turned the rude forests of nature into agreeable and fertile plains, and made the trackless and barren ocean a new fund of subsistence, and the great high road of communication to the different nations of the earth. The earth, by these labours of mankind has been obliged to redouble her

natural fertility, and to maintain a greater multitude of inhabitants (348-9; IV. i. 1. 10).

So far it will be observed that Smith has merely been describing a general tendency of human nature and some of its largely economic consequences, but he went even further in suggesting that the pursuit of the self-regarding goals already described was worthy of *moral* approval. Thus he commented that 'A person appears mean-spirited' who does not pursue the 'more extraordinary and important objects of self-interest', and contrasted the 'man of dull regularity' with the 'man of enterprise', going on to remark that 'Those great objects of self-interest, of which the loss or acquisition quite changes the rank of the person, are the objects of the passion properly called ambition; a passion which, when it keeps within the bounds of prudence and justice, is always admired in the world' (304; III. 6. 7). Later in the book the general position was further clarified, in a way which reminds us of the earlier discussion of self-command, when Smith stated that we also tend to approve of the *means* adopted to attain the *ends* of ambition. 'Hence', it is remarked, 'that eminent esteem with which all men naturally regard a steady persever- ance in the practice of frugality, industry and application, though directed to no other purpose than the acquisition of fortune.' Indeed Smith went further in arguing that it 'is the consciousness of this merited approbation and esteem which is alone capable of supporting the agent in this tenour of conduct', since normally the 'pleasure which we are to enjoy ten years hence interests us so little in comparison with that which we may enjoy today' (362-3; IV. i. 2. 8).

If we look back over this argument there is surely a great deal of material which is important with regard to our under- standing of Smithian economics, especially since it is here suggested that the pursuit of (self-interested) economic goals typically has a *social* significance, as do the means chosen to attain them, such as prudence and frugality. As we have seen, Smith suggests that it is the attempt to attain these ends which leads to the development of productive forces, and to a pattern of distribution of the product arising from the expenditure of riches. The emphasis in this respect at least is on self-regarding pursuits, although Smith was careful to argue

that the pursuit of such goals is only tolerable within a framework which reflects man's capacity for fellow-feeling; that is,
his sympathy for those whose interests may be damaged by
others. Thus, if the individual

> would act so as that the impartial spectator may enter into the principles
> of his conduct, which is what of all things he has the greatest desire
> to do, he must, upon this, as upon all other occasions, humble the
> arrogance of his self-love, and bring it down to something which other
> men can go along with. They will indulge it so far as to allow him to be
> more anxious about, and to pursue with more earnest assiduity, his own
> happiness than that of any other person. Thus far, whenever they place
> themselves in his situation, they will readily go along with him. In the
> race for wealth, and honours, and preferments, he may run as hard as
> he can, and strain every nerve and every muscle, in order to outstrip all
> his competitors. But if he should justle, or throw down any of them,
> the indulgence of the spectators is entirely at an end. It is a violation of
> fair play, which they cannot admit of (182–3; II. ii. 2. 1).

It is ultimately our tendency to sympathize with the
sufferer and to resent any damage caused to him that leads
to the approval of punishment and the imposition of certain
restraints on the actions of individuals. The same point also
leads back to Smith's thesis that the basic precondition of
social stability is a system of positive law embodying our
conception of the rules of justice which are administered by
some system of magistracy.

When we come to the economic analysis of the *Lectures*
many of the points made above are either repeated or taken
for granted. The analysis, for example, quite clearly proceeds
on the assumption of some system of security, and opens in
a manner which would have been immediately recognizable
to the students of the *Theory of Moral Sentiments*. Smith in
effect begins by reminding his auditors of the importance of
the 'natural wants' of man, and attributes the development
of agriculture, manufactures, and the useful arts (including
geometry and government) to the 'delicacy' of our tastes
rather than to the simpler desire to acquire 'our three humble
necessities, food, clothes and lodging'. In this way the general
theme of change and growth which so informs this aspect of
the discussion in the *Theory of Moral Sentiments* is continued,
although there are some differences: notably that the pursuit
of the sources of pleasure or satisfaction is now stated solely

in terms of self-interest and without further reference to the
sociological factors which had so dominated the argument of
the ethical work; a background with which his auditors would
certainly be expected to be familiar.

II

The arguments so far reviewed all come from work which
Smith had completed by 1759 when the first edition of the
Theory of Moral Sentiments appeared.

However, the *formal* analysis of economic phenomena is
to be found elsewhere — chiefly in Smith's *Lectures*, whose
content is such as to suggest that the more direct influences
working upon him at this stage were probably Hutcheson and
Hume. In the latter case the possibilities are considerable and
indeed acknowledged by Smith in relation to such topics as
the specie-flow doctrine, the treatment of interest, and the
association of liberty with the commercial stage of history.
But Hume's influence was probably still more pervasive, conscious as he was of the basic sectoral division of manufactures
and agriculture, and of the association between development
in the arts and the natural wants of man. There are certainly
enough areas of agreement between the two men to lend some
credence to Dugald Stewart's general assessment, namely
that 'The Political Discourses of Mr Hume were evidently
of greater use to Mr Smith, than any other book that had
appeared prior to his lectures' (Stewart, IV. 24).

The influence of the 'never to be forgotten' Hutcheson is
possibly of even greater significance — a point which has been
elaborated particularly by W.R. Scott.[3] It will suffice here to
recall that although Hutcheson may have had some 'mercan-
tilist' leanings, none the less his treatment of economics at
an analytical level unfolds in an order and in a form which
corresponds closely to the argument offered by Smith. We
find, for example, the same emphasis on the division of
labour, with attention drawn both to the phenomenon of

---

[3] W.R. Scott, *Francis Hutcheson* (1900), chapter xi. Hutcheson's role in relation to Smith was noted by Cannan in his introductions to the *Lectures on
Justice, Police, Revenue and Arms* (1896) and the *Wealth of Nations* (1904). The
most elaborate recent treatment will be found in W.L. Taylor, *Francis Hutcheson
and David Hume as Precursors of Adam Smith* (1965).

interdependence and to the sources of increased productivity, not to mention a similar emphasis on the importance of security as a basic pre-condition of social stability and economic growth. In dealing with price we find a distinction in effect between supply and demand prices — with the former defined in terms of labour cost and in a way which allows for the cost of materials, the skill of the artist, and even the social position which he may expect to maintain. The treatment of money follows, and contains, like Smith's, an interesting discussion of the measure of value before going on to treat such topics as interest and insurance under the general heading of 'The Principal Contracts in a Social Life'. There is certainly enough in all this to amply justify the general assessment offered by Scott and Cannan with respect to Hutcheson's role. The only point which should be added perhaps is that Hutcheson did *not* neglect the importance of self-interest — the point with which Smith took issue was Hutcheson's alleged denial that actions of a self-regarding type could ever be regarded as worthy of *moral* approbation.[4]

Smith's early writings on economics (apart from two short fragments on the division of labour) are contained in the two sets of lecture-notes currently available to us and in the document first discovered by W.R. Scott and described by him as an 'early draft' of the *Wealth of Nations*. The latter document belongs to the same broad period as the lectures which relate

[4] See above, 45n. Hutcheson was just as aware as Smith had been of the existence of self- and other-regarding propensities and of the need to attain some degree of control over the former. As this implies, he did not neglect the importance of self-interest. In the *System of Moral Philosophy*, Book I, chapter 2 (i. 28), it is remarked for example that 'A penetrating genius, capacity for business, patience of application and labour ... are naturally admirable, and relished by all observers; but with quite a different feeling from moral approbation'. Again, in Book I, chapter 8, it is noted that

Moral goodness indeed consists principally in the social and kind affections carrying us out beyond ourselves. But there is a natural subserviency of the private or selfish affections, while they are kept within certain bounds, not only to the good of the individual, but to that of the system; nor is anyone compleat in his kind without them. And as the happiness of a system results from that of the individuals, 'tis necessary to it, that each one have the selfish affections in that degree which his best state requires ... (i. 149).

He went on: 'Tis ... evident that the selfish affections may be excessive and vicious. But it ought also to be observed that there may be a degree of them too low and defective with respect to the intention of nature' (i. 150).

respectively to the sessions 1762-3 and 1763-4. There are of course differences between these documents: the first set of lecture-notes on economic topics is less complete than the second, for example, and excludes the discussion of Law's Bank, interest, exchange, and the causes of the slow progress of opulence. On the other hand, the topics covered in LJ(A) (which correspond approximately to sections 1-12 of Part 2 in Cannan's account) are typically handled with much greater elaboration — this is especially true of the treatment of the division of labour, the theory of price, and the problem of velocity. Again, LJ(B) is not only more complete but more highly polished; eschewing the passages of recapitulation with which Smith usually began his lectures. The *Early Draft*, on the other hand, while often seeming to follow the argument of LJ(A) rather than of LJ(B), features a coverage of the subject which matches that of the latter, although the topics are often handled only in note form. There are, however, perhaps two outstanding exceptions: the treatment of the origins and nature of the division of labour is much more elaborate in the *Early Draft* than in either version of the lectures (although the limitation imposed by the extent of the market is not mentioned),[5] and has the striking feature of beginning with a long polemic on the subject of inequality. Secondly, it is evident that the treatment of the causes of the slow progress of opulence is sometimes rather more elaborate than in LJ(B). But in all this there is no evidence of a major shift of analytical perspective, thus making it possible for us to take LJ(B) (i.e. the Cannan version) as providing a reasonable guide to Smith's system of economic analysis in the form in which it existed just prior to his visit to France.

The account which Smith provides in LJ(B) is concerned with an *economic* system which features the activities of agriculture, manufacture, and commerce (210, ed. Cannan, 160) where these activities are characterized by a division of labour (211-23, ed. Cannan, 161-72) with the patterns of exchange facilitated by the use of money (235-43, ed. Cannan, 182-90). There are three main features of the central analysis; the treatment of the division of labour, the analysis of price

[5] See below, Chapter 6.

and allocation, and the exposure of the mercantile fallacy. We may take these in turn, examining each topic with the minimum degree of elaboration which is consistent with coherence.

The division of labour is of course central to the analysis because it is by reference to this institution that Smith explains the growth in opulence which is associated with the development of the arts under the stimulus of the 'natural wants' of man (209-11, ed. Cannan, 159-61). Smith here rehearses points which have now become familiar, explaining the increase in productivity in terms of improved dexterity, the saving of time otherwise lost in passing from one function to another, and the scope given to the use of machines. But the second aspect of the argument is equally important in the sense that Smith draws attention to the high degree of interdependence which follows from the division of labour, and this in two ways. First, it is pointed out that in the modern state even a relatively simple product such as the labourer's woollen coat is the creation of a large number of different workmen including the wool-gatherer, the spinner, the dyer, weaver, tailor, etc. — not to mention the different processes involved in the manufacture of the tools required. Secondly, it is emphasized that in such a situation every man in effect acquires the goods he needs through exchange (218-22, ed. Cannan, 168-71); a point which leads directly to the discussion of price and allocation.

As in the case of the *Wealth of Nations*, Smith's handling of price theory is amongst the most successful aspects of the study, featuring as it does a clear distinction between natural and market price together with an examination of their interdependence. *Natural* price is defined in effect as the supply price of a commodity, where the latter refers to labour cost:

A man then has the natural price of his labour when it is sufficient to maintain him during the time of labour, to defray the expence of education, and to compensate the risk of not living long enough and of not succeeding in the business. When a man has this, there is sufficient encouragement to the labourer and the commodity will be cultivated in proportion to the demand (227, ed. Cannan, 176).

Market price, on the other hand, is the price which may prevail at any given point in time and will be determined, Smith argues, by the 'demand or need for the commodity',

its abundance or scarcity in relation to the demand (a point which is used to explain the 'paradox' of value), and, finally, the 'riches or poverty of those who demand' (227–8, ed. Cannan, 176–7). Smith then went on to suggest that although the two prices were logically distinct, they were also 'necessarily connected'. Thus in the event of market price rising above the natural level, the reward of labour in this employment will rise above its natural (long-run equilibrium) rate, leading to an inflow of labour and an expansion in supply (and vice versa). In equilibrium, therefore, the market and natural price will be the same; a point which allowed Smith to go on to argue that 'whatever police' tends to prevent this coincidence will 'diminish public opulence' (230, ed. Cannan, 178). The familiar examples which contributed to keep the market above the natural price include taxes on industry, monopolies, and the exclusive privileges of corporations — all of which affect price either through their impact on the supply of the commodity or on the flow of labour to a specific employment. Similarly, Smith criticized policies such as the bounty on corn, which kept market below the natural price. Now these examples refer of course to particular cases, but Smith may be said to have added a further dimension to the problem in grasping the fact that the economic system can be seen under a more general aspect. This much is evident in his objection to particular regulations of 'police' on the ground that they distorted the use of resources by breaking 'what may be called the natural balance of industry' and interfering with the 'natural connexion of all trades in the stock' (233–4, ed. Cannan, 180–1). He concluded: 'Upon the whole, therefore, it is by far the best police to leave things to their natural course' (235, ed. Cannan, 182).

The third main aspect of the argument relates to the issue of money — a concept whose relevance is implied in the previous discussion of price, but which is introduced at this point perhaps because it provided an easy means of transition to the discussion of a particular branch of police which attracted Smith's attention — the mercantile system. The subject is approached by way of a discussion of the role of money as the instrument of exchange, which enables Smith to demonstrate that natural opulence does not consist in

money and to expose the absurdity of policies which were designed to prohibit the free exportation of specie. The policy is shown not merely to involve an error, but also to have pernicious effects with regard to the use of resources — once again returning to the general theme stated in connection with the theory of allocation. The advantages of free trade are thus suggested to complement those of domestic economic freedom, and the argument closes with the claim that all policies in restraint of trade, whether based on misunderstanding or national jealousy (a point more than a little reminiscent of Hume), should be rooted out:

From the above considerations it appears that Brittain should by all means be made a free port, that there should be no interruptions of any kind made to forreign trade, that if it were possible to defray the expences of government by any other method, all duties, customs, and excise should be abolished, and that free commerce and liberty of exchange should be allowed with all nations and for all things (269, ed. Cannan, 209).

While this account of Smith's early work on economics is necessarily brief, it may be sufficient to confirm that Smith had in fact attained a sophisticated grasp of the interdependence of economic phenomena prior to his departure for France in 1764. The same account also suggests that Smith had succeeded in producing an organised, systematic discourse, which also had the merit of presenting his policy views as the logical outcome of an underlying understanding of economic laws. It certainly seems likely that a man who had developed the level of interest in, and knowledge of, economic problems which is disclosed in the *Lectures* and the *Theory of Moral Sentiments* would be well equipped to appreciate the significance of what the physiocrats were trying to do — a group whose classical texts were already in existence before Smith completed his last lecture course, and whose primary source, the *Tableau Economique*, had already gone through several editions before the *Theory of Moral Sentiments* appeared.

III

Although Smith's first visit to Paris was for a period of only ten days, he was resident there continuously from December 1765 until the following October. Smith thus came into con-

tact with the Physiocratic School when it was virtually at the zenith of its powers, and it is now well known that he had ready access to the literary salons of the time.[6] We have it on his own authority that he was acquainted with Turgot, enjoying the happiness, 'I flattered myself, even of his friendship and esteem'.[7] Smith was also known to Quesnay,. whom he described as 'one of the worthiest men in France',[8] while in addition we learn from Dugald Stewart that 'Mr Smith had once an intention (as he told me himself) to have inscribed to him his "Wealth of Nations" ' (Stewart, III. 12).

Smith of course recognized Quesnay as the main physiocratic figure, and as the founder of a numerous sect whose members all followed his doctrines without 'sensible variation'. In fact Smith could have come in contact with Quesnay's work before leaving for France, in the shape of the articles 'Fermiers' (January 1756) and 'Grains' (November 1757). Both were published in the *Encyclopédie* (which Smith purchased for Glasgow University Library while Quaestor), and the second of the two may be particularly important since it was here that Quesnay drew attention to Cantillon's recognition of certain 'fundamental truths'. It is at least quite possible that Cantillon, as Professor Meek has suggested, was 'one of the main *theoretical* influences' working on Quesnay,[9] and it is now well known that Mirabeau too had made considerable use of the *Essai* (1755) when preparing his *Ami des Hommes* (1756). In practice, however, Smith refers to the

---

[6] The familiar facts are recorded in John Rae's *Life*, chapter xiv, and the rise of the School is traced in R.L. Meek's *Economics of Physiocracy* (1962). Smith's interest in physiocracy is attested by the contents of his library, which contained works by Quesnay, Mirabeau, Mercier de la Riviere, and Le Trosne. Smith also possessed a run of the *Journal de l'Agriculture* and of the *Ephemerides du Citoyen*, which included at least the first two parts of Turgot's *Reflections on the Formation and Distribution of Riches*, written in 1766.

[7] Letter 248, addressed to La Rochefoucauld, dated 1 November 1785. The connection is carefully examined by P.D. Groenewegen in 'Turgot and Adam Smith', *Scottish Journal of Political Economy*, 16 (1969).

[8] While in Paris, Quesnay attended Smith's young pupil, Buccleuch, in his capacity as a doctor. In Letter 97, addressed to Lady Frances Scott, dated 15 October 1766, Smith, having made the remark quoted in the text, went on to describe Quesnay as 'one of the best Physicians that is to be met with in any country. He was not only the Physician but the friend and confident of Madame Pompadour a women who was no contemptible Judge of merit.'

[9] *Economics of Physiocracy*, 267.

'arithmetical formularies' of the 'Œconomical Table' as a major source of Quesnay's views, and to some 'subsequent formularies' which consider the working of the system 'in different states of restraint and regulation' (WN IV. ix. 27). This reference would suggest that Smith may have made use of Quesnay's articles on the first and second 'economic problems' and, if so, that he was relying on Dupont's *Physiocratie* where the latter problem first appeared.[10] Smith also cited the *Philosophie Rurale* (1763), a joint production of Quesnay and Mirabeau, together with Mercier de la Riviere's *Natural and Essential Order of Political Societies* (1767), a 'little book' which provided the 'most distinct and best connected account' of the doctrine (WN IV. ix. 38). While Cannan was no doubt correct in suggesting that Smith's report on physiocracy did not obviously 'follow any particular book closely', still Quesnay would appear to be the dominant source. At the same time, however, it must be noted that the formulation of the model offered by Smith includes an allowance for the distinction between wages and profits, and this, together with the greater emphasis placed on the *avances foncières* and the tendency for profit levels to reach equality in different employments, may suggest the influence of Mercier — and perhaps that of other 'revisionists' such as Baudeau and Turgot.[11]

Smith's account of the physiocratic system begins with the now time-honoured statement of the different classes which feature in the model — proprietors, cultivators, manufacturers, and merchants — and thus draws attention to the main sectors of the economy together with the functions of the various groups which are involved. The proprietors, for example, are stated to be responsible for the *avances foncières*, that is, for expenses devoted to the improvement of land, buildings, drains, enclosures, and 'other ameliorations, which they may either make or maintain upon it, and by means of which the cultivators are enabled, with the same capital, to raise a greater produce, and consequently to pay a greater rent' (IV. ix. 6). Smith went on to note that this enhanced payment need not be regarded as rent properly so called in stating that

---

[10] Ibid. 265.
[11] The term is R.L. Meek's: see, for example, his essay on the 'Physiocratic Concept of Profit' in *Economics of Physiocracy*.

'This advanced rent may be considered as the interest or profit due to the proprietor upon the expence or capital which he thus employs' (ibid.). The second class, that of the cultivators, is divided into two sections: farmers and country labourers (IV. ix. 5), with the former having responsibility for two types of advance: *original* and *annual*. Smith defines the former in terms of investment in the instruments of husbandry, in the stock of cattle employed, and in the maintenance of the farmer's family, servants, and cattle 'during at least a great part of the first year of his occupancy' (IV. ix. 7). The annual expenses were said to consist in covering, for example, the cost of the seed annually used up, in the wear and tear of the instruments of husbandry, and in the annual maintenance of the farmer's servants and cattle. Smith went on to observe that the produce which remains to the farmer after the payment of rent would have to be sufficient to replace to him the whole of his annual expenses together with the ordinary profits of stock, and to replace within 'a reasonable time' or the period of the lease the whole of the original expenses together with a rate of return on capital equal to the ordinary or usual rate of profit. It is thus suggested that *profit* is the relevant form of return as far as the undertaker engaged in farming is concerned, and that it also accrues to the proprietor in respect of his *avances foncières*. In addition, the latter also receives a distinct form of return in the shape of *rent* properly so called, which is 'no more than the neat produce which remains after paying in the compleatest manner all the necessary expences which must be previously laid out in order to raise the gross, or the whole produce' (IV. ix. 7). It is because the advances of the proprietors and farmers are capable of generating this 'neat produce' that they are described, Smith comments, as productive expenses.

As far as the third class is concerned, there is a division between manufacturers and merchants, and, in terms of the former group, between employers and labourers. The employers emerge as being responsible for certain advances, which include 'materials, tools, and wages' (IV. ix. 10) so that the goods produced must be sufficient to repay the maintenance which the employer advances to himself, 'as well as the materials, tools and wages which he advances to his workmen'. *Wages*

thus emerge as the payment which accrues to the workmen, and *profit* as the fund which 'is destined for the maintenance of their employer' (IV. ix. 10). The difference, however, between this type of activity and that carried on by the farmers is, of course, that the latter generates not only a profit on capital invested, but also a neat produce which accrues as *rent*. Smith duly went on to report that 'The expence, therefore, laid out in employing and maintaining artificers and manufacturers, does no more than continue, if one may say so, the existence of its own value, and does not produce any new value' (IV. ix. 10). Hence the 'humiliating' description of this class, together with that of the merchants, as unproductive — that is, literally unproductive of a neat produce.

At the same time, however, Smith pointed out that the physiocratic system did make allowance for the fact that the manufacturing sector could contribute to economic growth, but only through 'parsimony', or, 'as it is expressed in this system, by privation, that is, by depriving themselves of a part of the funds destined for their own subsistence' (IV. ix. 13). In constrast to the farmers, 'They annually reproduce nothing but those funds. Unless, therefore, they annually save some part of them, unless they annually deprive themselves of the enjoyment of some part of them, the revenue and wealth of their society can never be in the smallest degree augmented by means of their industry' (IV. ix. 13).

But in fact Smith went further than the enumeration of the classes and their functions in drawing attention to a salient feature of the analysis: namely the interdependence which was shown to exist between all the relevant groups in the system. The point is evident in Smith's emphasis on the replacement of the various advances by virtue of the purchases (by all groups) of the agrarian and manufactured goods which were produced within any annual period. The same point was made quite explicit in another way, when he drew attention to the fact that the main purpose of Quesnay's 'Œconomical Table' was to show 'In what manner . . . the sum total of the annual produce of the land is distributed among the three classes above mentioned, and in what manner the labour of

the unproductive class, does no more than replace the value of its own consumption' (IV. ix. 27).

Interestingly enough, Smith also chose to emphasize the issue of interdependence by focusing attention on the position of the unproductive class, who were shown to be ultimately dependent on the 'two other classes', whose purchases finally pay the wages of the labourers employed and the profits which accrue, while furnishing it 'both with the materials of its work and with the fund of its subsistence, with the corn and cattle which it consumes while it is employed about that work' (IV. ix. 14). At the same time, Smith indicates that one purpose of the model was to show that the proprietors and farmers were interdependent, and that both in turn depended on the 'sterile' group for the manufactured products which they required. Smith also indicated that the productive class would benefit from the *sectoral* division of labour postulated in the model, which 'increases the productive powers of productive labour, by leaving it at liberty to confine itself to its proper employment, the cultivation of land' (IV. ix. 15). The basic analysis also served to suggest, as Smith went on to note, that the interests of the different classes did not conflict. He thus observed that 'It can never be the interest of the proprietors and cultivators to restrain or to discourage in any respect the industry of merchants, artificers and manufacturers', since 'The greater the liberty which this unproductive class enjoys, the greater will be the competition in all the different trades which compose it, and the cheaper will the other two classes be supplied' (IV. ix. 16). Similarly, it can never be the interest of the unproductive class to oppress the other two, since the greater the agricultural surplus, the 'greater must likewise be the maintenance and employment of that class', leading to the conclusion that 'The establishment of perfect justice, of perfect liberty, and of perfect equality, is the very simple secret which most effectually secures the highest degree of prosperity to all the three classes' (IV. ix. 17).

Having stated these basic principles, Smith then proceeded to illustrate their application in a relatively neglected area of physiocracy — international trade — at least to the extent of showing that the pattern of interdependence which exists between classes in the domestic case also applies to different

nations. Thus, for example, in speaking of mercantile states such as Holland and Hamburg it is pointed out that their labourers are just as surely maintained by the proprietors and cultivators as any other:

The only difference is, that those proprietors and cultivators are, the greater part of them, placed at a most inconvenient distance from the merchants, artificers, and manufacturers whom they supply with the materials of their work and the fund of their subsistence, are the inhabitants of other countries, and the subjects of other governments (IV. ix. 18).

Thus it can never be the interest of a landed nation to 'discourage or distress the industry of such mercantile states by imposing high duties upon their trade': first, because the nation which follows this policy, 'by raising the price of all foreign goods and of all sorts of manufactures . . . necessarily sinks the real value of the surplus produce of its own land'. Secondly, because the nation thus acting 'raises the rate of mercantile and manufacturing profit in proportion to that of agricultural profit, and consequently either draws from agriculture a part of the capital which had before been employed in it, or hinders from going to it a part of what would otherwise have gone to it' (IV. ix. 25). It therefore follows that 'The most effectual expedient . . . for raising the value of that surplus produce, for encouraging its increase, and consequently the improvement and cultivation of their own land, would be to allow the most perfect freedom to the trade of all . . . mercantile nations' (IV. ix. 20).[12]

But there was another and equally interesting reason for this policy, at least as reported by Smith: namely, that a landed nation whose growth was sustained through concentration on agriculture would eventually find itself able to 'justle out' the manufacturers and merchants of those nations on which it might originally have relied. The argument rests on two propositions which are more than a little reminiscent

---

[12] It is noted at WN IV. ix. 49 that 'Those systems, therefore, which preferring agriculture to all other employments, in order to promote it, impose restraints upon manufactures and foreign trade, act contrary to the very end which they propose, and indirectly discourage that very species of industry which they mean to promote. They are so far, perhaps, more inconsistent than even the mercantile system.'

of Smith's own thesis regarding the 'natural progress of opulence': first, that the

continual increase of the surplus produce of their land, would, in due time, create a greater capital than what could be employed with the ordinary rate of profit in the improvement and cultivation of land; and the surplus part of it would naturally turn itself to the employment of artificers and manufacturers at home (IV. ix. 22).

Secondly, that this

continual increase both of the rude and manufactured produce of those landed nations would in due time create a greater capital than could, with the ordinary rate of profit, be employed either in agriculture or in manufactures. The surplus of this capital would naturally turn itself to foreign trade, and be employed in exporting, to foreign countries, such parts of the rude and manufactured produce of its own country, as exceeded the demand of the home market (IV. ix. 23).

While Smith's account is an interesting record of what he understood physiocracy to be, there were, of course, many points on which he disagreed with its teaching. He criticized Quesnay, for example, for seeming to have advanced the view that a society could 'thrive and prosper only under a certain precise regimen, the exact regimen of perfect liberty and perfect justice' (IV. ix. 28), and rejected the thesis that artificers, manufacturers, and merchants could be regarded as unproductive (IV. ix. 29-37): a proposition which is described as the 'capital error of this system'. At the same time he drew attention to the superior application of the division of labour in manufactures and to the point that parsimony was the route to the achievement of net savings and thus growth for *all* classes in the system, not merely the manufacturing group (IV. ix. 34). But, at the same time, there was obviously a great deal with which the Smith of the *Lectures* could agree, and he duly concluded that

in representing the wealth of nations as consisting, not in the unconsumable riches of money, but in the consumable goods annually reproduced by the labour of the society; and in representing perfect liberty as the only effectual expedient for rendering this annual reproduction the greatest possible, its doctrine seems to be in every respect as just as it is generous and liberal (IV. ix. 38).

IV

The task of reaching some conclusions with regard to Smith's sources of ideas or inspiration helps to focus attention not just on these sources but also on the critical importance of his early writings. For, as Edwin Cannan noted, and subsequent discoveries have confirmed, some knowledge of Smith's early work on economics 'enables us to follow the gradual construction of the work almost from its very foundation, and to distinguish positively between what the original genius of its author created out of British materials on the one hand and French materials on the other'.[13] Perhaps the issues are less clear cut than Cannan implied, although it surely can be said with confidence that the early writings on economics provide a valuable record of an edifice whose basic outlines survive in the *Wealth of Nations* itself.

Such topics as the division of labour, the discussion of money, and allocation, all find their place in the first book, albeit with the analysis of money now preceding that of price, and the doctrine of net advantages being accorded a separate section (as indeed was the discussion of impediments to the working of the allocative mechanism), while the treatment of banking was to find a place in Book II. The critique of the 'mercantile fallacy' is still the dominant feature of the opening chapters of Book IV — and the pattern is repeated when we consider those sections of the lectures which have not been examined in any detail here. The discussion of interest and exchange, for example, was to find a place in Book II, and the section dealing with the slow progress of opulence was to reappear in a more elaborate form as the main theme of Book III; taxation is of course featured in the concluding sections of the *Wealth of Nations*, while in addition Smith's comments on the social consequences of the division of labour and the section on 'arms' were to find their echoes in the analyses of defence and education. There are also interesting omissions from the *Wealth of Nations*, such as the thesis of natural wants, the treatment of stock-jobbing and 'Mr. Law's Bank'. Yet the overwhelming impression left from a comparison of the *Wealth of Nations* and LJ(B), such as

[13] *Lectures*, xxiv.

that undertaken by Edwin Cannan in his edition of the latter work, is of a pattern of gradual development in a basic scheme whose outlines were already clear by 1763.

Moreover, particular doctrines are present in the *Lectures*, in addition to those noted above, which were later to acquire an added significance. It is already stated in the *Lectures*, for example, that 'Agriculture is of all other arts the most beneficent to society' (289, ed. Cannan, 224). The concept of stock is also mentioned in a variety of contexts: in the discussion of the natural balance of industry, and the sections on interest and taxation. The necessity for the prior accumulation of stock is also noted in connection with the division of labour, with perhaps the clearest statement occurring where Smith remarks that 'till some stock be produced there can be no division of labour, and before a division of labour take place there can be very little accumulation of stock' (287, ed. Cannan, 223). Nor was the issue of growth ignored — a point which can be seen in the discussion of 'natural wants', their association with the division of labour, and with the development of the arts. Similarly, the discussion of the 'slow progress of opulence' in the *Lectures* throws a great deal of light on factors which influence the growth process, such as transport, legal impediments, and the changing attitudes to commercial activity.

But, at the same time, it is evident that there is a great deal missing from the *Lectures* when compared with the *Wealth of Nations*, and it is this fact which makes Smith's assessment of physiocracy so interesting, especially since many of the features which are absent from the *Lectures* were features which Smith himself associated with physiocratic analysis. In this connection Smith noted, as we have seen, the use of a clear separation of classes, together with the distinction drawn between employers and employed, and between categories of return such as rent, wages, and profit. Again, it is noteworthy that Smith underlined the physiocratic emphasis on capital, while drawing attention to the point that the rate of return on capital in different employments would tend to equality. It is certainly possible that Smith himself may have been led to clarify his own views as to the role of capital accumulation in the process of developing his criticism

of the physiocratic position on unproductive labour, and
clearly probable, as Cannan suggested, that he was led to introduce these concepts together with a theory of distribution
into his own work as a result of his contact with the School.[14]
A further important point, which may have received rather less
attention, arises from the fact that Smith evidently associated
the thesis of the 'natural progress of opulence' with physiocratic teaching, because this particular thesis may help to
explain two important changes in the *Wealth of Nations* as
compared to the *Lectures*. First, there is the point that the
thesis is stated at the beginning of Book III of the *Wealth of
Nations* as a direct development of the discussion of the
'different employments of capital' with which the preceding
Book had concluded. This in turn may explain Smith's decision to use material drawn from the lectures on public
jurisprudence in this place; that is, as a record of the *inversion*
of a 'natural order' which seemed to be suggested by the
history of Europe from the fall of the Western (Roman)
Empire to the present day. Secondly, it is worth noting that
Smith's critique of mercantilism in the *Wealth of Nations* acquires an added dimension from the level of debate contained
in LJ(B) in that the later version was largely dominated by
the desire to prove that mercantile policy had had the effect
of artificially diverting the use of capital from more to less
productive uses. It is indeed somewhat remarkable that the
analogy of the invisible hand is employed in the *Wealth of
Nations* in exactly this, essentially dynamic, context (IV. ii.
9). But perhaps the really important contrasts between the
Wealth of Nations and the *Lectures on Jurisprudence* are to
be seen not merely in relation to specific doctrines, but rather
in terms of the *system* of thought, and the economic *model*
of which these doctrines were the components.

[14] See, for example, *Lectures*, xxvii–xxix and WN (ed. Cannan, 1904), xxxvii–
xxxix. However, Dugald Stewart has stated that 'it appears from a manuscript of
Mr Smith's now in my possession, that the foregoing analysis or division (rent,
wages, profit) was suggested to him by Mr Oswald of Dunnikier'. *Works*, ix (1856),
6. While making this point, R.L. Meek has also drawn attention to the fact that a
similar division was stated by Hume in a letter to Turgot dated September 1766,
'Adam Smith and the Classical Concept of Profit', in *Economics and Ideolology,
and Other Essays* (1967), 29. See generally, pp.28–32, where the author offers
some interesting speculations as to the probable influence of physiocratic thought
with regard to distribution.

It is now widely recognized that the basic model of the *Tableau* represented an advance in economic theory so considerable as to justify comparison with Harvey's discovery of the circulation of the blood.[15] J.A. Schumpeter not unaptly described it as marking 'the great breach' and went on to point out that 'Only with the help of such an analysis was it possible for further knowledge of the economic life process of society to develop and were scholars enabled to survey all the general factors and their functions as well as all the elements which have to be considered in every individual problem as far as it is purely economic'.[16] Elsewhere, the same writer noted that the model opened up possibilities for numerical theory, and that it provided a means of conceptualizing the working of complex series of interrelated functions, while representing the 'first method ever devised in order to convey an *explicit* conception of the nature of economic equilibrium'.[17] But one need not agree with Schumpeter when he went on to state that Smith 'almost certainly . . . did not fully grasp the importance of the *tableau économique*'.

Now at first sight Smith's treatment of the *Tableau* was slight, for it is seemingly dismissed as 'some arithmetical formularies' (WN IV. ix. 27), which may indeed have jarred on a man well known for his distrust of 'political arithmetick' (IV. v. b. 30). In addition, Smith can hardly be said to have done justice to the basic model as represented, for example, by Quesnay's *Analyse* (1766) with its careful statement of the qualitative assumptions which were to be employed in demonstrating how a system with a particular level of production would function and sustain itself. Yet at the same time it seems unlikely that a man like Smith who was so acutely conscious of the role of analogy and system in scientific thought would fail to be struck by these qualities in physiocracy: an impression which is borne out by the fact that

[15] Henry Higgs, for example, remarked in his edition of Cantillon's *Essai* (1931) that 'I would put Cantillon's analysis of the circulation of wealth, trite as it may now appear, on the same level of priority as Harvey's study of the circulation of the blood' (p.388).

[16] J.A. Schumpeter, *Economic Doctrine and Method* (1954), 43. See generally chapter 2, 'The Discovery of the Circular Flow of Economic Life'.

[17] Schumpeter, *History of Economic Analysis*, 241–3. The statement immediately following will be found at p.232.

Smith's account of the system manifestly succeeds in con-
veying the *purpose* of the model, by demonstrating the interdependence of economic phenomena at the macro-economic
level. There is no irony in the passage where Mirabeau is cited
as having placed the discovery of the *Tableau* at least on a par
with the invention of writing and money (IV. ix. 38)), and
even some generosity in Smith's conclusion, namely, that
'This system, however, with all its imperfections is, perhaps,
the nearest approximation to the truth that has yet been
published upon the subject of political oeconomy, and is
upon that account well worth the consideration of every man
who wishes to examine with attention the principles of that
very important science' (IV. ix. 38).

That Smith benefited from his own examination of the
system may be seen both in terms of the basic model which
he employed, and with regard to specific doctrines, whose
use served to transform an older apparatus while at the same
time taking Smith well beyond the boundaries of physiocratic
teaching as a whole. Perhaps two examples can usefully be
cited here.

First, it may be worth noting that although the theory of
price and allocation which is developed in the *Wealth of
Nations* relies on distinctions already established in the *Lectures*, supply price is now defined in terms of the 'ordinary
or average' rate of payment for rent, profit, and wages. In this
way Smith made allowance for the existence of the three
factors of production, and also gave his analysis an explicitly
static aspect by treating the rates of return as given and the
factors as stocks rather than flows, at least in the short run. At
the same time, the earlier analysis of allocation is transformed
by the central role given to profit; a role which, as R.L. Meek
has noted, finally exposed the real significance behind Smith's
earlier, intuitive, preoccupation with the 'natural balance of
industry'.[18]

It is certainly clear that the division into wages, profit, and
rent had struck Smith forcibly and that it still possessed some
novelty — a point which may be seen in the attention given to
warning his readers against confusion between them (WN I. vi).

The second point relates to the discussion of macro-

---

[18] *Economics and Ideology*, 31–2.

economic problems and here again a number of issues may be noted. First, there is the fact that not only did the distinction between wages, profit, and rent transform the older discussion of allocation, it also provided Smith with a means of proceeding directly from the treatment of price to problems of a macro kind. Thus having pointed out that in equilibrium the price of each commodity must resolve itself into three parts,

it must be so with regard to all the commodities which compose the whole annual produce of the land and labour of every country, taken complexly. The whole price or exchangeable value of that annual produce, must resolve itself into the same three parts, and be parcelled out among the different inhabitants of the country, either as the wages of their labour, the profits of their stock, or the rent of their land (WN II. ii. 2).

Next, in examining the functioning of the economy from this point of view, Smith produced an argument which gives a great deal of prominence to the different employments of capital and to the distinction between fixed and circulating capital. But it is perhaps in his treatment of the 'division of stock' seen from the standpoint of *society at large* (II. ii), rather than from that of the individual entrepreneur, that physiocratic influence is to be seen at its strongest. For it is here that Smith divides the stock of society into fixed and circulating capital, where the latter included goods in process and those ready for sale during a particular period but which remain at the outset in the hands of the manufacturers, farmers, and merchants who compose the system. In this way Smith presented the functioning of the economy in terms of a process of *withdrawal* (through purchase) from the circulating capital of society, which was matched by the *replacement* of the goods thus used up, by virtue of current productive activity. It is surely this kind of perspective on the working of the system which shows just how clearly Smith had grasped the significance of what the physiocrats were trying to do.

Yet, of course, none of this should be interpreted to mean that Smith lacked originality. The treatment of resource allocation, for example, was not a strong feature of physiocratic writing and has, besides, a number of characteristics which might still commend it to the modern reader. Smith's

interest in the problems of space is one example, while in addition, as has recently been observed by George Richardson,

competition features within the *Wealth of Nations* in two distinct contexts; first, in the account given of the balancing of supply and demand in particular markets, and, secondly, in the explanation of structural and technological development. Smith offers us in effect both a theory of economic equilibrium and a theory of economic evolution; and in each of these competition has a key role to play. Within the *Wealth of Nations* no obvious tension exists between the two theories . . . [19]

A similar departure from physiocratic practice can be seen in the handling of the macro-economic model which in Quesnay's hands often had a 'static' aspect, at least to the extent of showing how an economy might open the period t + 1 under identical conditions to those which had prevailed in the period t. Smith worked in much more general terms in showing that goods currently withdrawn from the circulating capital of society by virtue of the purchases made by all classes could be either 'consumed' during the current (annual) period, or used to replace goods which had reached the end of their lives during the period, or added to the stock reserved for consumption and the fixed capital of society at large. In this way Smith drew attention to the problem of the *rates* at which goods are used or produced and, by implication, to the difficulty of defining static equilibrium conditions for the system. But at this level at least, static analysis was not Smith's concern, and his whole purpose might indeed be said to have been to expose the causes of economic growth and to present his model of the flow as a circle of constantly expanding dimensions. In this way Smith completed the logic of his own system and at the same time lent a new dimension to the preoccupation with growth already announced in the *Theory of Moral Sentiments* and the *Lectures on Jurisprudence*. It is also worthy of note in this context that Smith's last piece of finished work, Part VI of the *Theory of Moral Sentiments* which was published in 1790, should have *returned* to an area of interest first announced in the first edition — the psychological assumptions behind the pursuit of want satisfaction, and

[19] 'Adam Smith on Competition and Increasing Returns', in *Essays on Adam Smith*, 350–1. This article has the interesting feature of concentrating on Smith's concern with *dis-equilibrium*.

the moral approval of frugality, which he noted in remarking that

In the steadiness of his industry and frugality, in his steadily sacrificing the ease and enjoyment of the present moment for the probable expectation of the still greater ease and enjoyment of a more distant but more lasting period of time, the prudent man is always both supported and rewarded by the entire approbation of the impartial spectator . . . (TMS VI. i. 11).

Interestingly enough Smith went on to add that this quality 'never is considered as one, either of the most endearing, or of the most ennobling of the virtues', even if it is an important aspect of the drive to better our condition, as Book II of the *Wealth of Nations* makes plain (TMS VI. i. 14).

While recognizing the influence which Smith's completed system was to have on the future course of classical economics,[20] it would surely be unfortunate if our admiration for his 'gradual and beautiful progression of ideas' were to detract attention from his predecessors — and perhaps also unfair to Smith. For, as Dugald Stewart also noticed, and as an examination of the *Theory of Moral Sentiments* and the *Wealth of Nations* confirms, Smith's contributions were often as much synthetic as original. Stewart thus felt moved to add to his assessment of the *Wealth of Nations,* that:

The skill and the comprehensiveness of mind displayed in his arrangement, can be judged of by those alone who have compared it with that adopted by his immediate predecessors. And perhaps, in point of utility, the labour he has employed in collecting and methodizing their scattered ideas, is not less valuable than the results of his own original speculations: For it is only when digested in a clear and natural order, that truths make their proper impression on the mind, and that erroneous opinions can be combated with success (Stewart, IV. 27).

[20] The influence exerted by Smith on classical economics is one of the major themes of D.P. O'Brien's *The Classical Economists* (1975).

6

The Development of an Idea*

Most of the accounts hitherto given of the development of Adam Smith's ideas on the division of labour prior to the appearance of the *Wealth of Nations* have been based on a number of crucial assumptions made by early Smith scholars concerning the dating of the relevant documents — notably the so-called *Early Draft of the'Wealth of Nations'* and the two fragments on the division of labour discovered by Scott. The discovery of a new set of student's notes of Smith's Glasgow lectures on Jurisprudence, relating to the 1762-3 session, has made it possible to reconsider these assumptions. It will be our contention in the present chapter that in the light of the new evidence the documents should probably be placed in a date order very different from that which has up to now been accepted, and that if this is done the traditional picture of the way in which Smith's ideas on the division of labour developed is radically altered. In the Appendices we reproduce some of the more important of the materials upon which the argument rests, including extracts from the new lecture-notes and the text of the two fragments.

I

Let us begin with a brief review of the main documents which Scott had before him when he wrote his monumental *Adam Smith as Student and Professor* (1937) and the main assumptions which he made concerning their dates.

First, there were 'four documents, amounting to fifteen folio pages' which Scott discovered amongst letters kept by

* The article which forms this chapter was written jointly with R.L. Meek and appeared originally in the *Economic Journal*, 83 (1973), under the title 'The Development of Adam Smith's Ideas on the Division of Labour'. It was republished in R.L. Meek, *Smith, Marx and After* (1977).

Adam Smith.[1] One of these documents, as Scott himself
indicated, is very probably not by Smith, but a copy of a
paper on prices which he had received from Lord Hailes.[2] A
second, on moral philosophy, has recently been edited by
Professor Raphael, who has quite properly questioned Scott's
judgement as to date of composition, while indicating that it
was probably written before the first edition of the *Theory
of Moral Sentiments* in 1759.[3] The two remaining documents
— the really relevant ones so far as the present argument is
concerned — deal more or less exclusively with the division of
labour, and were thought by Scott to be of such interest as to
deserve reproduction in facsimile.[4] The longer of these two
pieces, which begins with a discussion of the interdependence
of the philosopher and the porter as representatives of distinct
trades, will henceforth be cited as 'Fragment A' (FA). The
second of the pieces (FB) is somewhat shorter, and opens
with a discussion of the relative merits of land and water
carriage. Upon examination, Scott concluded that these two
fragments were 'specimens of Adam Smith's earliest economic
work' (*ASSP* 59), and the captions to the facsimiles describe
them specifically as coming from 'one of the Edinburgh Lectures'. This judgement of Scott's was based in part upon his
interpretation of their content, but also, apparently, on the
very curious ground that the 'many avocations of Adam Smith
during the first eight years he was at Glasgow make it highly
improbable, if not impossible, that they [the four documents]
could have been written then, and thus they may be assigned
to the Edinburgh period' (*ASSP* 57-8).

Second, there was the well-known set of student's notes of
Smith's Glasgow lectures on Jurisprudence which Cannan had
discovered and published in 1896. On the basis of internal

---

[1] *ASSP* 57.

[2] In a letter (116) addressed to Hailes, dated 5 March 1769, Smith asked him
for 'the papers you mentioned upon the price of provisions in former times'.
Smith returned the original manuscript to Hailes after having 'taken a copy' of it,
on 23 May 1769.

[3] D.D. Raphael, 'Adam Smith and the Infection of David Hume's Society',
Journal of the History of Ideas, 30 (April–June 1969), republished in TMS, as
Appendix II.

[4] *ASSP* 379–85. The manuscripts themselves are located in the Bannerman
Papers, Glasgow University Library.

evidence, Cannan had opined that it was probable that 'the actual lectures from which the notes were taken were delivered either in the portion of the academical session of 1763–4 which preceded Adam Smith's departure [from Glasgow], or in the session of 1762–3, almost certain that they were not delivered before 1761–2, and absolutely certain that they were not delivered before 1760–1'.[5] On his title-page, however, Cannan had described the lectures as having been 'reported by a student in 1763'. Scott concluded that the lecture course concerned 'must have been given in the session 1762–3', apparently basing this judgement on 'an experiment made by an expert note-taker' which allegedly proved that it was 'not possible that the notes could have been taken in the part of the next session during which Adam Smith was at Glasgow' (*ASSP* 319).

Third, there was the so-called *Early Draft of the 'Wealth of Nations'* which Scott discovered among Charles Townshend's papers at Dalkeith House, and the text of which he published in an appendix to *Adam Smith as Student and Professor*. This document begins with an extended and fully written-out section on the division of labour (under the heading 'Chap. 2. Of the nature and Causes of public opulence') which occupies just over thirty pages of the manuscript; and the remaining eighteen pages are taken up with what appears to be a summary (under the heading 'Contents of the following Chapters') of the major part of the remaining 'economic' material in Smith's lecture course. Scott, asking himself the question 'Is this manuscript that of the *Glasgow Lectures* or an early revision of these?', answered that 'many reasons point to the latter' — among these reasons being, apparently, 'the very much greater prominence which is given to questions of Distribution here as compared with the report of the *Glasgow Lectures*'. Since in Scott's opinion, as we have just seen, the latter report must have related to lectures given in 1762–3, he concluded that 'the probable date of the revision, represented by this manuscript, would be 1763, probably the summer or later' (*ASSP* 319).

Summing up, the view put forward by Scott, which has

---

[5] LJ(B), xx.

been accepted by the great majority of later Smith scholars, was that FA and FB dated from the very early Edinburgh period; that the Cannan notes related to lectures delivered in the 1762–3 session; and that the *Early Draft* was probably written in 1763, fairly soon after these lectures had been delivered.

Our review of these assumptions in the remaining part of the present chapter is organized as follows. In Section II, we begin by provisionally ascribing the Cannan notes to the 1763–4 session. We then summarize the treatment of the division of labour in the newly discovered 1762–3 notes, and compare it with the treatment of this subject in the Cannan notes. Finally, we put the two sets of notes side by side and compare them with the *Early Draft*, arriving at the tentative conclusion that the latter was probably written before April 1763. In Section III, we turn to the two fragments. We first describe their form and content in more detail, and then compare them with the *Early Draft* on the one hand and Chapter III of Book I of the *Wealth of Nations* on the other, arriving at the conclusion that the fragments probably date from the 1760s rather than from the Edinburgh period. Finally, in Section IV, we survey some of the important *differences* between the fragments and the *Wealth of Nations*, drawing from this comparison certain conclusions regarding the nature and development of Smith's ideas on the division of labour.

II

The first thing which emerges as a result of the discovery of the new set of notes mentioned above is that the lectures to which the Cannan notes related (assuming that they were all of a piece) could not possibly have been given in the 1762–3 session. This is a point which is documented more fully in LJ(A):[6] here we need only say that so far as they go[7] they are very much fuller than the Cannan notes; that most of the

---

[6] See LJ(A), 5–22.
[7] The notes stop short a little over half-way through the 'economic' section of Smith's lectures. More specifically, the material in them corresponds roughly to that in the Cannan notes up to but not beyond p.208 of the 1896 edition.

lectures are separately reported *and dated*; that all the dates relate to the 1762-3 session; and that the whole order of treatment of the main subjects is radically different from that in the Cannan notes. The only question now really at issue, therefore, is whether the Cannan notes relate to 1761-2 or 1763-4. And on this point, fortunately, the reference to Florida on p.70 of the published edition of the Cannan notes would seem to be fairly decisive. A comparison of the passage in which this reference occurs with the corresponding passage in the 1762-3 notes shows that it must relate to the cession of Florida at the end of the Seven Years War, which could obviously not have been referred to in the 1761-2 session. It seems very likely indeed, therefore, *pace* Scott, that the lectures to which the Cannan notes refer were in fact delivered in 1763-4 — the session during which Smith left Glasgow, his course being continued and completed by Thomas Young.[8] If this is so, the intriguing question arises as to the extent, if any, to which Young's views as well as Smith's may be reported in the Cannan notes; but this is not a question which need concern us for the present.

Let us turn, then, to the treatment of the division of labour in the new 1762-3 lecture-notes, numbering the successive points made so as to facilitate later comparison with the other documents concerned.[9] After a discussion of the secular growth of wants, and a very interesting development of the idea that 'all the arts, the sciences, law and government, wisdom, and even virtue itself tend all to . . . the providing meat, drink, rayment and lodging for men' (LJ(A), vi. 20), Smith comes directly to the division of labour, dealing with it as follows:

1. The fact that the 'ordinary day-labourer' in Britain has a higher standard of living than 'an Indian prince at the head of 1000 naked savages' is due to the 'joint assistance' of hundreds

[8] If Young was in fact furnished by Smith with the latter's lecture-notes, as A.F. Tytler asserts (*Memoirs of the Hon. Henry Home of Kames*, vol. i (2nd edn., 1814), 272), and as would indeed seem very probable, it follows that the experiment by Scott's 'expert note-taker' proves nothing at all (see above, 132).

[9] In the quotations from the 1762-3 notes which follow and in Appendix A, a number of imperfections of grammar, punctuation, spelling, etc. in the student's report have been cleaned up in the interests of readability.

of different people who have in effect co-operated to produce his 'blue woollen coat', his tools, his furniture, etc. (vi. 21–2).

2.   It may not seem surprising that 'the moneyed man and man of rank' (vi. 23) should be so much better provided for than the most wealthy savage, since the 'labour and time of the poor is in civilized countries sacrificed to the maintaining the rich in ease and luxury' (vi. 26). Among the savages, however, there are 'no landlords, nor usurers, no tax gatherers', and we should therefore expect that 'the savage should be much better provided than the dependent poor man who labours both for himself and for others'. But the case is in fact 'far otherwise' (vi. 26).

3.   The difficulty in accounting for this is increased by the fact that labour is not 'equally proportioned to each', so that 'of 10,000 families which are supported by each other, 100 perhaps labour not at all'. The 'rich and opulent merchant' lives better than his clerks who 'do all the business' (vi. 27); the latter better than the artisans; and the latter in turn better than the 'poor labourer' who 'supports the whole frame of society'. How then can we account for 'the great share he and the lowest of the people have of the conveniences of life'? (vi. 28).

4.   The division of labour among different hands can alone account for this. Let us consider the effects the division of labour can have on 'one particular branch of business' — pin-making — with a view to judging from this the effect it will have on the whole. If one man had to do all the work of making a pin from beginning to end, it would take him at least a whole year to make a pin, so that its price would be £6, the value of a man's labour for a year. Even if he were given the wire ready made, he would not be able to make more than twenty pins a day, and the pins would sell at not less than one penny each. As things actually stand, however, the labour is normally divided among eighteen persons; 36,000 pins can be made in a day; and the pin-maker can as a result afford both to increase the workman's wages and to sell his pins more cheaply (vi. 29).

5.   Agriculture 'does not admit of this separation of employment in the same degree as the manufactures of wool or lint

or iron work' (vi. 30). Though an opulent state will no doubt far exceed a poorer one both in agriculture and in manufacture, 'yet this will not be so remarkable in the produce of the soil as the handycraft trades' (vi. 31).

6. When these improvements have been made, 'each branch of trade will afford enough both to support the opulence and give considerable profit of the great men, and sufficiently reward the industry of the labourer' (vi. 32). If, for example, the pin-maker can contrive that each man produces 2,000 pins per day, and if he sells these at one penny per hundred, he can pay the artisan fifteen pence and still have '5 for his share'.[10]

7. Thus 'the price of labour comes to be dear while at the same time work is cheap' — two things which 'in the eyes of the vulgar appear altogether incompatible'; and that 'state is opulent where the necessaries and conveniences of life are easily come at' (vi. 33).

8. The extension of the division of labour cheapens commodities. Thus we see that the price of almost all commodities has fallen since the Revolution, 'notwithstanding the supposed abundance of money'. 'We are not to judge whether labour be cheap or dear by the moneyed price of it, but by the quantity of the necessaries of life which may be got by the fruits of it' (vi. 36). Gold and silver, however, 'can not be so easily multiplied as other commodities'.

9. The increase in 'the stock of commodities' arising from the division of labour has three causes: '1st, the dexterity which it occasions in the workmen; 2dly, the saving of time lost in passing from one piece of work to another; and 3dly, the invention of machines which it occasions' (vi. 38).[11]

10. In relation to the invention of machines, those 'general observers whom we call philosophers' play an important role, as for example in the case of the fire-engine and wind- and water-mills. And in time 'philosophy itself becomes a separate

---

[10] This is in fact the second of two numerical examples which are given in this section. In the first, it is assumed that each man produces 1,000 (instead of 2,000) pins per day, and that these are sold at the rate of three-halfpence per 100. In this case 'the whole thousand will then be worth 15d., of which the artisan can afford 3 to his master and have 12 as the price of his labour'.

[11] This point and its illustrations occupy five pages of the manuscript.

trade . . . like all other subdivided into various provinces' (vi. 43).

11. The division of labour is not 'the effect of any human policy', but is rather 'the necessary consequence of a natural disposition altogether peculiar to men, *vis.*, the disposition to truck, barter, and exchange' (vi. 44). This disposition is never found in animals: the hounds which help each other when chasing a hare do not do so as the result of any contract between them. It is only men who enter into bargains, and who, when they want beer or beef, address themselves not to the humanity of the brewer or the butcher but to his self-love.

12. This 'bartering and trucking spirit' is the cause of the separation of trades and the improvements in arts. A savage, for example, who finds that he can make arrows 'better than ordinary', may become a full-time arrow-maker.

13. It is not the difference of 'naturall parts and genius' that occasions the separation of trades, but the separation of trades 'that occasions the diversity of genius', as is shown by the example of the philosopher and the porter (vi. 47).

The argument which we have just summarized takes us up to the end of the lecture which Smith gave on Tuesday, 29 March 1763. As we shall see directly, the argument was subsequently continued and developed — although in a very peculiar and significant manner — in the two following lectures on Wednesday, 30 March, and Tuesday, 5 April. Let us pause here, however, to draw a mental line under the thirteenth point, for, as will be emphasized later, the section of the *Early Draft* dealing with the division of labour more or less exactly mirrors the argument of the 1762–3 lectures *up to but not beyond* this point, whereas the Cannan notes in effect incorporate the subsequent material.

Under his date-heading for the lecture of Wednesday, 30 March, the student has — quite unusually — written a note which reads 'continues to illustrate former, etc.'. The notes of the lecture proper begin with Smith's customary summary of some of the main points in his previous lecture, which is fairly straightforward until he starts recapitulating point 11 above. Here he introduces some new material, of which there

is no trace at all in the student's notes of the previous lecture, concerning a law made by Sesostris to the effect that 'everyone should for ever adhere to his father's profession' (vi. 54). The student's report of this new material takes up 172 words. Smith then goes straight on to summarize point 12; and from there directly proceeds to make another new point, also not made in the previous lecture, to the effect that the 'disposition of trucking' is founded on 'the naturall inclination everyone has to persuade'. Men, the argument runs, 'always endeavour to persuade others to be of their opinion', and thus acquire 'a certain dexterity and address . . . in managing of men' (vi. 56-7). The activity of bartering, in which they 'address themselves to the self-interest of the person', is the result of their endeavours to do this 'managing of men' in the simplest and most effective manner.

Smith now leaves the subject of the division of labour, and announces the five main topics with which he is going to concern himself in the remaining part of the 'economic' section of the course. The first of these is 'the rule of exchange, or what it is which regulates the prices of commodities'; and he embarks immediately upon his discussion of this topic, continuing with it until the end of the lecture.

At the beginning of the *next* lecture, however, on Tuesday, 5 April, one is surprised to find Smith returning yet again, this time quite out of context, to the question of the division of labour, and developing for the first time (at any rate in the 1762-3 lectures) the crucial principle that the division of labour is limited by the extent of the market. This passage, which takes up nearly four pages of the student's manuscript, is clearly important, and is therefore reproduced in full in Appendix A at the end of this volume. After it is finished, Smith proceeds calmly on his way, picking up the threads of his previous discussion of 'the rule of exchange' and carrying on with his exposition of it.

Let us now make a comparison between the treatment of the division of labour in the 1762-3 notes, as outlined above, and the treatment of it in the Cannan notes (which, as we have seen, very probably relate to the lectures delivered in 1763-4), the purpose of this comparison being to detect the differences, if any, between what was actually said about the

division of labour in the lectures in 1762–3 and what was said about it in 1763–4.

One important point which must be stressed here is the enormous difference in the standard of note-taking as between the two sets of notes. The 1762–3 notes as a whole are extremely full, and so far as one can judge extremely accurate: in all probability they were a student's transcription of *shorthand* notes taken down by him in class, and the student evidently took great pains to make this transcription as correct as possible a rendering of the words actually used by Smith. The Cannan notes, by way of contrast, are in many places extremely sketchy, and in some places — as it now turns out — not at all reliable: they bear all the marks of being a copyist's later transcription of a set of rather abbreviated notes originally taken down by a student in *longhand*. Thus one frequently finds that a point which occupies a whole page of the 1762–3 notes is represented in the Cannan notes by no more than a single sentence — and sometimes a rather incomprehensible one at that. Thus whereas the absence of a particular point from the 1762–3 notes can normally be assumed to indicate that this point was not in fact dealt with in that session's lectures, the same assumption can *not* safely be made in relation to the Cannan notes.

Bearing this in mind, and putting the two sets of notes side by side,[12] there is no evidence to suggest that what was actually said about the division of labour in the 1763–4 lectures was *substantially* different from what had been said in 1762–3, *at any rate up to (and including) point 10 above.* Some of the points concerned are very baldly summarized in the Cannan notes, but most of them (with the possible exception of 6)[13] do in fact appear to be there, and they are presented in what seems to be the same order. The first difference which

---

[12] The relevant passages in LJ(B) will be found at 211–23, ed. Cannan, 161–72.

[13] The only counterpart of point 6 in the Cannan notes would seem to be a single sentence reading 'When labour is thus divided, and so much done by one man in proportion, the surplus above their maintenance is considerable, which each man can exchange for a fourth of what he could have done if he had finished it alone' (LJ(B), 214, ed. Cannan, 164). There is no trace of the two numerical illustrations from pin-making which Smith used in 1762–3 to illustrate the point. There are a number of possible explanations of this omission, but they need not concern us here. What is more interesting is the fact that these illustrations clearly

may be of importance occurs when we come to the counterpart in the Cannan notes of point 11.[14] Here the exposition begins with a discussion of that 'law made by Sesostris' of which we have already heard (above, 138), and only *after* this discussion does it proceed to the illustration of the hounds chasing a hare. In the 1762–3 lectures, by way of contrast, Smith when dealing with point 11 went straight to the hounds illustration, and as we have seen made no mention of the 'law made by Sesostris' until the recapitulation of the argument at the beginning of his next lecture on Wednesday, 30 March.

In the Cannan notes, the summary of point 11, expanded in this way, is followed immediately by a summary of points 12 and 13, and the notes then proceed directly to a discussion of the notion that the real foundation of the disposition to truck or barter is the 'principle to persuade'. This point was also made in the 1762–3 lectures, but only, as we have already seen, at the end of the recapitulation of the argument near the beginning of the lecture on Wednesday, 30 March. Immediately after this discussion, the Cannan notes proceed with a consideration of the crucial point that 'the division of labour must always be proportioned to the extent of commerce'. This point too, it will be remembered, was also made by Smith in the 1762–3 lectures, *but not at this place*: it was squeezed in, in a way which makes it look very like an afterthought, half-way through his exposition of the theory of price, at the beginning of his lecture on Tuesday, 5 April.

To sum up, then, the three additional points made by Smith in 1762–3 in his lectures on Wednesday, 30 March, and Tuesday, 5 April — the 'law made by Sesostris' point, the 'principle to persuade' point, and most important of all, the point that the division of labour depends on the extent of the market — were all incorporated *in their proper places* in the 1763–4 lectures.

How can we account for this difference? It *could* be argued, of course, that in his lecture on Tuesday, 29 March 1763,

display the division of the product between wages and profits, and that they were carried over into the *Early Draft*. If Scott had been able to compare the *Early Draft* with the 1762–3 notes as well as the Cannan notes, he would have found it much less easy, we think, to argue that the *Early Draft* 'contains much more on Distribution' than the lectures (*ASSP* 319–20).

[14] See LJ(B), 218–19, ed. Cannan, 168–9.

Smith did not have time, or perhaps forgot, to deal with the three points concerned; that he remembered to deal with the first two at the beginning of his next lecture; but that he forgot about the third until the beginning of the next lecture after that. This would have been very uncharacteristic, but it is at least possible. More likely, however, we believe, is the suggestion that at any rate the third of the three points concerned — the idea that the division of labour depends on the extent of the market — really was a genuine afterthought, appearing for the first time in the 1762-3 course and assuming its proper place only in 1763-4.

This suggestion is supported by a comparison between the two sets of lecture-notes and the *Early Draft*. The latter document evidently represented a preliminary and rather tentative attempt by Smith to translate the 'economic' material in his Jurisprudence lectures into book form. It is very much the sort of document which any of us today might produce for a publisher whom we were wanting to interest in a projected book and who had asked us to submit a sample first chapter plus a summary of the remaining chapters. And there is of course no doubt that the document is directly based on the material in *some* set of lectures: the only question really at issue is *which* set. The main point here is that the chapter on the division of labour, which is fully written out and with which the *Early Draft* begins, corresponds very closely indeed — argument by argument, and often sentence by sentence and even word by word — with the treatment in the 1762-3 lecture notes, *up to but not beyond the end of the lecture on Tuesday, 29 March*.[15] In other words, there is no mention

[15] The main differences between the relevant sections of the *Early Draft* and the 1762-3 notes are as follows:

(a) *Point 6*. In the 1762-3 notes the two numerical illustrations are based respectively on the assumptions that 1,000 pins and 2,000 pins are produced per day. In the *Early Draft* the corresponding assumptions are that 2,000 and 4,000 pins are produced per day.

(b) *Point 8*. In the *Early Draft* the substance of point 8 seems to have been transferred from the division of labour section to the summary of 'Chap. 4th. Of Money, its nature, origin and history' (cf. Scott, *ASSP* 347).

(c) At the end of the division of labour section of the *Early Draft*, after point 13, a new passage (not to be found, we believe, anywhere else in Smith's writings) is added. In this rather curious passage Smith discusses certain implications of the fact that almost everything we know is acquired second-hand from books.

It would take us too far out of our way to analyse these differences here: suffice it to say that in our opinion they are perfectly consistent with the view about the probable dating of the *Early Draft* given above in the text.

whatever in it of the 'law by Sesostris' point, the 'principle to persuade' point, or, more importantly, the point that the division of labour depends on the extent of the market. So far as the summary of the remaining chapters is concerned, it seems to us that this might equally have been based on the lectures as reported in 1762-3 or in 1763-4. But the absence from the first part of the *Early Draft* of any mention of the point about the extent of the market (to say nothing of the two other points concerned) surely suggests that it could not have been based on the 1763-4 lectures — and, indeed, that it could not have been based on the 1762-3 lectures either, *unless it was written prior to April 1763*. It does not seem at all plausible that the *Early Draft* should have omitted all mention of the idea that the division of labour depends on the extent of the market if Smith had in fact arrived at this idea, and appreciated its full economic significance, at the time when the document was drawn up. What does seem plausible is that the *Early Draft* was a revised version of the 'economic' part of Smith's lecture notes as they stood at some date shortly before April 1763; that while thinking about the division of labour and the way in which he would treat it in his projected book Smith arrived at certain new ideas, including that concerning the dependence of the division of labour on the extent of the market; and that he explained the latter idea to his students for the first time in his lecture on 5 April 1763.

III

The reader who has already had a look at Appendix A, in which the 1762-3 report of Smith's apparent afterthought on the dependence of the division of labour on the extent of the market is reproduced, will have noticed that it is divided roughly into two halves. In the first half Smith introduces and illustrates the general point that the division of labour is 'greater or less according to the market'; in the second half he goes on to talk about the relative effects of sea and land carriage upon 'the greatness of the market'. The curious thing is that these are precisely the two subjects dealt with respectively in the two fragments (FA and FB) mentioned on p.131 above. The fact that the only two unpublished economic

documents of Smith's (apart from the *Early Draft*) which have survived should deal with the same two subjects as the uncharacteristic 'afterthought' which we have just been considering can hardly be due to a mere coincidence, and cries out for some kind of explanation.

The text of FA and FB is reproduced in Appendices B and C. In physical appearance, FA consists of a single folio sheet of four pages with the text extending almost, but not quite, to the bottom of the last page. FB consists of a single folio sheet with the text covering rather more than two and one-half pages. Both fragments begin in the middle of a sentence. Each page has a broad margin at the left-hand side, and in FA there is in one case a lengthy insertion written in this margin and preceded by a signal which also appears in the text. Similar insertions appear on the first and third pages of FB. In both cases there are a number of words struck out in the text with new ones substituted — occasionally, it would seem (as in the case of the *Early Draft*), by Smith himself. The bulk of the insertions, however, are in the hand of the amanuensis, and generally occur above the line. In addition, there are a number of cancelled words (and parts of words) without corresponding insertions, indicating in all probability that Smith often changed his choice of expression during dictation. It is evident, therefore, that the two fragments, unlike the *Early Draft*, are not in a finished form.

The two folios have the same watermark and were written in the same hand. The watermarks are quite clear, and would appear to be the same as those found in the *Early Draft*. On one sheet there is a circular emblem containing the motto *Pro Patria Eiusque Libertate*, surmounted by a crown, the whole containing a lion 'rampant and regardant'. The lion seems to be grasping a weapon in one hand, and a sheaf of corn or arrows in the other. The animal stands on a pedestal whose base appears to bear the letters VRYHYT. On the facing page, the countermark consists of a single circle, enclosing the letters GR, which are flanked by laurel leaves and again surmounted by a crown.[16]

---

[16] Scott's description of the *Early Draft* watermarks (which is rather inaccurate) will be found in *ASSP* 322.

In other words, the paper on which the two fragments were written would appear to be the same as that used for the *Early Draft*, although the hand does differ.

Turning now from the physical appearance of the fragments to their actual content, we find that FA is mainly concerned with the relationship between the division of labour and the extent of the market. Smith here illustrates the point by reference to small communities such as those found in the 'mountainous and desart' Highlands of Scotland, where individuals are forced to exercise a number of different trades. His basic argument is that the extent of the market must be affected by the size of the community, and he goes on to provide further illustrations drawn from the experience of North American Indians, Tartars, Arabs, and Hottentots. In FB the same theme is considered from a rather different point of view: here the extent of the market is analysed in relation to ease of communication, especially by sea. Smith indicates that economic development was historically dependent on foreign or inland navigation, citing the experience of Greece and ancient Egypt as instances. Economic development round the coasts of the colonies in America is also mentioned in support of the general thesis; the colonies being likened (in the manner of King James's description of the county of Fife) to 'a coarse woollen coat edged with gold lace'.

Are these fragments in fact the work of the Edinburgh period, as Scott believed? Three main considerations seem to us to tell against the ascription of them to such an early date.

The first consideration is suggested by a comparison of the opening paragraph of FA with the concluding part of the section of the *Early Draft* dealing with the division of labour, which consists of a long analysis of the interdependence of, and mutual advantage to be derived from, the separate trades of the philosopher and the porter. The final portion of this concluding part of the section is reproduced in Appendix D; and a comparison with the opening paragraph of FA in Appendix B will show that the latter is virtually identical with a passage in the former. Starting with the words 'who, for an equal quantity of work' in the first line of FA and in the third sentence of the extract from the *Early Draft*, the two texts continue in more or less exact parallel down to the

sentence ending (in the *Early Draft*) 'usefull knowledge to diminish', so that there are about 25 lines of the *Early Draft* which reappear at the beginning of FA with only four very minor substantive changes and one handwritten alteration. At this point, however, the two texts part company: FA continues directly with a discussion of the dependence of the division of labour on the extent of the market, whereas the division of labour section of the *Early Draft* carries on with the general theme of the philosopher and the porter for a further 35 lines and then finishes. This final 35 lines constitutes that curious passage, mentioned in our footnote 15, in which Smith discusses certain implications of the fact that almost everything we know is acquired second-hand from books. What may have happened is that Smith decided to rewrite the final part of the division of labour section of the *Early Draft*, and in the process of revision judged it proper to omit the passage just mentioned. In other words, it seems at least possible that the fragments represent an alternative conclusion to the division of labour section of the *Early Draft*.[17]

The second consideration relates more directly to the question of the content of the fragments. It will be remembered that in the *Early Draft* Smith did not formally consider the relationship between market size and the division of labour at all. The subject *was* considered in the 1762-3 lectures, but only, apparently, as an afterthought, and not at any great length.[18] In the 1763-4 lectures it was also considered, this time in its proper place, but there is no evidence to suggest that it was then considered either more extensively than in 1762-3 or in any substantially different way. Certainly there

---

[17] The very fact that the fragments have survived, and that they were apparently found among letters kept by Smith, lends some support (although probably not very much) to the suggestion that they were linked in some way or other with the *Early Draft*. We are not prepared, however, to hazard any guess as to the exact reasons for their survival.

[18] In his lecture on 24 February 1763, however, Smith did discuss the importance of the 'opportunity of commerce' in the developmental process, relating the relative lack of advance in 'Tartary and Araby' to (*inter alia*) the fact that they are deprived 'in most places of the benefit of water carriage, more than any other nation in the world; and in some places where they would have an opportunity of it, the land carriage which would be necessary before it, debars them no less than the other' (LJ(A) iv. 62). And Smith went on from there to compare the situation of these countries with that of ancient Greece, which did not suffer from the same disadvantage. Cf. LJ(B), 31, ed. Cannan, 22.

is nothing in either set of lecture-notes suggesting a treatment of the subject which remotely approaches, either in length or in sophistication, the treatment found in the fragments, extending as the latter do over six and one-half closely written folio pages. If, therefore, we adopt the plausible hypothesis that work which is analytically more developed is likely to come later in time, the possibility begins to emerge that the fragments were in fact written *after* that version of the lecture-notes which contains the most elaborate account of the subject — that is, the version of 1762-3.

The third consideration is suggested by a comparison of FA and FB with Chapter III of Book I of the *Wealth of Nations*, which brings to light a close parallel as regards the order and content of the argument. In both cases, for example, we find the point about the extent of the market illustrated in terms of community size before Smith goes on to examine the issue of transportation and its contribution to the development of commerce. Moreover, the form of words employed in certain passages is very similar — so similar, indeed, as to suggest that the fragments may have served at least as a preliminary basis for the chapter. In the *Wealth of Nations*, for example, paragraphs 1 and 2 of Chapter III appear to follow FA from the sentence in the latter beginning 'As it is the power of exchanging' (with which the second paragraph commences) to the end of the second page of the manuscript; and paragraphs 3-7 show the same close connection with the whole of FB.

Although the apparent link between the fragments and the *Early Draft* tends to suggest that Smith, at the time he wrote these documents, had not yet decided to accord the point about the dependence of the division of labour on the extent of the market a separate chapter in his proposed book, the close parallel between the *Wealth of Nations* and the fragments may perhaps suggest that the latter represent not just an *alternative* conclusion to the division of labour section of the *Early Draft*, but rather a *substitute* for it. There is also of course the possiblity — which we would however regard as much less likely — that the fragments could be discarded pages from the manuscript of the *Wealth of Nations* itself. But however this may be, it seems fair to conclude from all the evidence that the balance of probability lies in favour of a

date in the 1760s for the fragments and rather against the Edinburgh period of 1748-51. In placing FA 'almost midway between Hutcheson and the *Glasgow Lectures*', Scott relied in part on the point that while this fragment considers 'the nature' of the division of labour, 'there has yet to be worked out "its causes"' (*ASSP* 59). He does not seem to have examined the documents in relation to Smith's other work, or to have considered the possibility that 'its causes' had been worked out already and elsewhere.

IV

Apart from the parallels which exist between the fragments and the *Wealth of Nations*, there are also some interesting differences: materials, for example, which are present in one version of the argument but not in the other.

(1) The opening passage of FA, illustrating the advantages of the division of labour in terms of the philosopher/porter example, was omitted from the analysis in the *Wealth of Nations* — most probably on the ground that it was redundant, that is, concerned with a point which was already adequately established. At the same time, Smith must have decided to expand the new material included in the fragments and to give it the dignity of a separate chapter, beginning with the second paragraph of FA, as noted above.

(2) As stated above, paragraphs 1 and 2 of Chapter III of the *Wealth of Nations* appear to follow FA from the sentence in the latter beginning 'As it is the power of exchanging' to the end of the second page of the manuscript, which takes us to about the middle of paragraph 2 of Chapter III. There is no counterpart in Chapter III of the material in pp. 3-4 of FA;[19] and the counterpart in it of FB begins at the eleventh word of the third sentence in paragraph 3. There is therefore a long passage in Chapter III, beginning 'Country workmen are almost everywhere' and ending 'a ship navigated by six', of which there is no counterpart in the fragments. This passage begins by elaborating on the theme of paragraph 1 in providing

---

[19] We deal with the omission of this material under the last heading in this section.

further illustrations of the point that rural communities are often too small to permit of a complete division of employments, and links the discussion of the relation between community size and the division of labour (the subject of FA, 1-2) with that of the relative merits of land and sea carriage (the subject of FB). The passage amounts to approximately 300 words, which would make about one folio page in the hand of the amanuensis used. It is thus quite possible that Smith, having decided to omit the material in the two final pages of FA, later inserted a single page of material (now lost) linking the two fragments together.

(3) Another addition to the *Wealth of Nations* is represented by the last paragraph of Chapter III, which continues a theme introduced in the previous part of the chapter. In FB the discussion of the importance of water carriage had reached a natural period in citing the examples of China and Egypt, but in the *Wealth of Nations* additional examples are provided — Africa, Austria, Bavaria, etc. From the standpoint of the discussion of the division of labour the new material is of limited significance, in that the point at issue had already been adequately established. But from other points of view the same material is important, and this for two reasons. First, it is interesting to note the weight of emphasis which Smith gave to ease of navigation as contributing to economic development and even as a pre-condition of it. It was in this place that Smith commented: 'All the inland parts of Africa, and all that part of Asia which lies any considerable way north of the Euxine and Caspian seas, the antient Scythia, the modern Tartary and Siberia, seem in all ages of the world to have been in the same barbarous and uncivilized state in which we find them at present' (WN I. iii. 8). Second, the point is also significant in relation to Smith's general theory of historical change, which features the use of four socio-economic stages through which communities are 'naturally' expected to pass in sequence over time. The emphasis on a sequence of stages tends to distract attention from the necessary pre-conditions of development (ease of defence, fertility, navigation) which Smith himself isolated, and thus from the point that socio-economic development may be arrested at a certain level — such as that reached by the Tartars.

(4) Interestingly enough, our final point is also connected with Smith's use of economic stages. We have already noted that the two final pages of FA were omitted from the *Wealth of Nations*, and that in this passage Smith had provided a number of historical illustrations of the point that community size must affect the scope for the extension of the division of labour. Smith probably had two reasons for making this omission: first, he had already illustrated the point at issue in terms of a modern example, so that additional material could be regarded as redundant; and second, the examples drawn from the experience of North American Indians, Tartars, Arabs, and Hottentots, while important of themselves, were all to receive attention elsewhere in the *Wealth of Nations*, most notably in Book V.[20] Yet this particular

[20] There may of course have been another more general reason for this omission, related to what Scott called Smith's 'epoch-making decision' to separate his economic material from 'the treatment of Jurisprudence in which it had been previously embedded' (*ASSP* 319). After making this decision, and as his economic work proceeded, it would have been natural for Smith to purge the more 'analytical' parts of his material of some of the 'sociological' illustrations with which they had hitherto been associated.

There may be an interesting parallel here with Smith's decision to omit paragraphs 2 and 3 of the *Early Draft* (the counterpart of points 2 and 3 in the 1762-3 notes) from the *Wealth of Nations*. In the first paragraph of the *Early Draft* he had already noted that in a modern society the unassisted labour of the individual could not supply him with his simple needs, and that the poor man was in fact able to command enjoyments which placed him nearer to the modern *rich* than 'the chief of a savage nation in North America' (Scott, *ASSP* 325). In the *Early Draft* this is presented as part of a problem to be explained, while in the *Wealth of Nations* the material is used to conclude the discussion of Chapter I. In the *Early Draft*, however, the second and third paragraphs continue with the theme that while it is an easy matter to explain why the rich of a modern state should be well provided as compared to the savage, it is not so easily understood why this should also apply to the modern poor. By way of illustration Smith proceeded to show that the peasants and labourers of the modern state were relatively badly off due to inequality in the distribution of wealth (and effort). Smith really warmed to his task in these two paragraphs: here we meet the 'slothful Landlord', the 'indolent and frivolous retainers' of the court, and the moneyed man indulging himself in 'every sort of ignoble and sordid sensuality' — and we are told that 'those who labour most get least', and of the 'oppressive inequality' of the modern state. From the standpoint of the analytical discussion of the division of labour the two paragraphs are probably redundant, thus explaining their omission; an omission which probably does improve the flow of the argument and which lends to it a modern air of technicality and detachment. Yet one wonders if the reaction of contemporary (and modern) readers might have differed, had they been introduced to an enquiry into the nature and causes of the *Wealth of Nations* by way of a by no means trivial polemic on the subject of inequality.

decision is less obviously an improvement, for a number
of reasons. First, in the passage omitted Smith explicitly
established a connection between mode of subsistence, size
of community, and division of labour, illustrating the point
in terms of three distinct economic types (hunting, pasturage,
and agriculture).[21] Second, Smith there provided hard evidence that the division of labour was practised in primitive
communities such as the Hottentots, pointing out in the latter
case that 'Even in each village of Hottentots ... there are
such trades as those of a smith, a taylor & even a phisician, &
the persons who exercise them, tho' they are not entirely, are
principally supported by those respective employments ...'.
Third, Smith's discussion, when taken in conjunction with the
previous chapters in the *Wealth of Nations*, helps to clarify
just what he meant by the term 'division of labour'. The point
made in the omitted passage of FA is really that even backward or barbarous communities will feature a division of
labour but not necessarily specialization in employments.
The Hottentots, for example, are 'principally', not 'entirely',
supported by their respective employments. But the division
of labour properly so called only exists where there is *specialization* both in terms of area of employment and process of
manufacture. For Smith, such specialization was the characteristic of the fourth socio-economic stage alone: a point
which he makes plain in remarking that while the first three
stages gave increasing scope to the division of labour, yet 'The
compleat division of labour ... is posteriour to the invention
even of agriculture'. In the *Wealth of Nations* Smith was of
course concerned with a form of economy characterized not
merely by the division of labour, but by the 'compleat' form
of that institution.

---

[21] See above, 69ff.

7

A Conceptual System*

I

Value

Although Smith's model, in its post-physiocratic form, has several distinct elements, the feature on which he continued to place most emphasis was the *division of labour*. In terms of the content of the model outlined in previous chapters, a division of labour is of course implied in the existence of distinct *sectors* or types of productive activity. But Smith also emphasized the fact that there was specialization by types of employment, and even within each employment. To illustrate the basic point, Smith chose the celebrated example of the pin; a very 'trifling manufacture' which none the less required some eighteen processes for its completion.

In Smith's hands, the argument was important for two main reasons. First, he was at some pains to point out that the division of labour (by process) helped to explain the relatively high productivity of labour in modern times; a phenomenon which he ascribed to:

(a) The increase in 'dexterity' which inevitably results from making a single, relatively simple operation 'the sole employment of the labourer'.

* The argument of this section is intended simply to convey an impression of the structure of Smith's system, *primarily* for the non-specialist. It is based upon section 3 of the introduction to the 1974 (Pelican) edition of the *Wealth of Nations*. The most exhaustive modern account is S. Hollander's *The Economics of Adam Smith* (1973). The *Essays on Adam Smith* contain sixteen articles on different aspects of Smith's system, for example value theory, the theory of distribution, money, international trade, and growth. Of these, that by A. Lowe on 'Adam Smith's System of Equilibrium Growth' comes closest to the intentions of this paper. I am grateful to R.L. Heilbroner for bringing Professor Lowe's work to my attention.

(*b*) The saving of time which would otherwise be lost in 'passing from one species of work to another'.

(*c*) The associated use of machines which 'facilitate and abridge labour, and enable one man to do the work of many'.[1]

He further observed that the existence of specialization (by employment) necessarily involves a high degree of interdependence, in that each separate *manufacture* tends to rely on the output of other industries for different goods and services. It thus follows that the individual consumer who purchases a single commodity must at the same time acquire, in effect, the separate outputs of a 'great variety of labour'. Smith added, 'If we examine . . . all these things, and consider what a variety of labour is employed about each of them, we shall be sensible that without the assistance and co-operation of many thousands, the very meanest person in a civilized country could not be provided, even according to, what we very falsely imagine, the easy and simple manner in which he is commonly accommodated' (WN I. i. 11).

However, the aspect of this discussion which is most immediately relevant is the light which it throws on the necessity of exchange. As Smith observed, once the division of labour is established, our own labour can supply us with only a very small part of our wants. He thus noted that even in the barter economy the individual can best satisfy the whole range of his needs by exchanging the surplus part of his own production, receiving in return the products of others. Where the division of labour is thoroughly established, it is then to be expected that each individual is in a sense dependent on his fellows, and that 'Every man thus lives by exchanging, or becomes in some measure a merchant' (I. iv. 1).

This observation brought Smith directly to the problem of value, and it is noteworthy that in order to simplify the analysis he in fact used the analytical (as distinct from historical) device of the barter economy. However, despite the attempt made to simplify and to be 'perspicuous', these

---

[1] For a useful comment on the various ways in which Smith used the term 'division of labour' see Jacob Viner's *Guide to John Rae's Life of Adam Smith* (1965), 103–9.

passages in the book remain somewhat obscure, very largely because Smith uses a single term, 'exchangeable value', in handling two distinct, but related, problems.[2]

The first problem concerns the forces which determine the *rate* at which one good, or units of one good, may be exchanged for another; the second is concerned basically with the means by which we can measure the value of the total *stock* of goods created by an individual, and which is used in exchange for others. We may take these issues in turn.

As regards the *rate* of exchange, Smith isolated two relevant factors: the usefulness of the good *to be acquired*, and the 'cost' incurred in creating the commodity *to be given up*. The first of the relevant relationships, then, is obviously that which exists between 'usefulness' and value, and the elements of Smith's argument become apparent in his handling of the famous paradox, namely that the 'things which have the greatest value in use [e.g. water] have frequently little or no value in exchange; and, on the contrary, those which have the greatest value in exchange [e.g. diamonds] have frequently little or no value in use'.[3]

The solution to this paradox can be stated in two stages, where the first involves an explanation as to why two such goods have *some* value, and the second an explanation as to why the two goods have *different* values.

Smith's handling of the first part of the problem is based on his recognition that both goods are considered to be 'useful' although noting that the 'utilities' of each are qualitatively different. In the former case (water) we place a value on the good because we can use it in a practical way, while in the latter case (diamonds) we place a value on the good because it appeals to our 'senses', an appeal which, as Smith observed, constitutes a ground 'of preference', 'merit', or 'source of pleasure'.[4] He concluded: 'The demand for the precious stones arises altogether from their beauty. They are of no use,

[2] The main discussion of value theory appears in WN I, v and vi.

[3] WN I. iv. 13. For a discussion of Smith's treatment of the paradox of value, see J.A. Schumpeter's *History of Economic Analysis* (1954), Part 2, chapter 6, section 3.

[4] LJ(B), 206–10; ed. Cannan, 157–60; cf. TMS IV. i ('Of the beauty which the appearance of UTILITY bestows upon all the productions of Art, and of the extensive influence of this species of Beauty').

but as ornaments' (I. xi. c. 32). The utilities of the two goods thus emerge as being qualitatively different, although the significant point is seen to be that *both* have *some* value precisely because they represent sources of satisfaction to the individual.

Smith was then left with the second part of the initial problem, namely the explanation as to why the two goods have *different* values. Here again, the answer provided, while simple, is clear, embodying in effect the argument that merit (value) is a function of scarcity. As Smith put it, 'the merit of an object which is in any degree either useful or beautiful, is greatly enhanced by its scarcity' (I. xi. c. 31). Even more specifically he remarked: 'Cheapness is in fact the same thing with plenty. It is only on account of the plenty of water that it is so cheap as to be got for the lifting, and on account of the scarcity of diamonds (for their real use seems not yet to be discovered) that they are so dear' (LJ(B) 205-6, ed. Cannan, 157).

Smith introduced the second major element in the problem by observing that the rate at which the individual will exchange one good for another must be affected not only by the utility of the good to be acquired, but also by the 'toil and trouble' involved in creating the good exchanged. In this connection he clearly recognized that in acquiring the means of exchange (goods in the barter case), the individual must undergo the 'fatigues' of labour and thus 'lay down' a 'portion of his ease, his liberty, and his happiness' (WN I. v. 7).

In dealing with the rate of exchange, Smith placed most emphasis on this side of the problem, and explicitly argued that in the case of the barter economy 'the proportion be-tween the quantities of labour necessary for acquiring different objects seems to be the only circumstance which can afford any rule for exchanging them for one another' (I. vi. 1). Thus he suggested that if it takes twice the labour to kill a beaver that it does to kill a deer, then 'one beaver should naturally exchange for or be worth two deer'. Smith left the analysis at this point, although it will be apparent from the previous argument that the rate of exchange above mentioned can only prevail where the ratios of the relevant utilities and disutilities are the same for the respective hunters. This is

plainly one way of looking at the problem of exchange value, but Smith seems to have treated it, not as an end in itself, but as a means of elucidating those factors which govern the value of *the whole stock of goods* which the individual creates, and which he proposes to use in exchange.

Looking at the problem *in this way*, Smith then went on to argue that

The value of any commodity . . . to the person who possesses it, and who means not to use or consume it himself, but to exchange it for other commodities, is equal to the quantity of labour which it enables him to purchase or command. Labour, therefore, is the real measure of the exchangeable value of all commodities (I. v. 1.).

Smith's meaning becomes clear when he remarks that the value of a stock of goods must always be in proportion to 'the quantity . . . of other men's labour, *or, what is the same thing, of the produce* of other men's labour, which it enables him to purchase or command. The exchangeable value of every thing must always be precisely equal to the extent of this power' (I. v. 3; italics supplied). In other words, Smith is here arguing that the real value of the goods which the workman has to dispose of (in effect his income) must be measured by the quantity of goods (expressed in terms of labour units) which he can command, and which he receives once the whole volume of (separate) exchanges has taken place.

If we remain for the moment with the primitive state, we may clarify the conclusion just mentioned, and at the same time show a connection between this and the preceding analysis. In the case of the barter economy, it will be recalled that the individual is assumed to create a single (complete) product, which then becomes his personal (disposable) property. Now if, as Smith suggested, the *rate* of exchange between goods is always equal to the ratio of the labour embodied in them, then it follows that the exchangeable value of the whole *stock* of goods must be equal to the labour required to make it. In other words, the labour embodied in the stock of goods made by the individual must be equal to the labour embodied in the goods received; that is, the quantity of goods which the original stock enables the possessor to purchase or command.

Given this, it will now be apparent that the argument thus

far has two important features. First, Smith suggests that in the barter economy, the labour which the individual expends, and which is embodied in the goods *he* creates, must exchange for, or command, an equal quantity. In short, in this state, labour embodied equals labour commanded, the essential premisses being that *all* goods exchange at a given (previously defined) rate and that labour is the sole factor of production. Secondly, Smith suggests that the extent to which the individual can satisfy his needs through exchanging his produce for that of others must be determined by the quantity of other men's output (in labour units) which he receives in exchange. This is one way of measuring the economic welfare (command over goods) of individuals, and one which indicates the necessity of measuring welfare in real terms.

It is evident that in the modern economy labour is no longer the sole factor of production, and that in 'this state of things, the whole produce of labour does not always belong to the labourer' (I. vi. 7). This means of course that the labour commanded by virtue of our possession of a stock of goods must always exceed the (*direct*) labour embodied in them, by virtue of the allowance which must be made for the contribution of capital and land. In short, the equality between labour embodied and labour commanded appears to be relevant to the primitive (barter) economy and to no other. However, Smith did not consider that the recognition of this truth did any violence to his second result; namely, that the real value of income must be determined by the produce of other men's labour (measured in labour units) which it enables the recipient to purchase or command.

As Smith observed, a clear difference between the barter and modern economies is to be found in the fact that, while in the former, goods are exchanged for goods, in the latter, goods are exchanged for a sum of money, which may then be expended in purchasing other goods. Under such circumstances the individual, as Smith saw, very naturally estimates the value of his receipts (received in return for undergoing the 'fatigues' of labour) in terms of money, rather than in terms of the quantity of goods he can acquire by virtue of his expenditure. However, Smith was at some pains to insist that the real measure of welfare (that is, our ability to satisfy our wants)

was to be found in 'the money's worth' rather than the money, where the former is determined by the quantity of products (labour 'commanded') which either individuals or groups can purchase.[5] On this basis, Smith went on to distinguish between the nominal and the real value of income, pointing out that if the three original sources of (monetary) revenue in modern times are wages, rent, and profit, then the real value of each must ultimately be measured 'by the quantity of labour which they can, each of them, purchase or command' (I. vi. 9).

II

Price

It will be apparent from the previous argument that Smith regarded rent, wages, and profit as the types of return payable to the three 'great constituent orders' of society, and as the price paid for the use of the three factors of production. The revenues which accrue to individuals and groups in society, and which permit them to purchase commodities, thus appear to be costs incurred by those who create commodities. These points were made quite explicitly by Smith when he remarked:

As the price or exchangeable value of every particular commodity, taken separately, resolves itself into some one or other or all of those three parts; so that of all the commodities which compose the whole annual produce of the labour of every country, taken complexly, must resolve itself into the same three parts, and be parcelled out among different inhabitants of the country, either as the wages of their labour, the profits of their stock, or the rent of their land (WN I. vi. 17).

This argument obviously raises the problem of price and its determinants, and it is to this area of analysis (following Smith) that we now turn.

To begin with, Smith assumes the existence of given 'ordinary' or 'average' rates of wages, profit, and rent; rates which may be said to prevail within any given society or neighbourhood, during any given (time) period. This assumption is of considerable importance, for two main reasons. First, it indicates that in dealing with the problem of price,

---

[5] See especially M. Blaug, *Economic Theory in Retrospect* (1962), 48–52.

Smith was implicitly using the analytical device of a static system, and working in terms of a given (stable) stock of factors together with a given (stable) level of aggregate demand for them. Secondly, the assumption of given rates of return is important in that these rates determine the supply price of commodities.[6]

With these two points forming Smith's major premisses, he proceeded to examine the determinants of price, and to produce a discussion which seems to involve two distinct, but related, problems. First, Smith set out to show those forces which determine the prices of particular commodities, elucidating in the process the nature of partial equilibrium. Secondly, he would appear to have used the above analysis as a means of explaining the phenomenon of general inter-dependence, and thus those forces which determine the manner in which a (given) stock of factors of production is allocated between different uses or employments.

In dealing with the first aspect of the problem, Smith implicitly examines the case of a single commodity manufactured by a number of sellers, opening the analysis by establishing an important distinction between 'natural' and 'market price'. *Natural price* is defined as that amount which is 'neither more nor less than what is sufficient to pay the rent of the land, the wages of the labour, and the profits of the stock . . . according to their natural rates' (I. vii. 4). In other words, where natural price prevails, the seller is just able to cover his costs of production, including a margin for 'ordinary or average' profit. By contrast, *market price* is defined as that price which may prevail at any given point in time, being regulated 'by the proportion between the quantity which is actually brought to market, and the demand of those who are willing to pay the natural price of the commodity' (the 'effectual demanders'; I. vii. 8). Now these two 'prices' are interrelated, the essential point being that while in the short run market and natural price may diverge, in the long run they will tend

---

[6] In fact Smith's argument suggests that in the long run manufactures could be produced at constant cost. This means that the position of the cost curve facing the firm will be determined by factor costs. With a given cost 'curve', the position of the demand curve will then determine the *amount* produced, with *price* determined by cost of production.

to coincide. Natural price thus emerges as an *equilibrium* price, which will obtain when the commodity in question is in fact sold at its cost of production. The latter point may be illustrated by examining the consequences of divergences between the two prices.

If, for example, the quantity offered by the seller was less than that which the consumers were prepared to take at a particular (natural) price, the consequence would be a competition among the consumers to procure some of a relatively limited stock. Under such circumstances, Smith argued that the 'market' will rise above the 'natural' price, the extent of the divergence being determined by 'the greatness of the deficiency' and varying 'according as the acquisition of the commodity happens to be of more or less importance' to the buyer (I. vii. 9). In making the latter point, Smith took due note of the fact that where a relative shortage occurs of goods which are 'necessaries' of life, the extent of the divergence between the two prices (in effect the demand and supply prices) would be greater than that which would occur in other cases (for example, luxuries).

Under such circumstances, the price received by the seller must exceed the natural price (cost of production), with the result that rates of return accruing to factors in this employment also rise above their 'ordinary' level. The consequence of such a divergence between the returns paid in a particular employment, and the 'natural' rates prevailing must then be an inflow of resources to this relatively profitable field, leading to an expansion in the supply of the commodity, and a return to that position where the commodity is sold at its natural price. Given a relative shortage of the commodity in the market, Smith concluded: 'The quantity brought thither will soon be sufficient to supply the effectual demand. All the different parts of its price will soon sink to their natural rate, and the whole price to its natural price' (I. vii. 14).

Smith's second case is one where the quantity brought to market exceeds that which the consumers are willing to take at a particular (natural) price. Under these circumstances, he argued, the supply offered cannot be disposed of at the natural price, so that part of the total output must be sold 'to those who are willing to pay less, and the low price which

they give for it must reduce the price of the whole' (I. vii. 10). In such a case, the market must fall below the natural price with the degree of divergence determined by the extent of the excess supply. It will also vary according to the degree of competition generated among the sellers and 'according as it happens to be more or less important to them to get immediately rid of the commodity' (I. vii. 10). Once again, Smith noted that the type of good involved would be important as regards the competition engendered by a relative excess, and observed that over-supply of a perishable commodity 'will occasion a much greater competition than in that of durable commodities' (ibid). However, given some divergence between market and natural price, the consequence in this case must be that the rates of return payable to factors in this employment fall below their 'ordinary' rates, thus prompting labourers and entrepreneurs to 'withdraw a part of their labour or stock from this employment. The quantity brought to market will soon be no more than sufficient to supply the effectual demand. All the different parts of its price will rise to their natural rate, and the whole price to its natural price' (I. vii. 13). Taking the two cases of divergence, it thus becomes apparent that the price paid by the consumers in purchasing a particular quantity of some commodity will tend to coincide with that price which the seller requires to cover his costs for a specific level of output. In short, the 'natural price' emerges as the equilibrium or 'central' price, 'to which the prices of all commodities are continually gravitating'.[7]

Smith also observed that the result attained (namely that commodities in the long run are sold at their cost of production) can only hold good where there is perfect liberty; in the absence of monopoly powers, transport problems, or secrets in manufacture. The cost of production solution is, in short, only to be expected where free competition prevails.[8]

The first stage of the discussion establishes that in the case of any one commodity, equilibrium will be attained where

---

[7] It is worth noting that Smith's interest was in the processes by virtue of which positions of equilibrium tended to be attained rather than in the state of equilibrium *per se*.

[8] The policy implications of this position are examined in chapter 9 below.

the good is sold at its natural price, and where each of the (relevant) factors is paid for at its natural rate. Under these circumstances, equilibrium obtains precisely because there can be no tendency for resources to increase or decrease in this particular type of employment.

Now it is evident that if this process, and this result, holds good for all commodities taken separately, it must also apply to all commodities 'taken complexly', at least where a competitive situation prevails. That is, where the conditions which form the assumptions of the partial equilibrium case are satisfied *over the whole economy*, a position of equilibrium will be attained where each different type of good is sold at its natural price, and where each factor in each employment is paid at its natural rate. The economy can then be said to be in a position of 'balance', since where the above conditions are satisfied there can be no tendency to move resources within or between employments, and because, where the necessary conditions are not satisfied (for example, as a result of changes in tastes) they will naturally tend to be re-established as a result of (simultaneous) adjustments in the factor and commodity markets, which are analogous to those considered in the 'partial' case. It will be observed that departure from, and reattainment of, a position of (*general*) equilibrium depends upon the essentially self-interested actions and reactions of consumers and producers.[9] Smith's treatment of price and allocation thus provides one of the best examples of his emphasis on 'interdependence' and one of the most dramatic examples of his thesis of the Invisible Hand.

However, while this argument would appear to express the logic of Smith's treatment, he did modify the conclusions reached in two important respects.

First, while Smith certainly conceived of general equilibrium in terms of a situation where there was no tendency for resources to move between employments, he also recognized that a position of 'balance' need not involve an equality between monetary rates of return. The point follows directly from Smith's recognition of the fact that employments differ

---

[9] However, cf. WN I. vii. 17 where Smith discusses the problems of supply with special reference to agriculture.

qualitatively and that such differences may serve to explain why, even in a position of 'balance', different money rates prevail. As Smith put it, 'certain circumstances in the employments themselves ... either really, or at least in the imaginations of men, make up for a small pecuniary gain in some, and counter-balance a great one in others' (I. x. a. 2).[10] Thus, for example, he noted that money wage rates would tend to vary between different types of employment according to the difficulty of learning the trade, the constancy of employment, and the degree of trust involved. Similarly, he observed that both wages and profits would vary with differences in the agreeableness of the work, and with the probability of success in particular fields. In short, he was suggesting that money rates of return would only tend to equality within employments of similar kinds, and that over the whole economy the relevant balance would be one involving net advantages (I. x. a. 1). It will be seen that this argument involves an important modification to the definition of (general) equilibrium previously used, and that, as Smith pointed out, the (modified) result will only hold good where there is perfect liberty for labour and stock to move between employments (ibid.).[11]

Secondly, Smith observed that in the real world the conditions necessary for the attainment of equilibrium (as previously defined) were unlikely to be satisfied in fact, placing most emphasis on the problems presented by current

[10] See especially A. Rees, 'Compensating Wage Differentials', in *Essays on Adam Smith* and E.H. Phelps-Brown, 'The Labour Market', in *The Market and the State*, ed. T. Wilson and A. Skinner (1976).

[11] The other necessary assumptions are: 'First, the employments must be well known and long established in the neighbourhood; secondly, they must be in their ordinary, or what may be called their natural state; and, thirdly, they must be the sole or principal employments of those who occupy them' (I. x. b. 40).

It is worth noting that the argument concerning 'net advantages' provides a clear link with the analysis of man's psychology contained in the *Moral Sentiments*. This is very obvious in Smith's discussion of the agreeable or disagreeable nature of employments, and of the effect which this must have on pecuniary rates of return. He noted, for example, the impact of fashion, and of what is considered by men in general to be honourable or disgraceful, the point being that where an occupation is generally approved of, this fact alone constitutes an important part of the reward. Where on the contrary it is considered disgraceful to make a parade of certain abilities, this fact means that a higher rate of monetary reward is required; required, that is, to induce men to suffer the penalty of disapproval. See, for example, WN I. x. b. 25.

'regulations of police'. Of these, he singled out monopoly powers, since the 'price of monopoly is upon every occasion the highest which can be got' (I. vii. 27) and thus unlikely to be regulated by cost of production. He was also a bitter critic of the privileges of corporations, which effectively served to hinder the movement of capital between areas; of the Poor Laws, which had a similar effect with respect to labour; and of the Statutes of Apprenticeship, which artificially controlled the numbers of workmen in particular types of employment.[12] Smith deplored all such regulations, both because they were violations of man's 'natural liberty', and because they break 'what may be called the natural balance of industry' (LJ(B), 233, ed. Cannan, 180), thus constraining productive activity in an 'unatural [less beneficial] channel' (LJ(B), 319, ed. Cannan, 246).

III

Distribution

Abstracting from the fact of legislative obstacles and qualitative differences in employments, it will be recalled that Smith's theory of price was built up on the assumption of given rates of factor payment. Following on from this argument, Smith's next task was to elucidate the forces which determine the *level* of ('ordinary or average') rates of return during any given time period, and over time, applying to the problem the simple 'demand and supply' type of analysis just considered. We may take the relevant issues in turn, reviewing them only in such detail as may be necessary for the present argument.

(*a*) Smith observed that payment for the use of the factor labour was a feature of modern society; a payment which is made by those classes who require the factor (undertakers, farmers) and which is necessary to compensate the disutility of work. The process of wage determination may then be viewed as a kind of bargain or contract:

What are the common wages of labour depends every where upon the contract usually made between ... two parties, whose interests are by

---

[12] On this subject, see below, chapter 9.

no means the same. The workmen desire to get as much, the masters to give as little as possible. The former are disposed to combine in order to raise, the latter in order to lower the wages of labour (WN I. viii. 11).

In Smith's judgement, the balance of advantage in determining the terms of this 'contract' must generally lie with the 'masters', the reason being that while the law permitted their 'combinations', it prevented those of the workers. However, Smith was careful to point out that the bargaining strength of the two parties would itself be affected by demand and supply relationships, irrespective of legal privileges. Thus, for example, where labour is relatively abundant, wage rates will tend to be low, partly because individuals will have to compete for such employment as is available, and partly because, while in 'the long-run the workman may be as necessary to his master as his master is to him . . . the necessity is not so immediate' (I. viii. 12). On the other hand, where labour is relatively scarce, 'The scarcity of hands occasions a competition among masters, who bid against one another, in order to get workmen, and thus voluntarily break through the natural combination of masters not to raise wages' (I. viii. 17).

Having come thus far, Smith clarified the argument by pointing out that wage rates may be relatively high or low, depending on the available supply of labour and the size of the funds (or capital stock) available for its purchase. He did not in fact set out to define some upper limit for wages, but he did suggest that the lowest limit, in the long term, must be determined by the needs of subsistence, since 'A man must always live by his work, and his wages must at least be sufficient to maintain him. They must even upon most occasions be somewhat more; otherwise it would be impossible for him to bring up a family, and the race of such workmen could not last beyond the first generation' (I. viii. 15). In Smith's analysis, the importance of the 'subsistence wage' lies in the fact that it constitutes the long-run supply price of labour, the argument being in effect that over time labour may be produced at constant cost, leading to the conclusion that the subsistence wage could be regarded as a kind of 'natural' or equilibrium rate. Smith in fact made use of three cases to illustrate an argument which is analogous to the previous treatment of equilibrium price.

To begin with, it will be apparent that in a position of long-run equilibrium the demand for, and supply of, labour must be such that a particular level of population is in receipt of a subsistence wage. Under such circumstances, we find a position of equilibrium in the sense that there can be no tendency for population to increase or diminish; a condition which will obtain so long as there is no change in the size of the wages fund. This is Smith's example of the stationary state, as illustrated by the experience of China. Secondly, Smith examined a case, again starting from a position of equilibrium, where there is a fall in the demand for labour either in any one year, or continuously over a number of years.

Under such circumstances, the actual wage rate paid must fall below the subsistence rate, resulting in a fall in population until the level is such as to permit subsistence wages to be paid. This example represents Smith's 'declining' state, the cases cited being Bengal and certain East Indian colonies; areas where the decline in the wages fund had led to want, 'famine, and mortality', until 'the number of inhabitants . . . was reduced to what could easily be maintained by the revenue and stock which remained' (I. viii. 26). Finally, we have Smith's 'advancing state' where an increase, or series or (annual) increases in the size of the wages fund, causes rates in excess of the subsistence level to be paid at least for as long as it takes to increase the level of population; an increase which, he said, would inevitably follow from the higher standard of living involved. However, Smith also pointed out that the feature of the 'advancing state' would be a continuous improvement in the demand for labour, thus making it possible for high wage rates to be paid over a number of years, and at least for as long as the *rate* of increase in the demand for labour exceeded the rate of increase in supply. Smith considered the case of North America to be a good example of the trend, but also that many European countries, including Great Britain, showed the same tendency, albeit to a lesser degree. In the case of Britain, for example, Smith pointed out that (real) wages had increased during the eighteenth century, and that as a matter of fact they were well above subsistence level at the time of writing (I. viii. 28). It is interesting to observe that Smith felt that high wages were to be approved of, on

the grounds of both equity and the improved productivity of labour which results.[13]

Now while this argument runs in terms of an analysis of equilibrium similar in kind to that used in dealing with the theory of (commodity) price, it will be apparent that it examines adjustments very much longer-term in character than those so far considered. On the other hand, the argument *is* important as regards the static aspects of Smith's analysis in the sense that it helps to elucidate the forces which determine the level of wages during the course of a single time period, such as a year, and thus the level of the 'ordinary or average' rates which Smith took as given in handling the problem of price. Certainly, what has been said so far serves to show that in any one time period (such as a year) wage rates may be equal to, above, or below the subsistence rate; that such rates are a function of the size of the wages fund and the level of population, and that particular rates, once established, will remain stable so long as there is no change in any of the relevant aggregates.

(*b*) As far as *profit* is concerned, it is interesting to observe that Smith did not consider this form of return to be the reward payable for undertaking the managerial function of 'inspection and direction' but rather as the compensation for the trouble taken, and the risks incurred, in combining the factors of production. As he put it 'As soon as stock has accumulated in the hands of particular persons, some of them will naturally employ it in setting to work industrious people, whom they will supply with materials and subsistence, in order to make a profit by the sale of their work, or by what their labour adds to the value of the materials' (WN I. vi. 5). Looked at in this way, the profits which accrue to individual producers must obviously be affected by the selling price of the commodity and costs of production (including wages). Profits are thus likely to be particularly sensitive to changes in the direction of demand, together with the 'good or bad

---

[13] 'It is but equity, besides, that they who feed, cloath and lodge the whole body of the people, should have such a share of the produce of their own labour as to be themselves tolerably well fed, cloathed and lodged' (I. viii. 36). For Smith's views on the causes of the increase in productivity which high wages involve, see I. viii. 44.

fortune' of rivals and customers; facts which make it difficult to speak of an 'ordinary or average' rate of return (I. ix. 3). However, Smith did suggest that the rate of interest would provide a reasonably accurate index of profit levels at any one time, basically on the ground that the rate payable for borrowed funds would reflect the profits to be gained from their use: 'It may be laid down as a maxim, that wherever a great deal can be made by the use of money, a great deal will commonly be given for the use of it; and that wherever little can be made by it, less will commonly be given for it' (I. ix. 4).

In this connection Smith was careful to argue that the rate of interest payable would be in proportion to the 'clear or neat' profit, rather than *gross* profit, that is, to the profit remaining after making allowance for the necessary risk premium required by the entrepreneur (I. ix. 18).

At least as a broad generalization, Smith felt able to suggest that the rate of profit accruing at any one point in time (other things remaining equal, and with wage rates given) would be determined by the quantity of stock (capital) available, taken in conjunction with the volume of business to be transacted by it, or the extent of the outlets for profitable investment. It thus followed that over time the rate of profit will tend to decline, partly in consequence of the gradual increase of stock, and partly because of the increasing difficulty of finding 'a profitable method of employing any new capital'. As he wrote in another passage, 'When the stocks of many rich merchants are turned into the same trade, their mutual competition naturally tends to lower its profit; and when there is a like increase of stock in all the different trades carried on in the same society, the same competition must produce the same effect in them all' (I. ix. 2). It then follows that 'the diminution of profit is the natural effect of . . . prosperity' (I. ix. 10).

In the long term, Smith concluded that just as wages would sink towards subsistence levels, so profit would progressively decline until the rate of 'clear' profit was just sufficient to meet the necessary interest payments, including a risk premium for the lender (I. ix. 22). Historically, the pattern of events involves a progression from the 'advancing' to the 'stationary' state (such as China), although Smith did observe that two sets of circumstances might serve to reverse the associated

trend of profits. First, he suggested that a declining state (such as Bengal) would feature a gradual reduction in capital stock and thus a tendency to *increased* rates of profit. Secondly, he pointed out that even in advancing states the tendency for profits to fall might be reversed or temporarily halted, due to the acquisition of new investment outlets, or of new territories as a result of conquest. For example, in the case of Great Britain, Smith pointed out that the acquisitions made after 'the late war' must necessarily have increased the rate of profit, despite the advancing tendency of the country, since so 'great an accession of new business to be carried on by the old stock, must necessarily have diminished the quantity employed in a great number of particular branches, in which the competition being less, the profits must have been greater' (I. ix. 12).

However, the basic points which Smith was endeavouring to establish seem clear. If we look at the long-term trends of the economy, the tendency is for profits (like wages) to fall. If we look at the economy at a particular point in time (say a single year), then it appears that the 'ordinary or average' rate of profit prevailing must be a function of the quantity of stock, and the 'proportion of business' to which it can be applied. However, Smith made an important qualification to the latter point when he indicated that even where the quantity of stock remains the same (say, in two different time periods), other things remaining equal, the rate of profit will also be related to the prevailing wage rate. Thus for example, if labour is relatively abundant in relation to a given capital stock (that is, the wages fund), the rate of profit will be higher, and wage rates lower, than they would be where labour was relatively scarce.

(c) Smith formally defined *rent* as the 'price paid for the use of land' (WN I. xi. a. 1); a price paid because land is of itself productive, part of the property of individuals, and (presumably) scarce. Looking at the question in this way, Smith was careful to argue that rent constitutes a surplus in the sense that it accrues to the owner of land independently of any effort made by him, so that the proprietors emerge as 'the only one of the three orders whose revenue costs them neither

labour nor care, but comes to them, as it were, of its own accord' (I. xi. p.8). Moreover, Smith suggested that rent payments are somewhat akin to a 'monopoly price' at least in the broad sense that they are generally the highest which can be got in the 'actual circumstances of the land' (I. xi. a. 1). The reference to 'actual circumstances' is important, since Smith recognized that rent payments would vary with both the fertility and the situation of the land involved.

Smith generally took the view that land used for the production of human food would always yield a rent, and indeed computed that rent would be of the order of one third of the gross produce. Moreover, he suggested that in the long term, rent payments would tend to increase, at least absolutely, due to the increased use of the available stock (of land) which the growth of population inevitably involves. 'The extension of improvement and cultivation tends to raise it directly. The landlord's share of the produce necessarily increases with the increase of the produce' (I. xi. p.2). He added that the real value of the landlords' receipts would also tend to increase over time, since all 'those improvements in the productive powers of labour, which tend directly to reduce the real price of manufactures, tend indirectly to raise the real rent of land' (I. xi. p.4).

However, two aspects of Smith's argument would appear to be of particular importance in the present context. First, the analysis serves to suggest that at any point in time, or during any given annual period, rent payments will be a function of the proportion of the fixed stock (of land) used, where the latter is in turn a function of the level of population. Secondly, Smith's argument indicates that during any given annual period rent payments will be related, not only to the fertility of the soil, but also to the prevailing rates of wages and profit.

Rent, it is to be observed . . . enters into the composition of the price of commodities in a different way from wages and profit. High or low wages and profit, are the causes of high or low price; high or low rent is the effect of it. It is because high or low wages and profit must be paid, in order to bring a particular commodity to market, that its price is high or low. But it is because its price is high or low; a great deal more, or very little more, or no more, than what is sufficient to pay

those wages and profit, that it affords a high rent, or a low rent, or no
rent at all (I. xi. a. 8).

While we will have occasion to return later to Smith's
theory of distribution taken as a whole, two of its features
may be worth emphasizing before going further.

1. In explaining the forces which determine rates of return,
the argument throughout has a static element (linking it to
the theory of price) at least in so far as Smith was concerned
to elucidate those forces which determine the 'ordinary or
average' rates of return which prevail in any given (annual)
period. It will be observed that in this case Smith treats factors of production as fixed stocks (quantities), and that he
suggests a certain interdependence with respect to the rates
of return prevailing in the course of a single year. As we have
seen, rent payments are affected by the prevailing rates of
profit and wages, while, in addition, profits are affected by
the existing wage levels.

2. The argument just reviewed also has a dynamic element, at
least in the sense that Smith was partly concerned with long-
run trends in rates of return, treating factors as flows rather
than stocks. Once again it will be recalled that these trends are
interrelated and that they apparently depend on the process
of capital accumulation. Thus Smith suggests that profits will
decline as the size of the capital stock (wages fund) increases;
that high rates of accumulation will generate high market
wage rates, leading to an increase in the level of population,
a movement back towards subsistence levels, and changes in
rent payments which reflect the inevitable increase in the
output of food. However, it is interesting to note that at this
stage of the argument no explanation is offered as to the
source of the increase in capital; a lack which is supplied in
the predominantly macro-economic analysis of Book 2.

IV

A Macro-Economic Model

The 'static' and 'dynamic' themes which are present in the
theory of distribution are continued in the second book; the
former in the attempt made to show the working of the

economy *as a whole* during a particular annual period; the
latter in the analysis of trends over a number of years.
Specifically, the first theme is developed in the form of an
analysis of the 'circular flow', which shows the connection
between *aggregate* income, output, and expenditure, while
the second is developed in the form of a theory of growth.
These (macro-economic) areas of analysis may be seen to be
interrelated, while in addition both would appear to be connected with the previous treatment of price and distribution.
We may take these issues in turn.

Smith's analysis of the 'circular flow' may be seen as a
direct development of certain results already stated in connection with the theory of price. To begin with, it will be
recalled that costs of production are incurred by those who
create commodities, thus providing individuals with the
means of exchange. It therefore follows that if the price of
each good (in a position of equilibrium) comprehends payments made for rent, wages, and profit, according to their
natural rates, then 'it must be so with regard to all the
commodities which compose the whole annual produce of
the land and labour of every country, taken complexly' (WN
II. ii. 2). On this basis, Smith concluded that 'The whole price
or exchangeable value of that annual produce, must resolve
itself into the same three parts, and be parcelled out among
the different inhabitants' (ibid.). If for the moment we ignore
the problem of distribution (that is of a given level of income
between rent, wages, and profit), the result which Smith is
here endeavouring to establish may be stated to involve a
relationship between aggregate output and aggregate income.
In his own words, 'The gross revenue of all the inhabitants of
a great country, comprehends the whole annual produce of
their land and labour' (II. ii. 5).

Now it will be evident that a particular level of income,
created by a particular level of (aggregate) output, represents
that power to purchase goods which is available to all the
members of 'a great society'. Smith then went on to observe
that this level of purchasing power would be divided into two
funds, consumption and saving. In fact, Smith offered no
formal explanation of the forces which would determine the
actual distribution of (aggregate) income or purchasing power

between these two uses, at any particular point in time. He did however suggest that the proprietors and labourers would tend to devote a high proportion of their income to consumption, the latter by virtue of the size of their receipts (in relation to their basic needs), and the former by virtue of the habits of 'expence' associated with that class. The problem of balancing future against present enjoyments thus appears to be mainly relevant for the entrepreneurial group: a group whose functions and objectives necessarily dispose it to frugality.

But Smith did clarify the problems here considered from the standpoint of expenditure. For example, he duly noted that the proportion of annual income earmarked for consumption, taking all groups 'complexly', would be used to purchase consumption goods both perishable and durable in character. He also noted that this type of expenditure could involve the purchase of services; services of a kind which do not directly contribute to the annual output of commodities (in physical terms) and which thus cannot be said to contribute to that level of income associated with it. Smith formally described such labour as 'unproductive', but did not deny that services of this kind are useful. For example, he pointed out that the services of 'players, buffoons, opera singers, and musicians' have a certain value because they represent sources of satisfaction to those who pay for them. Similarly, he pointed out that the services provided by governments, and which are paid for out of taxes, have a value, the reason being that society could not subsist without them. However all such services are by definition unproductive: 'The sovereign . . . with all the officers both of justice and war who serve under him, the whole army and navy, are unproductive labourers. They are the servants of the publick, and are maintained by a part of the annual produce of the industry of other people' (II. iii. 2).

As regards the use of savings, Smith suggested that the proportion of income devoted to this purpose would provide or contribute to the 'capitals' used by the undertaker, and that these capitals could be divided into two categories. *Fixed Capital* he defined as that portion of savings used to purchase 'useful machines' or to improve, for example, the productive

powers of land, the characteristic feature being that goods are created, and profits ultimately acquired, by using and retaining possession of the investment goods involved. *Circulating Capital* Smith defined as that portion of savings used to purchase investment goods other than 'fixed' implements, such as labour power or raw materials, the characteristic feature being that goods are produced through temporarily 'parting with' the funds so used. Smith also noted that different trades would use different proportions of fixed and circulating capital, and that 'No fixed capital can yield any revenue but by means of a circulating capital' (II. i. 25).

Although Smith is here describing the activities of individual entrepreneurs, the distinctions just mentioned were also to appear in his (threefold) division of the *total* stock of capital of society at large.

The relevant components are, first, that part of total stock which is reserved for immediate consumption, and which is held by *all* consumers (capitalists, labour, and proprietors). The characteristic feature of this part of the total stock is that it affords no revenue to its possessors since it consists in 'the stock of food, cloaths, household furniture, &c. which have been purchased by their proper consumers, but which are not yet entirely consumed' (II. i. 12).

Secondly, there is that part of the total stock which may be described as 'fixed capital' and which will again be distributed between the various groups in society. This part of the stock, Smith suggested, is composed of the 'useful machines' purchased in preceding periods and held by the undertakers engaged in manufacture; the quantity of useful buildings and of 'improved land' in the possession of the 'capitalist' farmers and the proprietors, together with the 'acquired and useful abilities' of all the inhabitants (II. i. 13–17): that is, human capital.

Thirdly, there is that part of the total stock which may be described as 'circulating capital' and which again has several components, these being:

(*a*) The quantity of money necessary to carry on the process of circulation. In this connection Smith observed that

The sole use of money is to circulate consumable goods. By means of it, provisions, materials, and finished work, are bought and sold, and

distributed to their proper consumers. The quantity of money, therefore, which can be annually employed in any country must be determined by the value of the consumable goods annually circulated within it (II. iii. 23).

(*b*) The stock of provisions and other agricultural products which are available for sale during the current period, but which are still in the hands of either the farmers or merchants.

(*c*) The stock of raw materials and work in process, which is held by merchants, undertakers, or those capitalists engaged in the agricultural sector (including mining etc.).

(*d*) The stock of manufactured goods (consumption and investment) created during a previous period, but which remain in the hands of undertakers and merchants at the beginning of the period examined (II. i. 19–22).

Perhaps the logic of the process can be best represented by artificially splitting up the activities involved much in the manner of the physiocratic model with which Smith was familiar (above, 116). Let us suppose at the beginning of the time period in question that the major capitalist groups possess the total net receipts earned from the sale of products in the previous period, and that the undertakers engaged in agriculture open by transmitting the total rent due to the proprietors of land, for the use of that factor. The income thus provided will enable the proprietors to make the necessary purchases of consumption (and investment) goods in the current period, thus contributing to reduce the stocks of such goods with which the undertakers and merchants began the period. Secondly, let us assume that the undertakers engaged in both sectors, together with the merchant groups, transmit to wage labour the content of the wages fund, thus providing this socio-economic class with an income which can be used in the current period. It is worth noting in this connection that the capitalist groups transmit a fund to wage labour which formed a part of their *savings*, providing by this means an income (wages) which is available for current *consumption*. Thirdly, the undertakers in agriculture and manufactures will make purchases of consumption and investment goods from each other (through the medium of retail and wholesale merchants) thus generating a series of expenditures linking

the two sectors. Finally the process of circulation may be
seen to be completed by the purchases made by individual
undertakers within their own sectors. Once again these
purchases will include consumption and investment goods,
thus contributing still further to reduce the stocks of commodities which were available for sale when the period under
examination began, and which form part of the circulating
capital of the society in question.

Given these points, we can represent the working of the
system in terms of a series of flows whereby money income
(accruing in the form of rent, wages and profit) is exchanged
for commodities in such a way as to involve a series of
withdrawals from the 'circulating' capital of society. As
Smith pointed out, the consumption goods thus withdrawn
from the existing stock may be entirely used up within the
current period, used to *increase* the stock 'reserved for immediate consumption', or to replace the more durable goods
(for example, furniture or clothes) which had reached the
end of their lives in the course of the same period. Similarly,
the undertakers as a result of their purchases may *add* to
their stocks of raw materials and/or their fixed capital, or
replace the machines which had finally worn out in the current period, together with the materials used up as a result
of current productive activity. Looked at in this way, the 'circular flow' may be seen to involve a certain level of purchases
which take goods from the circulating capital of *society*,
which is matched by a continuous process of replacement by
virtue of current production of materials and finished goods
— where both types of production require the use of the fixed
and circulating capitals of *individual* entrepreneurs. It is indeed
an essential part of Smith's argument that all available resources are used.

In all countries where there is tolerable security, every man of common
understanding will endeavour to employ whatever stock he can command in procuring either present enjoyment or future profit. If it is
employed in procuring present enjoyment, it is a stock reserved for
immediate consumption. If it is employed in procuring future profit,
it must procure this profit either by staying with him, or by going from
him. In the one case it is a fixed, in the other it is a circulating capital.
A man must be perfectly crazy who, where there is tolerable security,
does not employ all the stock which he commands, whether it be his

own or borrowed of other people, in some one or other of those three ways (WN II. i. 30).

V

Growth

In choosing to examine the working of the economy during a given time period such as a year, Smith gave his model a broadly static character although it is obviously one which included a time dimension. At the same time Smith did not seek to formulate *equilibrium* conditions for the model (as Quesnay had done), at least in the sense that he did not try to develop a model using specified assumptions of a quantitative kind as a means of showing what must happen before the next time period could open under identical conditions to those prevailing in the period actually examined. Indeed, Smith's lack of concern, not with macro-statics, but with macro-static *equilibrium* was to some extent announced by the fact that, in developing his model of the flow, he made allowance for the problem of the different *rates* at which goods are used up.

Nor in dealing with the 'flow' did Smith suggest that the level of output attained during any given period would be exactly sufficient to replace the goods used up in it. On the contrary, he argued that output levels attained in any one year would be likely to exceed previous levels: an important reminder that Smith's predominant concern was with economic growth. In this connection, Smith noted that 'The annual produce of the land and labour of any nation can be increased in its value by no other means, but by increasing either the number of its productive labourers, or the productive powers of those labourers who had before been employed' (WN II. iii. 32). Smith also observed that both the above sources of increased output required an 'additional capital' devoted either to increasing the size of the wages fund or to the purchase of 'machines and instruments which facilitate and abridge labour'; an additional capital which can only be acquired through extra (net) savings, which naturally tend to enhance the exchangeable value of the annual produce of the

land and labour of the country, the real wealth and revenue of all its inhabitants' (II. iii. 13).

It will be observed that net savings attained during the course of a single (annual) period will lead indirectly to higher output and income, where the latter become available either during the course of the period examined or in subsequent years. The argument can of course be extended from this point in that the higher levels of output and income attained in any one year make it possible to reach still higher levels of savings and investment in subsequent years, thus generating still further increases in output and income. Once started, the process of capital accumulation and thus economic growth may be seen as self-generating, indicating that Smith's 'flow' is to be regarded as a spiral, rather than as a circle of given dimensions. This indeed is the burden of Smith's argument in Book 2; a fact which helps to explain three of its recurrent themes. First, Smith frequently argues that net savings will always be *possible* during each annual period; that such savings will be made by virtue of 'frugality', and prompted by 'the desire of bettering our condition, a desire which, though generally calm and dispassionate, comes with us from the womb, and never leaves us till we go into the grave' (II. iii. 28). Secondly, he argues that savings once made will always be *used* either to make purchases of investment goods or to employ productive (output-creating) labour: 'What is annually saved is as regularly consumed as what is annually spent, and nearly in the same time too; but it is consumed by a different set of people' (II. iii. 18). Thirdly, Smith consistently suggests that savings when used must create successively higher levels of output, since

Parsimony, by increasing the fund which is destined for the maintenance of productive hands, tends to increase the number of those hands whose labour adds to the value of the subject upon which it is bestowed. It tends therefore to increase the exchangeable value of the annual produce of the land and labour of the country. It puts into motion an additional quantity of industry, which gives an additional value to the annual produce (II. iii. 17).

Smith's basic theme is that economic growth depends on the accumulation of capital, and he went on from this point to draw attention to a number of factors which might affect

its rate. In this connection he noted the importance of the level of resources needed to support a fixed capital: a support which must absorb 'a certain portion' of the produce (II. ii. 7). In the same vein, he drew attention to the incidence of commercial failure in observing that 'Every injudicious and unsuccessful project in agriculture, mines, fisheries, trade, or manufactures, tends . . . to diminish the funds destined for the maintenance of productive labour' (II. iii. 26). Likewise the size of the government sector was seen to be important, since 'The whole, or almost the whole publick revenue, is in most countries employed in maintaining unproductive hands' (II. iii. 30).

This was in fact only one aspect of a more general point, namely, that the rate of growth must be determined by the extent to which available resources are used to support productive, or unproductive, hands:

According . . . as a smaller or greater proportion . . . is in any one year employed in maintaining unproductive hands, the more in the one case and the less in the other will remain for the productive, and the next year's produce will be greater or smaller accordingly; the whole annual produce, if we except the spontaneous productions of the earth, being the effect of productive labour (II. iii. 3).

Elsewhere, Smith observed that this proportion 'depends very much in every country upon the proportion between that part of the annual produce, which . . . is destined for replacing a capital, and that which is destined for constituting a revenue' (II. iii. 8).

The basic principle just stated led Smith to a further refinement of the argument in stating that the rate of growth would also be affected by the area of investment to which a specific injection of capital was applied.[14]

More specifically, it was Smith's contention that the four main fields of investment which were mentioned in the account of the 'flow' would support, directly or indirectly, very different quantities of productive labour. For example, the *retailer* replaces the stock of the merchant from whom he purchases goods, thus supporting a certain quantity of productive labour even though the retailer himself is the only

[14] On this subject, see WN II. v.

productive labourer directly employed. In the same way, the *wholesaler* replaces the capitals of the farmers and merchants with whom he does business, and 'of whom he purchases the rude and manufactured produce which he deals in, and thereby enables them to continue their respective trades' (II. v. 10). Both indirectly and directly, the merchant supports a larger number of productive hands than the retailer.

(Smith went further in noting that different kinds of wholesale trade would vary in their contribution to the maintenance of productive labour at the *domestic* level. In this connection he asserted that the home trade of consumption was to be preferred since it served to replace only domestic capitals. The foreign trade of consumption was ranked second in that the exchange of domestic for foreign goods at least replaced *some* domestic capitals. The carrying-trade was held to replace foreign capitals only and thus to make a limited contribution to domestic *industry*.)

If the wholesale trade was preferred to the retail, *manufactures* emerge as still more important since investment in this area would indirectly support a relatively large amount of productive labour by replacing the capitals of those who supply machinery and materials, while at the same time tending directly to employ a relatively significant number of men. But undoubtedly Smith's preference was for agriculture: 'No equal capital puts into motion a greater quantity of productive labour than that of the farmer' — leading to the conclusion, that 'Of all the ways in which a capital can be employed, it is by far the most advantageous to the society' (II. v. 12).

Smith advanced two additional propositions which *seem* to follow from the argument just stated. First, he asserted that where the total stock available is insufficient for all three main purposes (agriculture, manufacture, trade) the growth rate will be maximized by first concentrating on agriculture. He believed as a matter of fact that the rate of growth in Europe was lower than it might be and that 'Agriculture . . . is almost every where capable of absorbing a much greater capital than has ever yet been employed in it' (II. v. 37). By contrast, 'It has been the principal cause of the rapid progress of our American colonies towards wealth and greatness, that

almost their whole capitals have hitherto been employed in agriculture' (II. v. 21). Secondly, he argued that men would generally prefer a certain *sequence* of investment, in part because of differences in the degree of security involved. He therefore concluded: 'According to the natural course of things . . . the greater part of the capital of every growing society is, first, directed to agriculture, afterwards to manufactures, and last of all to foreign commerce' (III. i. 8).

While these two propositions are logically distinct, and not essential to the understanding of Smith's conceptual system, they were to provide him with apparently significant weapons in his critique of mercantilism in general, and of the existing colonial relationship with America in particular.

VI

In conclusion, three points are worth noting. First, it will be remembered that the process of growth here outlined, and to which Smith devoted so much attention, depends upon the decisions taken, and the efforts made, by individuals; that is, by the entrepreneurial groups. If the combination of the factors of production leads to the creation of output and thus increasing levels of income, Smith never lost sight of the fact that it all depended on the pursuit of gain; on the pursuit of 'vulgar' fortune and the desire to better one's condition materially and socially.[15] Indeed, he felt that 'It is this effort, protected by law and allowed by liberty to exert itself in the manner that is most advantageous, which has maintained the progress of England towards opulence and improvement in almost all former times, and which, it is to be hoped, will do so in all future times' (WN II. iii. 36). Once again we find a

---

[15] It is to be observed that this argument is directly linked to the psychology of the *Moral Sentiments*, where Smith explains the drive to better one's condition (fortune) in terms of the desire to become an object of approval to one's fellows. On this subject, see above, chapter 5. Smith also argued that the personal qualities necessary for the acquisition of fortune were objects of approval to mankind thus stimulating individuals to acquire them. The end (fortune) is thus seen by Smith to be quite as 'natural' as the means (prudence and frugality, for example), since both represent activities or qualities with which the 'spectator' is likely to sympathize. In this connection Smith made two points. First, he suggested that the man of enterprise is always approved of, while ambition too 'is always admired in the world' — provided that this passion is kept 'within the bounds of

reminder of the ubiquitous thesis of the 'Invisible Hand' and of the reiterated truth that the whole pattern of events depends upon the condition of personal security.

Secondly, it should be observed that the area of analysis just noticed is inseparably connected with other areas of Smith's thought. As we have seen, the theory of price and distribution helps Smith to handle the analysis of the 'circular flow', just as the latter model enables him to move on to the theory of accumulation. It will now be evident that the treatment of accumulation (of stock) also completes the logic of the earlier analysis of long-run trends in the rates of wages, profits, and rent, by providing an explanation of the motor force involved.

Finally, it must be recalled that Smith's theory of growth is linked not only to the thesis of accumulation, but also to the oldest part of the whole edifice, namely his treatment of the division of labour. The point is of course a simple one, namely that as the process of economic growth unfolds, so in turn the increasing size of the market gives greater scope to the division of labour, thus increasing productivity and at the same time giving greater scope to technical change in the shape of the flow of invention (I. i), so that the economy he describes is one subject to increasing returns.

It may now be apparent that the concept of the philosophical (analytical) system as a kind of 'imaginary machine' is particularly apt as a description of Smith's contribution to theoretical economics. As we have just seen, Smith's argument makes it possible to proceed from one area of analysis to another in a fairly clear and logical order; from the analysis of price to that of distribution, from the analysis of distribution to the treatment of the 'circular flow' and thus to the

prudence and justice'. On this subject, see Part 3, chapter 6. Secondly, Smith argued that the willingness of individuals to forgo present enjoyments, and thus to accumulate stock through frugality, was also an admired quality since it involved the virtue of self-command. He added: 'Hence arises that eminent esteem with which all men naturally regard a steady perseverance in the practice of frugality, industry, and application, though directed to no other purpose than the acquisition of fortune' (TMS IV. 2. 8). Very similar points are made in TMS VII. ii. 3. 16 where Smith suggests, 'The habits of oeconomy, industry, discretion, attention, and application of thought, are generally supposed to be cultivated from self-interested motives, and at the same time are apprehended to be very praiseworthy qualities, which deserve the esteem and approbation of every body.'

explanation of growth. Moreover, it is apparent that Smith advances through the work by dealing with distinct logical problems in a particular sequence, and in a form which successfully demonstrates the interdependence of economic phenomena. Now it is certainly *not* true that Smith's 'system' is a perfect, logical whole, just as it is probably not true to suggest that his handling of particular problems is always superior to that found in the works of contemporaries, such as Turgot or Hume. What *is* true is that the form and content of Smith's 'imaginary machine' shows a grasp of the interdependence of economic phenomena which was not equalled by other great system-builders of the period, with the possible exception of Turgot. It is indeed in this respect that the true measure of Smith's contribution is to be found. As Professor Viner has pointed out, the source of Smith's originality lies in his 'detailed and elaborate application to the wilderness of economic phenomena of the unifying concept of a co-ordinated and mutually dependent system of cause and effect relationships which philosophers and theologians had already applied to the world in general'.[16] Interestingly enough, the basic point at issue was grasped by writers much closer to the event than Professor Viner. Governor Pownall of Massachusetts, who was one of Smith's most trenchant critics, was none the less quick to appreciate that the *Wealth of Nations* constitutes 'an INSTITUTE OF THE PRINCIPIA *of those laws of motion*, by which the operations of the community are directed and regulated, and by which they should be examined'.[17] Writing a little later, Dugald Stewart also noted that 'it may be doubted, with respect to Mr Smith's Inquiry, if there exists any book beyond the circle of the mathematical and physical sciences, which is at once so agreeable in its arrangement to the rules of a sound logic, and so accessible to the examination of ordinary readers' (Stewart, IV. 22). These were certainly compliments which Smith would have appreciated, conscious as he was of the value of systems which connect together 'in the fancy those different

[16] *Adam Smith, 1776–1926* (1928), 116, 118. See also Jacob Hollander's comments in the same volume, at pp. 15–19.
[17] *A Letter from Governor Pownall to Adam Smith, LL.D. F.R.S., being an Examination of Several Points of Doctrine* . . . (London, 1776), § 41, Corr., 354.

movements and effects which are already in reality performed'
(Astronomy, IV. 19) and of the 'beauty of a systematical
arrangement of different observations connected by a few
common principles (WN V. i. f. 25).

8

Mercantilist Policy: The American Colonies*

It is well known that Adam Smith addressed himself to the whole question of colonial power in his *Wealth of Nations*,[1] and hardly surprising that his views on America should have continued to attract attention.[2] After all, Smith was one of those who hoped for union between Britain and America as a solution to current difficulties, while recognizing that total separation was the more likely solution in fact. He also noticed the possibility of a special relationship between the two countries, based on a common cultural and political heritage, while pointing out that in the long run America would reach a position of economic and political dominance, with or without union with the 'mother country'. Smith also lent a real touch of originality to the debate by showing that the differing rates of growth in the two countries must inevitably cause some change in the relationship (currently defined by the regulating acts of trade and navigation) which had originally existed between them.

Points such as these are sufficient reason to restate the elements of Smith's position, and adequate justification for

* An earlier version of this paper was given at a Seminar in Edinburgh University's Institute for the Advanced Study of the Humanities. I am grateful to the members of that Seminar, and in particular to Dr. Keith Hampson, for a number of helpful comments. The paper in its present form was given to the Scottish Section at the Fourth International Congress on the Enlightenment in July 1975 and published in the *Journal of the History of Ideas*, 37 (1976).

[1] The main body of the argument appears at IV. vii.

[2] For comment, see esp. E.A. Benians, 'Adam Smith's Project of an Empire', *Cambridge Historical Review*, 1 (1923-5); C.R. Fay, 'Adam Smith, America, and the Doctrinal Defeat of the Mercantile System', *Quarterly Journal of Economics*, 48 (1934); R. Koebner, *Empire* (1961); D. Winch, *Classical Political Economy and the Colonies* (1965); also David Stevens, 'Adam Smith and the Colonial Disturbances', in *Essays on Adam Smith*.

going over some familiar ground. However, this chapter will seek to meet three further objectives. First, it is proposed to restate Smith's argument in the general form of an exercise in theoretical history; a form of enquiry which Smith used a great deal and which has the distinguishing characteristic of starting from a given environment or situation and then examining the way in which certain forces of development, released within it, must ultimately impinge upon it.[3] Secondly, it is hoped that such a restatement of Smith's position may clarify the steps of an argument which are largely implicit and at the same time permit us to isolate some of the more obvious forms of criticism to which it may be subject. Finally, our argument taken as a whole may allow us to offer some speculations as to Smith's purpose in including so extensive a treatment of the colonial problem in his major work. More specifically, we shall suggest that this section of the *Wealth of Nations* may have been designed as an essay in *persuasion*; that Smith may have set out to produce a single argument composed of a number of separate parts organized in such a way that each component gained strength and ·plausibility from its association with the others.[4]

The main components of the analysis would appear to be:

1. A statement of the purposes of the laws of trade and navigation, which defined the relationship between the mother country and the colonies.

2. An examination of the possibilities for economic development within the legal framework thus defined.

3. A consideration of the contradictions which, Smith felt, must ultimately emerge as between the future economic development of both countries and the restrictions currently imposed upon them.

4. An account of the actual situation faced by Great Britain in the 1770s, which is represented as making some change in the colonial relationship inevitable.

5. Smith's assessment of the form which that change was likely to take in the actual circumstances of the time.

---

[3] See above, chapter 4.   [4] See below, n. 42.

We may briefly review these individual sections before examining their implications with regard to Smith's purpose, thus dividing the argument into two main parts.

I

1. In describing the objectives of colonial policy, Smith concentrated mainly on its economic aspects and duly reported on the extensive range of restrictions which Britain had imposed on trade and manufactures, domestic as well as American. To begin with, the regulating acts of navigation required that trade between the colonies and Great Britain had to be carried on in British ships, and that certain classes of commodities were to be confined initially to the market of the mother country. These, so-called 'enumerated' goods were of two types: those which were either the peculiar produce of America or were not produced in Britain, and those goods which were produced in Britain but in insufficient quantities to meet domestic demand. Examples of the first type were molasses, coffee, and tobacco; of the second, naval stores, masts, pig-iron, and copper. The first broad category of goods was not of a kind which could harm British industry, and here the object of policy, as reported by Smith, was to ensure that British merchants could buy cheaper in the colonies with a view to supplying other countries at higher prices, and at the same time establish a useful carrying trade. In the second case, the objectives were to ensure essential supplies and, through the careful use of duties, to discourage imports from other countries 'with whom the balance of trade was supposed to be unfavourable'. Smith also took notice of another feature of British policy, namely, that the production of the more 'advanced or more refined manufactures' was discouraged in the colonies (WN IV. vii. b. 40). Thus woollen manufactures were forbidden, and although they were encouraged to export pig-iron, the colonists were prevented from erecting slitt-mills which might have led ultimately to the development of manufactures competitive with those of Great Britain. There was a certain ingenuity in these arrangements (no doubt, as Smith suggests, as much the product of accident as design) in that the colonial relationship could be

seen to benefit *both* parties at least in the short run. For example, the relationship with the colonies, as defined by the regulating acts, had the effect of creating a self-supporting economic unit whose main components provided complementary markets for each others' products, and in addition helped to minimize gold flows abroad (IV. viii. 15). By the same token, the colonial relationship gave Britain access to *strategic* materials, and thus contributed to national defence (IV. ii. 30), through the encouragement given to her mercantile marine.

2. Smith also argued that there were considerable opportunities for economic growth within the framework of the colonial relationship. In this connection, he placed most emphasis on American experience, and drew attention to three factors which contributed to explain her rapid rate of expansion. First, Smith isolated what may be described as 'institutional' forces in pointing out that the colonies possessed political institutions derived from the British model, which encouraged economic activity by guaranteeing the security of the individual (WN IV. vii. b. 51).

In the same way he pointed out that the colonists had brought to an underdeveloped territory the habit of subordination and a 'knowledge of agriculture and of other useful arts' (IV. vii. b. 2), the legacy of the more developed economies from which they had often come. Smith also emphasized that certain features were absent from the colonies, of a kind which contributed to slow up the rate of growth in Europe: for example, high rents, tithes, and taxes, together with legal arrangements such as laws of entail which hindered the sale of lands to those whose object was to improve them.[5]

Secondly, he drew attention to the economic situation of the colonial territories in pointing out that 'A new colony must always for some time be more under-stocked in proportion to the extent of its territory, and more under-peopled in proportion to the extent of its stock, than the greater part of other countries' (WN. I. ix. 11). This meant that the rates of both wages and profits were likely to be high, thus contributing to a level of activity which explained the 'con-

---

[5] WN III. iv. 19; cf. LJ(B) 285–307, ed. Cannan, 222–36.

tinual complaint of the scarcity of hands in North America. The demand for labourers, the funds destined for maintaining them, increase, it seems, still faster than they can find labourers to employ' (I. viii. 23).

Thirdly, Smith argued that the legislative arrangements governing trade with the mother country had contributed most materially to colonial development even though this had not always been the motive behind them. In this connection he drew attention to the fact that 'the most perfect freedom of trade is permitted between the British colonies of America and the West Indies', thus providing a 'great internal market' for their products (IV. vii. b. 39). In addition, the relative freedom of trade in non-enumerated commodities provided a further market for the primary products involved, while Britain also gave preferential treatment to American products which were confined to her own domestic market. Again, Britain provided a large European market (albeit indirectly) for the enumerated items — for example, goods like tobacco which were largely re-exported. Taken as a whole, the colonial policy had the effect of encouraging what Smith described as 'Agriculture . . . the proper business of all new colonies; a business which the cheapness of land renders more advantageous than any other' (IV. vii. c. 51). This point is of great importance, since on Smith's argument agriculture was the most productive of all forms of investment,[6] capable of generating a large surplus which could sustain further growth. He even argued that the restrictions imposed on the introduction of manufactures had benefited the colonies by ensuring that they bought from the cheaper European markets and therefore avoided diverting any part of the available capital into less productive employments. He concluded:

Unjust, however, as such prohibitions may be, they have not hitherto been very hurtful to the colonies. Land is still so cheap, and, consequently, labour so dear among them, that they can import from the mother country, almost all the more refined or more advanced manufactures cheaper than they could make them for themselves. Though they had not, therefore, been prohibited from establishing such manufactures, yet in their present state of improvement, a regard to their

---

[6] See above, 123, 179-80.

own interest would, probably, have prevented them from doing so (IV. vii. b. 44).

There is no doubt as to the buoyancy of Smith's tone in describing the growth rate of North America: a country where the benefits available, natural, artificial, and accidental, were such as to prompt the conclusion that 'though North America is not yet so rich as England, it is much more thriving, and advancing with much greater rapidity to the further acquisition of riches (I. viii. 23).

Yet at the same time, it cannot be said that Smith minimized the benefits to Britain from the standpoint of economic growth. In this connection he pointed out that Britain (together with her neighbours) had as a matter of fact acquired, through the control of the colonies, a 'new and inexhaustible market' which had given occasion to 'new divisions of labour and improvements of art' (IV. vii. c). Indeed, it can be said that Smith's assertion of benefit accruing to Great Britain as a result of the colonial relationship simply reflects his own grasp of the gains from trade (IV. i. 31).

Taken as a whole, Smith's argument seems designed to suggest that for a time at least the colonial relationship had both contributed to, and proved compatible with, a relatively high rate of growth in both the colonies and the mother country.

3. The relationship between mother country and colonies is thus represented as beneficial to the two parties, both as regards the politico-economic objectives of the regulating acts and the stimulus given to economic growth. But at the same time Smith evidently believed that there were contradictions inherent in the colonial relationship which must begin to manifest themselves over time. For example, while Smith took pains to emphasize the great stimulus given to the growth of the colonies, he also pointed out that the high and rapid rate of growth which they had attained must ultimately come in conflict with the restrictions imposed on colonial trade and manufactures; restrictions which could be regarded as the 'principal badge of their dependency' (WN IV. vii. c. 64) and as a 'manifest violation of one of the most sacred rights of mankind'. He also pointed out: 'In their

present state of improvement, those prohibitions, perhaps, without cramping their industry, or restraining it from any employment to which it would have gone of its own accord, are only impertinent badges of slavery . . . In a more advanced state they might be really oppressive and insupportable' (IV. vii. b. 44). Smith quite clearly considered that in the long run some change must come in the colonial relationship for the reason just stated, although he did place most emphasis on the more immediate problems faced by Britain herself.

As far as Great Britain was concerned Smith contended that although the colony trade was 'upon the whole beneficial, and greatly beneficial' (IV. vii. c. 47), still the rate of growth was necessarily less than it would have been in the absence of the regulating acts. He quite clearly believed that 'If the manufactures of Great Britain . . . have been advanced, as they certainly have, by the colony trade, it has not been by means of the monopoly of that trade, but in spite of the monopoly' (IV. vii. c. 55). Smith advanced a number of points in support of this contention. First, he suggested that the monopoly of the colony trade had inevitably increased the volume of business to be done by a relatively limited amount of British capital and, therefore, the prevailing rate of profit. In this connection he argued that high rates of profit would affect the improvement of land (IV. vii. c. 58) and the frugality of the merchant classes (IV. vii. c. 61), while ensuring that available capital would be partly drawn, and partly driven, from those trades where Britain lacked the monopoly (that is, drawn by the higher profits available in the colony trade, and driven from them by a poorer competitive position). But Smith especially emphasized that the pattern of British *trade* had been altered in such a way that her manufactures, 'instead of being suited, as before the act of navigation, to the neighbouring market of Europe, or to the more distant one of the countries which lie round the Mediterranean sea, have, the greater part of them, been accommodated to the still more distant one of the colonies' (IV. vii. c. 22). Smith's point was that the existing legislation had drawn capital from trades carried on with a near market (Europe), and diverted it to trade carried on with a distant market (America), while forcing a certain amount of capital

from a direct to an indirect foreign trade: all with consequent effects on the rate of return, the employment of productive labour, and, therefore, the rate of economic growth.[7]

Smith also added that the pattern of British trade had been altered in such a way as to make her unduly dependent on a single (though large) market:

Her commerce, instead of running in a great number of small channels, has been taught to run principally in one great channel. But the whole system of her industry and commerce has thereby been rendered less secure; the whole state of her body politick less healthful, than it otherwise would have been. In her present condition, Great Britain resembles one of those unwholesome bodies in which some of the vital parts are overgrown, and which, upon that account, are liable to many dangerous disorders scarce incident to those in which all the parts are more properly proportioned (IV. vii. c. 43).

In sum, the colonial relationship could be represented as compatible with a high rate of growth in America, but a suboptimal rate of growth as far as Great Britain was concerned. In the former case Smith argued that a difficulty must be faced in the long run when a rapid rate of growth came in conflict with the restrictions imposed on American manufactures. In the case of Great Britain, Smith argued that a suboptimal rate of growth must ultimately affect her ability to sustain those imperial pretensions of which the regulating acts were the reflection, by adversely affecting her level of taxable capacity. Indeed, Smith roundly asserted that 'the present system of management' ensured that Britain derived nothing but loss from the dominion assumed over the colonies (IV. vii. c. 65) at the *present* time and that costs incurred *now* exceeded the profits actually gained. Looked at from this point of view, the colonial policy emerged as essentially contradictory, at least in the long run, and as attractive only to the 'undiscerning eye of giddy ambition' (IV. vii. c. 85).

4. Smith's account of the problem currently facing Great Britain is largely dominated by that of fiscal need. In Smith's opinion Britain's needs seemed to be growing more rapidly than her resources, and he noted in this connection that by January 1775 the national debt had reached the then

---

[7] See WN II. v. and III. i.

astronomical figure of 130 millions (absorbing 4.5 millions in interest charges), much of which was due to the acquisition of the colonial territories.[8]

This was a matter of some moment since it meant that a country whose rate of growth had been adversely affected by the colonial relationship had to face a large and probably growing tax burden which would itself affect the rate of economic expansion, and thus compound the problem. Smith therefore concluded that Great Britain must either tax the colonies or give them up, and by this means either solve the fiscal problem or abandon it by accommodating 'her future views and designs to the real mediocrity of her circumstances' (WN V. iii. 92).

However, Smith quite plainly believed that Britain both could and should tax the colonies, partly as a means of relief from the growing burden of the national debt and partly as a means of making the colonies pay for benefits received from the imperial connection. It is worth noting that Smith did not defend colonial taxation on the ground that Britain had planted the colonies; on the contrary, he pointed out that they had been originally peopled largely as the result of religious persecution (IV. vii. b. 61). Nor did he suggest that taxation was justified on the ground that the mother country had originally invested in their improvement; on the contrary, he insisted that policy to regulate the colonies had only been implemented after the original colonists had made significant economic progress (IV. vii. b. 63). He simply argued:

It is not contrary to justice that both Ireland and America should contribute towards the discharge of the publick debt of Great Britain. That debt has been contracted in support of the government established by

---

[8] Smith pointed out elsewhere that Britain's two most expensive wars, i.e. the Spanish and French wars, 'were undertaken, the one chiefly, the other altogether on account of the colonies'. He went on to point out that at one time the British had complained of involvement with the affairs of Hanover 'with which we should, otherwise, have had nothing to do. But we, surely, have had much more reason to complain, upon the same account, of our connexion with America.' This comment appears in a memorandum submitted by Smith to Alexander Wedderburn, Solicitor-General in Lord North's administration, after the loss of Saratoga (*Memorandum*, § 12, Corr., p. 382). The memorandum appears in G.H. Guttridge, 'Adam Smith on the American Revolution', *American Historical Review*, 38 (1932–3), and is now reprinted in Smith's *Correspondence*, appendix B.

the Revolution, a government to which the protestants of Ireland owe, not only the whole authority which they at present enjoy in their own country, but every security which they possess for their liberty, their property, and their religion; a government to which several of the colonies of America owe their present charters, and consequently their present constitution, and to which all the colonies of America owe the liberty, security, and property which they have ever since enjoyed. That publick debt has been contracted in the defence, not of Great Britain alone, but of all the different provinces of the empire; the immense debt contracted in the late war in particular, and a great part of that contracted in the war before, were both properly contracted in defence of America (V. iii. 88).

Having made a point which commanded a good deal of support in contemporary Britain, Smith went on to consider how such a policy might be implemented and what its consequences might be. To begin with, he suggested that the colonies might be taxed by their own assemblies, a proposition no sooner stated than rejected on the ground that colonial assemblies cannot be supposed to be the proper judges of the needs of the empire as a whole (IV. vii. c. 70). Secondly, he suggested that taxes might be levied by requisition, which was the current practice: 'the parliament of Great Britain determining the sum which each colony ought to pay, and the provincial assembly assessing and levying it in the way that suited best the circumstances of the province' (IV. vii. c. 71). Such a system had some obvious advantages in Smith's opinion, especially in that it left the central and colonial governments with important and appropriate areas of control. But this solution too was rejected, partly because he felt that the mother country might face some difficulty in actually extracting the revenue required (a point confirmed by British experience during the war with France), and partly because central control of taxation might have adverse repercussions as a result of its political consequences in America itself. Taxation by requisition and without representation would, Smith felt, effectively reduce the power and status of the colonial assemblies, and, therefore, that of 'all the leading men of British America'.[9]

---

[9] Smith made much of this point, both in the *Memorandum* and in the *Wealth of Nations*, where he added: 'The leading men of America, like those of all other countries, desire to preserve their own importance. They feel, or imagine, that

Finally, Smith suggested that the British government should retain the right of assessment but extend the British system of taxation to all the colonies. The concluding sections of the *Wealth of Nations* are largely concerned with the technical problems of this aspect of harmonization, and Smith saw no reason to suppose that the major British taxes (land tax, stamp duties, customs, and excise) could not be successfully applied to both America and Ireland. He added that such a change of policy should be accompanied by freedom of trade between all parts of the empire (V. iii. 72) and, most dramatically, that it would require a form of union which would give the colonies representation in the British parliament and in effect create a single state:

This, however, could scarce, perhaps, be done, consistently with the principles of the British constitution, without admitting into the British parliament, or if you will into the states-general of the British Empire, a fair and equal representation of all those different provinces, that of each province bearing the same proportion to the produce of its taxes, as the representation of Great Britain might bear to the produce of the taxes levied upon Great Britain (V. iii. 68).

5. Smith's discussion of Union emerges directly from his examination of Britain's fiscal needs and his acceptance of the constitutional rule that there should be no taxation without representation. It is thus an essentially logical solution, although Smith did add a further dimension to his discussion in examining some of the political problems which contributed to make union unlikely, and which reflected the fact that the colonies were already in a state of revolt. There can be no doubt that Smith regarded union as desirable in the sense that it would have given both Britain and the colonies considerable economic and political advantages. In the case of Britain, for example, Smith believed that the great internal market thus created (that is, embracing the former colonies) would stimulate economic growth, solve the problem of im-

if their assemblies, which they are fond of calling parliaments, and of considering as equal in authority to the parliament of Great Britain, should be so far degraded as to become the humble ministers and executive officers of that parliament, the greater part of their own importance would be at an end. They have rejected, therefore, the proposal of being taxed by parliamentary requisition, and like other ambitious and high-spirited men, have rather chosen to draw the sword in defence of their own importance' (IV. vii. c. 74).

balance, and at the same time dramatically increase the taxable capacity of the Union.[10] Politically, this solution would have the advantage of avoiding dismemberment[11] of the empire while representing a logical development of British political experience. Indeed Smith believed that

there is not the least probability that the British constitution would be hurt by the union of Great Britain with her colonies. That constitution, on the contrary, would be completed by it, and seems to be imperfect without it. The assembly which deliberates and decides concerning the affairs of every part of the empire, in order to be properly informed, ought certainly to have representatives from every part of it (WN IV. vii. c. 77).

As far as America was concerned, Smith's argument suggests that the colonies would benefit from free trade and the removal of restrictions on manufactures, while, in addition, membership of the Imperial Parliament (at Westminster) would open up 'a new and more dazzling object of ambition' (IV. vii. c. 75) to the leading men of each colony.[12] In fact the advantages to America would appear to have been overwhelming, since in Smith's judgement her rapid progress 'in wealth, population and improvement' had been such that 'in the course of little more than a century, perhaps, the produce of American might exceed that of British taxation. The seat of the empire would then naturally remove itself to that part of the empire which contributed most to the general defence and support of the whole' (IV. vii. c. 79).

However, Smith recognized that union was in fact no longer really likely as a solution to Britain's current problems and that it commanded very little support on either side of the Atlantic:[13] 'We, on this side the water, are afraid lest the

---

[10] Since Smith was somewhat sceptical about the likelihood of free trade, in fact, he may have approved of union with America as a means of creating a free trade area of immense potential.

[11] It is interesting that the term 'dismembering the empire', so much used in the nineteenth-century debate over Ireland, should have been such a feature of the *Memorandum*; see, e.g., § 13, Corr., p. 383.

[12] In the *Memorandum* Smith comments: 'The leading men of America, we may believe, wish to continue to be the principal people in their own country. After a union with Great Britain, they might expect to continue to be so; in the same manner as the leading men of Scotland continued to be the principal people of their own country after the union with England' (§ 14, Corr., pp. 383–4).

[13] In the *Memorandum*, Smith suggested that such a plan as 'would certainly

multitude of American representatives should overturn the balance of the constitution' (IV. vii. c. 78), while the 'people on the other side of the water are afraid lest their distance from the seat of government might expose them to many oppressions (IV. vii. c. 79).

But some form of change was inevitable and Smith went on to consider the possible alternatives open. One such was that Britain should simply give up her pretensions to dominion, and by this generous act create a special relationship while acquiring all those advantages which the existing colonial structure seemed to deny her:

By thus parting good friends, the natural affection of the colonies to the mother country, which, perhaps, our late dissentions have well nigh extinguished, would quickly revive. It might dispose them not only to respect, for whole centuries together, that treaty of commerce which they had concluded with us at parting, but to favour us in war as well as in trade, and, instead of turbulent and factious subjects, to become our most faithful, affectionate, and generous allies (IV. vii. c. 66)[14]

Smith added with regret that these advantages too were un-likely of realization, since such a voluntary withdrawal rep-resents a policy which 'never was, and never will be adopted, by any nation in the world' because of the damage done to national pride (IV. vii. c. 66). The only alternative, from a British point of view, was the subjection of the colonies by force. However, this too was a solution which Smith rejected as unlikely to succeed (IV. vii. c. 75), partly because of the

tend most to the prosperity, to the splendour, and to the duration of the empire, if you except here and there a solitary philosopher like myself, seems scarce to have a single advocate' (§ 11, Corr., pp. 381-2). Smith considered that the Americans, especially in 'their present elevation of spirits', were unlikely to agree to union even on terms advantageous to themselves. As to British opinion, Smith believed that the most popular solution was military victory (§ 11).

[14] Smith pointed out in the *Memorandum* that with emancipation on these terms, the colonists' 'antient affection for the people of this country might revive, if they were once assured that we meant to claim no dominion over them', and added that 'the similarity of language and manners would in most cases dispose the Americans to prefer our alliance to that of any other nation' (§ 12, Corr., p. 383). But he felt that in the meantime, 'tho' this termination of the war might be really advantageous, it would not, in the eyes of Europe appear honourable to Great Britain; and when her empire was so much curtailled, her power and dignity would be supposed to be proportionably diminished. What is of still greater im-portance, it could scarce fail to discredit the Government in the eyes of our own people ... [it] ... would have every thing to fear from their rage and indignation at the public disgrace and calamity, for such they would suppose it to be, of thus dismembering the empire' (§ 13, Corr., p. 383).

spirit of the colonists and partly on account of the fact that while a professional standing army, such as the British, was always likely to be the superior of a militia, experience suggested that this need not be the case where the latter was long in the field: 'Should the war in America drag out through another campaign, the American militia may become in every respect a match for that standing army, of which the valour appeared, in the last war, at least not inferior to that of the hardiest veterans of France and Spain (V. i. a. 27).[15] Complete separation thus emerges as the most likely outcome, given the actual circumstances of the time.

II

1. The argument which we have just reviewed, with its division into five interrelated components, provides us with a common basis from which to proceed to our second main problem: the assessment of Smith's purpose in devoting so much attention to the case of America. This is not an idle question when we recall Smith's zeal in American affairs, and the belief, shared by some of his friends at the time, that the publication of the *Wealth of Nations* had been delayed because of it.[16] In this respect it would probably be agreed that the *content* of Smith's argument has given rise to three main interpretations with regard to his *purpose*.

(*a*) First, we may regard Smith's views on the American problem simply as a comment on the economic, political, and constitutional crisis which faced Britain at the time of writing. This interpretation rests mainly on the first, fourth, and fifth components of Smith's argument as stated above; components which do, as we have seen, contain a good deal of information as to events of immediate relevance. It is in this connection that we meet the acts of trade and navigation, the problems

---

[15] It is pointed out in the *Memorandum* that even if the British did win by force of arms, the colonists 'would be ten times more ungovernable than ever; factious, mutinous and discontented subjects in time of peace, at all times, upon the slightest disobligation, disposed to rebel' (§14, Corr., p. 383). In any event, Smith seems to have felt, writing in 1778, that the most likely (and the most expensive) outcome would be the loss of part of America, i.e. the colonies excluding Canada (§17, Corr., pp. 384–5).

[16] Winch, op.cit. 6.

of debt and taxation, together with Smith's assessment of the outcome of the current crisis. There is evidently a great deal of such material, and it is this fact which justifies the student of the times in regarding Smith as a useful source both as regards the interpretation of facts and as a record of informed, contemporary opinion on the British case. The same material also justifies the opinion of those who consider that Smith's purpose was to deliver a statement and interpretation of the current crisis. This was the view taken by Hugh Blair, for example, who remarked that Smith had given American affairs 'a representation etc. which I wish had been omitted, because it is too much like a publication for the present moment. In Subsequent editions, when publick Measures come to be Settled, these pages will fall to be omitted or Altered.'[17] This is an interesting reaction precisely because Blair recognized that the purpose of the *Wealth of Nations* was to state and apply principles of universal validity and that it ought not, therefore, to include material of passing relevance, however important.

(*b*) The second main line of interpretation concentrates mainly, although not exclusively, on the first, second, and third components of Smith's argument and purports to show that these parts of the *Wealth of Nations* were not changed precisely because they *were* designed to illustrate theses for which Smith *did* claim universal validity. Thus, for example, Smith's treatment of the American experience would appear to confirm his general thesis regarding the relationship between political freedom and economic performance, while his analysis of the benefits accruing to both the colonies and mother country illustrates the 'gains from trade'.[18] In the same way his explanation of the differing rates of growth between the two countries runs very much in terms of the 'natural progress of opulence' (WN III. i) and Smith's ranking of the various forms of investment in terms of productive labour used (WN II. v). All of these arguments may be said to

[17] Letter 151, dated 3 April 1776, addressed to Smith: also quoted in Koebner, op.cit. 358; cf. Winch, op.cit. 20–1.
[18] For comment: Winch, op.cit. 7–9; S. Hollander, *The Economics of Adam Smith*, ch. 9; H. Myint, 'The Classical Theory of International Trade and the Underdeveloped Countries', *Economic Journal*, 68 (1958).

be featured separately, yet at the same time it will be evident that they are combined in such a way as to justify Koebner's view that Smith's treatment of the colonial issue is 'organically woven into the context of his great systematic work' to provide 'a single important instance of the general problem of colonial monopolies and the economic fallacies bound up with them'.[19]

Interestingly enough, one of Smith's contemporaries, William Robertson, viewed Smith's purpose in a rather similar way when he somewhat pompously recorded that 'Many of your observations concerning the Colonies are of capital importance to me. I shall often follow you as my Guide and instructor. I am happy to find my own ideas concerning the absurdity of the limitations upon the Colony trade established ~uch better than I could have done myself.'[20]

The third line of interpretation differs from the first two in so far as it finds in Smith's account a single whole ~h begins with the acts of trade and navigation and ends with an assessment of Britain's difficulties in the 1770s. In short, Smith's analysis may be seen to include both an exposé of the mercantile fallacy *and* an account of contemporary events, where the former is stated in such a way as to imply that the problems which Britain faced at the time were the inevitable outcome of that fallacy. When looked at from this point of view, the two main facets of Smith's argument would appear to be linked by his discussion of the problems of debt and taxable capacity; linked in that the exposé of the mercantile fallacy is designed to explain an adverse effect on Britain's rate of growth and, therefore, her need to tax the colonies — the point at which her real difficulties began.

This is an attractive thesis in that it does not call in question the arguments used to support either of the other two, but merely ascribes to them a more equal weighting. It is also a plausible interpretation of Smith's intention since it offers a reasonable explanation as to why this material was included in the book, while taking account of the degree of elaboration

---

[19] Koebner, op.cit. 229.
[20] Letter 153, dated North Murchiston, 8 April 1776.

which Smith brought to each of the main sides of his argument. This (third) thesis may also gain some support from the realization that it ascribes to Smith a purpose which conforms to the requirements of his own historical method, by suggesting that he offered an account of current events in terms of their long-run (economic) and immediate (political) causes.[21]

Now the argument thus far would appear to establish: first, that there are several possible ways in which Smith's purpose may be interpreted; and, second, that all these interpretations are based, in one way or another, on the existence of two main sides to Smith's argument, that is, the exposé of the mercantile fallacy and the concern with current events.

2.   Given the above, we can now take a step further in that once we consider it possible to reach some conclusion with regard to Smith's purpose it then becomes appropriate to assess the degree of success which he enjoyed. Let us begin by agreeing that both sides of Smith's argument are open to some criticism.

(*a*) For example, Smith's analysis of the long-run causes of change in the nature of the imperial relationship would appear to rest on two trends: the relatively slow rate of growth attained by Britain in the face of self-imposed costs and restrictions, and the relatively high rate attained in America which in part at least had *resulted from* these restrictions. It is also evident that Smith's explanation of British economic performance at the time rests very heavily on his thesis of the natural progress of opulence and the consequent belief that any derangement of the natural balance of industry would slow down the rate of growth. In particular, it would appear that Smith made much of the point that the colonial trade transferred capital from a near to a distant market where the rate of return was slower, and that he relied heavily on the (relative) decline in Britain's taxable capacity, as the source of her problems. However, there is remarkably little by way of *verification* of these critical points. As Koebner has pointed out, Smith 'did not take the trouble to check' many of his

---

[21] Smith elaborates on the methodology of historical writing in lecture 17 • the *Lectures on Rhetoric and Belles Lettres*; see above, 91 ff.

suppositions,[22] and a similar criticism was voiced by a contemporary of Smith's, Governor Pownall of Massachusetts. The Governor questioned Smith's assertion that the rate of return was slower in the American as compared to the European trade and insisted that the matter of diversion of stock from Europe to America was 'a matter of fact, which must not be established by an argument, *a priori* − but on an actual deduction of facts. . . . I did not find the latter in your book. . . .'[23]

Pownall made an even shrewder point when he recognized that Smith was using theses established in one part of the book as proven principles in another. For example, he recognized the central importance of Smith's views on the productivities of investment: 'In that part, however, which explains the different effect of different employment of capital . . . I will beg to arrest your steps for a moment, while we examine the ground whereon we tread: and the more so, as I find these propositions used in the second part of your work as data; whence you endeavour to prove, that the monopoly of the colony trade is a disadvantageous commercial institution.'[24] The Governor also drew attention to the *style* of Smith's argument in the course of a discussion of Britain's potential losses arising from the colonial relationship:

It strikes me as material, and I am sure, therefore, you will excuse me making, in this place, one remark *on the manner* of your argument, and how you *stretch your reasoning nicely*. You in words advance upon the ground of *probable reasons for believing* only, you prove by probable suppositions only; yet most people who read your book, will think you mean to set up an absolute proof, and your conclusion is drawn as though you had.[25]

Writing much later, Richard Koebner made a similar point in adverting to the fact that Smith often presents views on the colonial issue in such a way that they appear, at first sight, to be 'unavoidable inferences' from his argument as a

[22] Koebner, op.cit. 229-30.
[23] *A letter from Governor Pownall to Adam Smith , LL.D. F.R.S.* (London, 1776), § 88; Corr., p. 369.
[24] Pownall, op.cit. § 41; Corr., p. 354; Winch op.cit. 8-9.
[25] Pownall, op.cit. § 84; Corr., p. 369.

whole.[26] Too much need not to be made of the latter point, at least for the moment. But it is important to observe that while Smith may have been correct as to the matter of fact, his explanation of differing rates of growth between the two countries, and the problem of taxable capacity, was based on theses whose validity has since been questioned and which Smith himself did not seek to confirm by reference to the available evidence.

(b) Nor do we need to look far in discovering apparent shortcomings in Smith's treatment of contemporary events. For example, while Smith did emphasize the problems of colonial paper money, he did not give his readers any inkling as to the depth of colonial reaction when the British government was forced to prohibit it in 1764.[27] If he did concentrate attention on the controls introduced by the British Parliament after 1763, he cannot be said to have explained the extent to which these controls were the result of the inability of the colonies to co-operate among themselves (never mind with the British) during the recent major war with France.[28] Again, while Smith did have a good deal to say about the fiscal problem facing Britain after the war, he hardly managed to provide an account of the legislative programme which had been implemented by Grenville and which had been designed to raise taxes in America: 'for defraying the expense of defending, protecting, and securing the same'.[29]

[26] This may be the significance of Koebner's remark that 'Adam Smith took care to have his reflections on the American problem organically woven into the context of his great systematic work. They could appear *at first sight* as unavoidable inferences of [a] consistent and comprehensive argument . . .' (op.cit. 227; italics supplied).

[27] WN II. ii. 101; G.L. Beer, *British Colonial Policy 1754–1765* (1933), 180, 187.

[28] Beer has emphasized that the colonies fought among themselves during the war with France and that they also contributed to Britain's difficulties by actively trading with the enemy (87). The problems of co-operation also led to the system of levying money by requisition: a system which was largely an expensive failure and which contributed to the greatly increased size of the national debt (87). The difficulties faced during the war with France were also evident in the face of the Pontiac Uprising of the 1760s; both contributing to convince the British Government 'that Parliamentary taxation was the sole and only means of obtaining from the colonies their just share of the cost of their own defence' (270).

[29] The statement comes from the Revenue (or Sugar) Act of 1764 and is quoted in D.B. Rutman, *The Morning of America 1603–1789* (1971), 155. For

Moreover, while Smith emphasized the debt owed by the colonists to British political institutions, he did not provide us with any guidance as to the widening gulf between the British and colonial interpretation of a common body of constitutional law.[30] There was a classic confrontation between the colonial belief in 'no taxation without representation',[31] and the British assertion of parliamentary sovereignty as contained in the Declaratory Act of 1766.[32] It might even be suggested that the state of conflict with America confirmed a contradiction in addition to the economic problem with which Smith was concerned; namely, the contradiction inherent in the dogma of parliamentary sovereignty, which was to Britain an affirmation of her freedom from absolutism, but in the territories to which it was applied, evidence of their subjection to it.

It is also relevant to observe that Smith's account of the mercantile system in the context of America gave a great deal of emphasis to the acts of trade and navigation, and that he judged the success of the mercantile policy in terms of the contribution made by the colonies to imperial revenue and defence. In presenting the matter in this way Smith helped to obscure the fact that post–1763 policy marked a major (and perhaps inevitable) shift of emphasis away from a

American reaction to the taxation measures see *The American Revolution, 1763–1783*, ed. R.B. Morris (1970), and M. Beloff, *The Debate on the American Revolution, 1761–1783* (2nd ed., 1960).

[30] This point is especially emphasized by Beloff, op.cit. 6: 'There was a single political tradition of opposition to arbitrary government which went back to the political struggles of the seventeenth century. In Great Britain it had come to serve as the foundation for a theory of Parliamentary sovereignty, in America as the basis of a theory of limited government.'

[31] A typical reaction was probably that of Benjamin Franklin in his examination before the House of Commons on 13 February 1766 where he stated the views of the colonists: 'They understood it thus: by the same charter, and otherwise, they are entitled to all the privileges and liberties of Englishmen ... that one of the privileges of English subjects is, that they are not to be taxed but with their common consent.' Quoted in Morris, op.cit. 85.

[32] The Declaratory Act of 18 March 1766, which accompanied the repeal of the Stamp Act, took occasion to state, despite the repeal, that the King in Parliament 'had, hath, and of right ought to have, full power and authority to make laws and statutes of sufficient force and validity to bind the colonies and people of America, subjects of the crown of Great Britain, in all cases whatsoever'. Morris, op.cit. 87. The 'imperial' nature of such sentiments has been emphasized by C.M. Andrews, *The Colonial Background of the American Revolution* (1924), 143; cf. Rutman, op.cit. 160.

mercantile policy based on trade regulation and towards an *imperial* policy of which the Declaratory Act may be representative.[33]

In addition it should also be emphasized that the regulating acts which were so typical of mercantile policy, and which were regarded by Smith as unjust violations of natural liberty, were not at the time seen in this light by the colonists themselves.[34] It is certainly interesting to observe in this connection that neither the Declaration of Colonial Rights and Grievances nor the Declaration of Independence (which included a comprehensive indictment of British policy) contained any critical reference to them.[35] As Oliver Dickerson has pointed out, the colonial objection to British regulations after 1763 was 'not because they were trade regulations *but because they were not laws of that kind'*.[36]

It should also be said that some of the views which the student of Smith is apt to find most striking (such as the advocacy of union and the grasp of the long-run dominance of America) were not of themselves unusual at the time.[37] For example, in September 1774, even while Smith was supposedly writing his account of the colonial problem, the First Continental Congress debated and narrowly defeated Joseph Galloway's plan for a 'grand legislative union' — and

[33] Andrews in particular has emphasized that after 1763 there was a shift away from a mercantile policy based on trade towards an imperial policy based on territorial aggrandizement and control; that 'imperialism not mercantilism . . . was the first cause of the eventual rupture': op.cit. 122, 128–9, and see generally ch. 3; Rutman, op.cit. 136. Such an interpretation reflects American sentiment of the time, as contained, for example, in the text of the Continental Association of 18 October 1774, whose members found 'that the present unhappy situation of our affairs is occasioned by a ruinous system of colony administration, adopted by the British ministry about the year 1763, evidently calculated for enslaving these colonies, and with them, the British Empire'. Morris, op.cit. 135.

[34] As Franklin pointed out in his examination: 'The authority of Parliament was allowed to be valid in all laws, except such as should lay internal taxes. It was never disputed in laying duties to regulate commerce.' Cf. J.C. Miller, *Origins of the American Revolution* (1943). The first chapter especially deals with the economic background to the dispute.

[35] Beer, op.cit. 305–6. Oliver Dickerson has pointed out: 'There was an almost universal acceptance of the desirability of the trade regulations in both England and America as one of the essential foundations of British commercial and industrial prosperity.' *The Navigation Acts and the American Revolution* (1951), 296.

[36] Ibid. 295.

[37] Winch, op.cit. 17–19.

this was only another version of Benjamin Franklin's 'Albany Plan' of 1754.[38] Similarly, the thesis that America would ultimately dominate Britain in economic terms finds its precedents. Pownall, for example, had already noted that America would become the dominant partner in his 'grand marine dominion',[39] and so too had Franklin, both in correspondence with Lord Kames and in his *Observations* of 1751.[40]

It would, however, be rash to conclude that Smith's views are unchecked, incomplete, and unremarkable. Criticism of the type we have considered, although perhaps justifiable given the elaboration of Smith's argument, only teaches us caution in reading Smith's account and confirms its positive value. For example, if Smith did fail to provide a sufficient 'detail of particulars' with regard to current events and if he did employ theses which went unchecked, such 'facts' do not of themselves qualify his contention that at some point there must be a fundamental change in the nature of colonial policy and in the relationship with America. Moreover his emphasis on the problems presented by differential rates of growth quite clearly adds a significant dimension both to the discussion of the American problem, and to Smith's own 'economic' interpretation of historical events. At the same time it must be said that in advocating union (with its attendant breakdown of controls between Britain and America) in the context of an *economic* problem, Smith clearly showed that the idea of an imperial connection could be distinguished from what Koebner has described as the 'postulate of commercial monopoly'.[41] Nor need one qualify the fact that Smith's views on the colonial question still have a certain

[38] Beer, op.cit. 20–2. The issue of union and the arguments for and against are extensively reviewed by Koebner, op.cit., ch. 4.

[39] Benians, op.cit. 263; Koebner, op.cit. 176.

[40] In a letter to Lord Kames, dated 11 April 1767, Franklin remarked: 'Scotland and Ireland are differently circumstanced. Confined by the sea, they can scarcely increase in numbers, wealth and strength, so as to overbalance England. But America, an immense territory, favoured by Nature with all advantages of climate, soil, great navigable rivers, and lakes, &c. must become a great country, populous and mighty; and will, in less time than is generally conceived, be able to shake off any shackles that may be imposed on her, and perhaps place them on the imposers.' Morris, op.cit. 195; also I.S. Ross, *Lord Kames and the Scotland of his Day* (1972), 340–1. As Ross points out, Franklin's sentiments were shared by Kames.

[41] Koebner, op.cit. 220.

interest for the student of European and American politics at the present time. In this connection it may be suggested that Smith attains some degree of interest for the modern student in dramatizing the repercussions of a vast debt on the performance of the economy, in linking the concept of union with freedom of trade, in advocating commercial and political union as a means of stimulating the growth rate in Great Britain, and in perceiving that such a union could involve technical problems of harmonization especially with regard to taxation.

3. Yet criticism of the kind reviewed above must seriously qualify each one of the three interpretations of Smith's purpose which we have already considered. For example, the conjectural element which Pownall noted must affect the validity of Smith's critique of mercantilism and its particular manifestation in the American case. The absence of certain important points must limit the usefulness of Smith's account of contemporary events, while in addition both forms of criticism are relevant if we interpret Smith's purpose as being to provide an explanation for the current crisis in terms of its long-run and immediate causes.

These are important points of themselves — they are even somewhat perplexing, especially when we consider the depth of Smith's interest in the colonial problem, his acquaintance with men such as Burke and Townshend, and the fact that he resided in the Capital during a period of developing crisis. Indeed, such facts are so striking as to combine to suggest that Smith's purpose may have been different from those so far considered and of such a type as to make the kinds of criticisms we have examined largely irrelevant. Looked at from one point of view it seems quite plausible to suggest that Smith was *not interested* in any detail of particulars in excess of that actually provided, and that he may have used certain facts (consciously or unconsciously) in such a way as to convince his readers of the validity of principles in which he believed and which he considered to be important. For example, as we have seen, there are two main sides to Smith's argument, which he expounds in turn: the critique of the mercantile fallacy and the examination of current events. Although these two main sides of the argument are not always

linked with the precision we might expect, it is interesting to observe the degree of elaboration which each receives and the juxtaposition in which they are placed, for, by so doing, Smith lent additional weight to each. The analysis of the mercantile fallacy with its emphasis on the natural progress of opulence gains in plausibility from the existence of the difficulties currently faced by Great Britain, just as these difficulties gain an additional dimension from being presented as the inevitable consequence of the fallacy itself. Smith may, in short, have written to *persuade* by producing an argument cast in such a way 'that the several parts, being thus connected, gain a considerable strength by the appearance of probability and connection'.[42] It would seem to be entirely possible, moreover, that Smith's analysis, developed as it is in terms of a gradually changing focus (thus allowing us to divide it into five component sections and two main parts) was organized in such a way as to attract the agreement of the reader. In the manner of some advocate appealing to the jury, Smith may be seen to have presented his case in such a way that 'though he can bring proof of very few particulars, yet the connection there is makes them easily comprehended and consequently agreeable, so that when the adversary tries to contradict any of these particulars it is pulling down a fabric with which we are greatly pleased and are very unwilling to give up'.[43]

If this conclusion seems somewhat finely drawn, two points should be borne in mind. First, as the citations above remind us, Smith was the author of a sophisticated series of lectures on Rhetoric which were designed to illustrate the powers of the human mind and the manner in which we organize discourse in order to appeal to those whom we wish to teach,

---

[42] LRBL ii. 205–6, Lothian, 172. Smith commented at length on the proper style of judicial oration in lecture 28 and made the interesting point: 'It is in the proper ordering and disposal of this sort of arguments that the great art of an orator often consists. These when placed separately have often no great impression, but if they be placed in a natural order, one leading to the other, their effect is greatly increased' (LRBL ii. 196, ed. Lothian, 167). For comment, see W.S. Howell, 'Adam Smith's Lectures on Rhetoric: an Historical Assessment', *Speech Monographs*, 36 (1969); now reprinted in *Essays on Adam Smith*. Smith's lectures show a sophisticated grasp of the problems of communication and contain an analysis of the forms assumed by various sorts of discourse including the scientific forms which reflect the purposes in hand; see e.g. T.D. Campbell, *Adam Smith's Science of Morals* (1971), and above, 9.

[43] LRBL ii. 196, ed. Lothian, 167.

persuade, or otherwise influence.[44] Secondly, it may be recalled that Smith was acutely aware of the fact that the connection with America had brought the mercantile system a degree of 'splendor and glory which it could never otherwise have attained to'(WN IV. vii. c. 81). This key fact is not denied, so that even if Smith did regard mercantile policy as but the reflection of the mean and parochial habits of second-rate shopkeepers he may well have recognized, *writing in the early 1770s*, that it was necessary to rely on more convincing arguments in disposing of its claims. If Smith did delay publication in order to add to or modify his section on America, it is little wonder. He may well have perceived the exciting possibility of using the difficulties of the moment to 'confirm' the 'truth' of his own principles while at the same time striking a telling blow where he believed it was most needed. In 1776 Smith was still seeking to persuade and still on the offensive. By 1783, the year of the third edition and of peace with America, he could write *as if* his case had been confirmed by events, and with a degree of confidence which would have been inappropriate ten years earlier when he was in London: 'It is unnecessary, I apprehend, at present to say any thing further, in order to expose the folly of a system, which fatal experience has now sufficiently exposed' (IV. viii. 15).

America, in short, had acquired the status of an experiment which confirmed Smith's theses; one which could be allowed to remain in the *Wealth of Nations* as a kind of permanent exhibit. Of course, no such conclusion can be established beyond a shadow of doubt, but if the case is plausible it counsels caution in the interpretation of this part of Smith's work. It may also be useful in that it is often easier to recognize in others the arts which we practise ourselves.

[44] See above, 8, 16.

9

The Functions of Government*

I

In a section entitled 'Liberalism and the Decline of Political Philosophy', Sheldon S. Wolin remarked on two strands of thought which existed in the post-Hobbesian atmosphere of the 'rediscovery of society'. The first of these, he suggested, can be represented by figures such as Montesquieu and Burke, who emphasize that 'the authority of political institutions was founded upon a myriad of social authorities and nourished by a variety of private loyalties'. The second strand is represented by the economists (including Locke) who are associated with 'a non-political model of a society, which, by virtue of being a closed system of inter-acting forces, seemed to sustain its own existence without the aid of an outside political agency'. Wolin added that it was this 'last quality that tinted the economists' model of society with anti-political overtones'.[1]

There is a good deal of truth in these remarks especially as applied to Smith when treated as an *economist*; a field in which his considerable achievements may have reached their highest level. In a formal sense, Smith's work on economics was designed to explain the working of a set of institutional arrangements which he regarded as the last of four stages of economic development,[2] and to elucidate these 'laws of motion' which governed their operations.[3]

These laws of motion, once elucidated, were designed to

* This chapter is based on ideas which were originally developed in *Adam Smith and the Role of the State* (1974), a lecture delivered in Kirkcaldy on 5 June 1973, at a symposium to celebrate the 250th anniversary of Smith's birth, and in a separate lecture which was given at the International Political Studies Association's conference in 1976.

[1] S.S. Wolin, *Politics and Vision* (1961), 290, 292.
[2] See above, chapter 4.
[3] See above, chapter 7.

show that the control of resources could be left to the market and to explain the source of their increase. As Wolin implies, this kind of perspective led directly to the demand that governments ought not to interfere with the economy; a claim which, while it may owe a good deal to Hume,[4] is also a dominant feature of Smith's *Lectures on Jurisprudence* and perhaps one of those 'leading principles' for which he claimed some degree of originality in a paper delivered in 1755. Dugald Stewart informs us that Smith expressed himself 'with a good deal of that honest and indignant warmth, which is perhaps unavoidable by a man who is conscious of the purity of his own intentions, when he suspects that advantages have been taken of the frankness of his temper' (Stewart, IV. 25).

The same sentiments appear in the *Wealth of Nations*, albeit expressed with even greater force, when Smith calls upon the sovereign to discharge himself from a duty 'in the attempting to perform which he must always be exposed to innumerable delusions, and for the proper performance of which no human wisdom or knowledge could ever be sufficient; the duty of superintending the industry of private people, and of directing it towards the employments most suitable to the interest of the society' (IV. ix. 51).

Yet at the same time it must be recalled that Smith had a very wide range of intellectual interests and that his ambition was to complete a wider system of social science embracing ethics and jurisprudence, as well as economics — all subjects on which he had lectured in Glasgow,[5] and which were to have a profound impact on the way in which he handled the functions of government and his analysis of government itself. Such subjects are obviously important in their own right. In the present context, they have the additional advantage of permitting us to draw together some of the separate strands of argument developed in the previous chapters.

Smith's views as to the functions of government are clearly related to his unequivocal belief that its duty is to further the interests of the citizens, thus calling in effect not only for a

---

[4] See above, chapter 5.   [5] See above, chapter 1.

considerable degree of knowledge as to how these interests can best be served, but also for an 'extensive public benevolence'. But given this, it is noteworthy that the specification of what the state should do is related to the same historical argument which, as we have seen, defines the broad nature of government and the socio-economic environment within which it must work. Smith's handling of public services thus has the interesting feature of explaining why a service is needed in a specific historical context, and the manner in which it should be organized in order to ensure effective provision. By way of illustration we may take the main topics of justice, police, revenue, and arms, but without confining the discussion to this precise order of subjects.

II

The General Functions of Government

(1) Justice

As previous discussion indicates,[6] justice is the most obvious service which must be provided, and there is no area of analysis where the historical argument is more obvious and, perhaps, more important. Here it may be sufficient to observe that Smith took the view that a separation of powers, with regard to organization, was a basic pre-condition for effective and equitable provision:

When the judicial is united to the executive power, it is scarce possible that justice should not frequently be sacrificed to, what is vulgarly called, politics. The persons entrusted with the great interests of the state may, even without any corrupt views, sometimes imagine it necessary to sacrifice to those interests the rights of a private man. But upon the impartial administration of justice depends the liberty of every individual, the sense which he has of his own security. In order to make every individual feel himself perfectly secure in the possession of every right which belongs to him, it is not only necessary that the judicial should be separated from the executive power, but that it should be rendered as much as possible independent of that power. The judge should not be liable to be removed from his office according to the caprice of that power. The regular payment of his salary should not

---

[6] Above, chapters 3 and 4.

depend upon the good-will, or even upon the good œconomy of that power (WN V. i. b. 25).

As Alan Peacock has pointed out, Smith's efficiency criteria are sharply distinguished from this basic issue of organization,[7] the argument being, in effect, that the services provided by attorneys, clerks, or judges should be paid for in such a way as to encourage productivity, since he believed that 'Publick services are never better performed than when their reward comes only in consequence of their being performed, and is proportioned to the diligence employed in performing them' (V. i. b. 20). Indeed, Smith ascribed the 'present admirable constitution of the courts of justice in England' to the use of a system of court fees which had served to encourage competition between the courts of kings's bench, chancery, and exchequer (WN V. i. b. 20, 21). A further interesting and typical feature of the discussion is found in Smith's argument that although justice is a service to the whole community, none the less, the costs of handling specific *causes* should be borne by those who give occasion to, or benefit from them. He therefore concluded that the 'expence of the administration of justice . . . may very properly be defrayed by the particular contribution of one or other, or both of those two different sets of persons, according as different occasions may require, that is, by fees of court' (V. i. i. 2), rather than by a charge on the general funds.

(2) *Defence*

The treatment of this topic is also clearly related to the discussion of stages of history, an important part of the argument being that a gradual change in the economic and social structure had necessitated the formal provision of an army. Thus for example in primitive stages, such as that of hunting and pasture, almost the whole male community is fitted and available for war by virtue of their occupations and the mode of subsistence which happens to prevail, while the same is also basically true of the stage of agriculture. In short, the

[7] A.T. Peacock, 'The Treatment of the Principles of Public Finance in the *Wealth of Nations*', *Essays on Adam Smith*, 553–67.

provision of this necessary service is basically costless until the stage of commerce or civilization is reached. It is in this context that the form of economic organization, the greater complexity of modern war (WN V. i. a. 9, 10), and the high costs associated with the introduction of fire-arms[8] lead to a situation where the 'wisdom of the state' (V. i. a. 14) must arrange for provision and payment; an expence which, since laid out 'for the general benefit of the whole society', ought to be 'defrayed by the general contribution of the whole society, all the different members contributing, as nearly as possible, in proportion to their respective abilities' (V. i. i. 1).

Of the options open to government, Smith preferred a standing army to a militia as likely to be more effective. While admitting the political dangers which such armies present, as exemplified by Caesar and Cromwell, Smith noted that

where the sovereign is himself the general, and the principal nobility and gentry of the country the chief officers of the army; where the military force is placed under the command of those who have the greatest interest in the support of the civil authority, because they have themselves the greatest share of that authority, a standing army can never be dangerous to liberty (WN V. i. a. 41).

On the contrary, he added, such an army

may in some cases be favourable to liberty. The security which it gives to the sovereign renders unnecessary that troublesome jealousy, which, in modern republicks, seems to watch over the minutest actions, and to be at all times ready to disturb the peace of every citizen. . . . That degree of liberty which approaches to licentiousness can be tolerated only in countries where the sovereign is secured by a well-regulated standing army. It is in such countries only, that the publick safety does not require, that the sovereign should be trusted with any discretionary power, for suppressing even the impertinent wantonness of this licentious liberty (ibid.).

(3) *Public Works*

A further major task of government is the provision and organization of certain 'public works and institutions for facilitating the commerce of the society' which were 'of such a nature, that the profit could never repay the expence to

---

[8] Above, 90.

any individual or small number of individuals, and which it, therefore, cannot be expected that any individual or small number of individuals should erect or maintain' (WN V. i. c. 1). The examples of public works which Smith provided include such items as roads, bridges, canals, and harbours, but although the list is short by modern standards the discussion of the principles of provision is interesting for two main reasons. First, Smith argued that in general such public works should be provided only where the market mechanism will fail, or has failed to do so. Secondly, he suggested that the main problems with regard to provision were those of equity and efficiency; problems which could only be solved by ensuring that the provision of such services was organized, here as elsewhere, in such a way as to take account of the market on the one hand and the principles of human nature on the other.

With regard to *equity*, Smith argued that public works such as highways, bridges, and canals should be paid for by those who use them and in proportion to the wear and tear occasioned. At the same time, he argued that the consumer who pays the charges generally gains more from the cheapness of carriage than he loses in the charges incurred:

The person who finally pays this tax, therefore, gains by the application, more than he loses by the payment of it. His payment is exactly in proportion to his gain. It is in reality no more than a part of that gain which he is obliged to give up in order to get the rest. It seems impossible to imagine a more equitable method of raising a tax (WN V. i. d. 4).

In addition, he suggested that tolls should be higher in the case of luxury goods so that by this means 'the indolence and vanity of the rich is made to contribute in a very easy manner to the relief of the poor, by rendering cheaper the transportation of heavy goods . . .' (V. i. d. 5).

Smith also defended the principle of direct payment on the ground of *efficiency*. Only by this means, he argued, would it be possible to ensure that services are provided where there is a recognizable need; only in this way, for example, would it be possible to avoid building roads through a desert for the sake of some private interest; or a great bridge 'thrown over a river at a place where nobody passes, or merely to embellish the view from the windows of a neighbouring palace: things which sometimes happen, in countries where works of this

...d are carried on by any other revenue than that which
...ey themselves are capable of affording' (V. i. d. 6). In the
...ame vein he argued against government 'taking the management of the turnpikes into its own hand', and settling the
charges, on the ground that the tolls levied would come to reflect the needs of the state rather than of the roads; that such
charges would be highly regressive, and that 'it would be still
more difficult, than it is at present, to compel the proper
application of any part of the turnpike tolls' (V. i. d. 14).

Smith also argued that while governments must be responsible for establishing major public works, care should be taken
to ensure that the services were administered by such bodies
or under such conditions as made it in the interest of individuals to do so effectively.[9] Smith tirelessly emphasized the
point, already noticed in the discussion of justice, namely,
that in every trade and profession 'the exertion of the greater
part of those who exercise it, is always in proportion to the
necessity they are under of making that exertion' (V. i. f. 4).
On this ground he approved of the expedient used in France,
whereby a construction engineer was made a present of the
tolls on a canal for which he had been responsible — thus ensuring that it was in his interest to keep the canal in good re-
pair. In fact Smith used a number of such devices: advocating
for example that the administration of roads would have to
be handled in a different way from canals because of course
...ey are passable even when full of holes. Here he suggested
...isdom of parliament' would have to be applied to
...ntment of proper persons, with 'proper courts of
...n' for 'controuling their conduct, and for reducing
...ls to what is barely sufficient for executing the work
done by them' (V. i. d. 9).

...mith also recognized that such services could not always
paid for by those who used them, arguing that in such
...ses 'local or provincial expences of which the benefit is
...ocal or provincial' ought, so far as possible, to be no burden
on general taxation, it being 'unjust that the whole society
should contribute towards an expence of which the benefit

---

[9] See especially Nathan Rosenberg, 'Some Institutional Aspects of the Wealth
of Nations', *Journal of Political Economy*, 68 (1960), and above, 6.

is confined to a part of the society' (V. i. i. 3). But here ag
it is argued (in the interests of efficiency) that such servic
'are always better maintained by a local or provincial revenue
under the management of a local and provincial administration,
than by the general revenue of the state, of which the executive power must always have the management' (V. i. d. 18).

It is also worth noting that even where recourse has to be
made to general taxation, Smith argued that such taxes should
be imposed in accordance with the generally accepted canons
of taxation;[10] that so far as possible such taxes should avoid
interference with the allocative mechanism, and that they
ought not to constitute disincentives to the individual effort
on which the working of the system has been seen to depend
(for example, taxes on profits).[11]

III

Economic Policy

(1) *Reform*

A further major task of the state is to ensure that the conditions of economic freedom are in fact satisfied, by sweeping
away all legal and institutional impediments to it. Broadly
speaking these impediments can be reduced to four main
categories. First, there is the problem that in every society
subject to a process of transition, 'Laws frequently continue
in force long after the circumstances, which first gave occasion
to them, and which could alone render them reasonable, a
no more' (WN III. ii. 4). In such cases Smith suggested tha
arrangements which were once appropriate but are now n
longer so should be removed, citing as examples the laws of
succession and entail: laws which had been appropriate in the
feudal period but which now had the effect of limiting the
sale and improvement of land. Secondly, Smith drew attention
to certain institutions which had their origin in the past but
which still commanded active support; for example, the
privileges of corporations with regard to the governance of
trades and the control of apprenticeship. Such regulations

---

[10] WN V. ii. b.   [11] WN V. ii. f.

were criticized on the ground that they were both impolitic and unjust: unjust in that controls over qualification for entry to a trade were a 'violation of this most sacred property' which every man has in his own labour (I. x. c. 12); impolitic in that regulations of apprenticeship, like University degrees, encourage idleness and constitute no guarantee of competence: 'The privileges of graduates are a sort of statutes of apprenticeship, which have contributed to the improvement of education, just as the other statutes of apprenticeship have to that of arts and manufactures' (V. i. f. 11). But Smith especially emphasized that such regulations adversely affect the market mechanism, and pointed out in this connection that 'The statute of apprenticeship obstructs the free circulation of labour from one employment to another, even in the same place. The exclusive privileges of corporations obstruct it from one place to another, even in the same employment' (I. x. c. 42). In a very similar vein Smith commented on the problems presented by the Poor Laws and laws of settlement and summarized his appeal to government in these words:

break down the exclusive privileges of corporations, and repeal the statute of apprenticeship, both which are real encroachments upon natural liberty, and add to these the repeal of the law of settlements, so that a poor workman, when thrown out of employment either in one trade or in one place, may seek for it in another trade or in another place, without the fear either of a prosecution or of a removal (IV. ii. 42).

Thirdly, Smith objected to positions of privilege, such as monopoly powers, which he regarded as essentially creatures of the civil law. The institution is again represented as impolitic and unjust: unjust in that a monopoly position was one of privilege and advantage, and therefore 'contrary to that justice and equality of treatment which the sovereign owes to all the different orders of his subjects' (IV. viii. 30); impolitic in that the prices at which goods so controlled are sold are 'upon every occasion the highest that can be got', so that 'The monopolists, by keeping the market constantly under-stocked, by never fully supplying the effectual demand, sell their commodities much above the natural price, and raise their emoluments, whether they consist in wages or profit, greatly above their natural rate' (I. vii. 26). He added that monopoly is 'a great enemy to good management' (I. xi. b. 5) and that it

had the additional defect of restricting the flow of capital to the trades affected because of the legal barriers to entry which were involved.

Finally, we may usefully distinguish Smith's objection to monopoly in general from his criticism of one expression of it; namely, the mercantile *system* which he described as the 'modern system' of policy, best understood 'in our own country and in our own times' (IV. 2). Here Smith considered regulations which defined the trade relations between one country and another and which, he felt, often reflected the state of animosity between them. In this context Smith examined a policy which sought to produce a net inflow of gold by means of such 'engines' as bounties on exportation, drawbacks, and controls over imports. But his main emphasis fell on one of the chief features of the system from a British point of view, the old colonial relationship with North America, which was currently breaking up[12] and which had sought to create a self-supporting economic unit which would give Britain access to strategic goods and raw materials; a ready market for her own manufactured products, and the monopoly of trade to Europe in colonial produce. Smith once again objected to such a policy of control and restraint, because it artificially restricted the extent of the market and, therefore, the possibilities for further extension of the division of labour and economic growth. In particular Smith insisted that this pattern of infringement of liberty was liable to 'that general objection which may be made to all the different expedients of the mercantile system; the objection of forcing some part of the industry of the country into a channel less advantageous than that in which it would run of its own accord' (IV. v. a. 24). The belief that regulation will always distort the use of resources by breaking the 'natural balance of industry' dates back, as we have seen, to Smith's days as a lecturer in Glasgow and represents his main criticism both of monopoly in general and its manifestation in mercantile policy as a whole. The general position is usefully summarized in the statement that

[12] See above, chapter 8.

No regulation of commerce can increase the quantity of industry in any society beyond what its capital can maintain. It can only divert a part of it into a direction into which it might not otherwise have gone; and it is by no means certain that this artificial direction is likely to be more advantageous to the society than that into which it would have gone of its own accord (IV. ii. 3).

The functions of the state in this respect are therefore something other than minimal: Smith here calls for the abolition of institutions and customs which are remnants of the past, for the abolition of positions of monopoly and privilege, and, finally, for a major reform of national policy. All this is done in the name of liberty and economic efficiency, and must be done before the system of *economic* liberty can be realized in its entirety: 'All systems either of preference or of restraint . . . being thus completely taken away, the obvious and simple system of natural liberty establishes itself of its own accord' (IV. ix. 51).

(2) *Specific Economic Policies*

Even in the absence of the kind of restraints we have just discussed there is still, on Smith's own admission, a wide range of governmental activity which may be necessary if the economy is to function efficiently. In this connection Smith was quite prepared to justify modifications to the general principle of non-intervention,[13] and indeed accepted the very general principle that 'those exertions of the natural liberty of a few individuals, which might endanger the security of the whole society, are, and ought to be, restrained by the laws of all governments; of the most free, as well as of the most despotical' (WN II. ii. 94).

The most famous set of modifications arise from Smith's well-known dictum that ultimately defence is of more importance than opulence, but there are many others albeit less well known. Thus for example he was prepared to countenance a legal rate of interest, set in such a way as to ensure that 'sober people are universally preferred, as borrowers, to prodi-

---

[13] See Jacob Viner, 'Adam Smith and Laisser-Faire', section 5, in *Adam Smith 1776–1926, Lectures to Commemorate the Sesquicentennial of the Publication of the Wealth of Nations* (1928).

gals and projectors' (II. iv. 15),[14] and he was also prepared to regulate the small note issue in the interest of a stable banking system. To those who objected to this proposal, he replied that the interests of the community demand it, adding that 'The obligation of building party walls, in order to prevent the communication of fire, is a violation of natural liberty, exactly of the same kind with the regulations of the banking trade which are here proposed' (II. ii. 94). Likewise Smith advocated use of stamps on plate and linen as the most effectual guarantee of quality (I. x. c. 13), the compulsory regulation of mortgages (V. ii. h. 17), the legal enforcement of contracts (I. ix. 16), and government control of the coinage. Again in the name of the public interest, he supported taxes on the retail sale of liquor in order to discourage the multiplication of alehouses (V. ii. g. 4) and differential rates on ale and spirits in order to reduce the sale of the latter (V. ii. k. 50). To take another example, Smith advocated higher taxes on those who demanded rents in kind, as a means of discouraging a policy which was injurious to the tenant, and on those leases which prescribe a certain form of cultivation; a condition which 'is generally the effect of the landlord's conceit of his own superior knowledge (a conceit in most cases very ill founded)'. In the same way we find Smith suggesting that the practice of selling a greater future revenue for a relatively small sum of ready money, reflecting what we would now describe as a defective telescopic faculty, ought to be discouraged through taxation. Here the object was to discourage a practice which in effect reduced the working capital of the tenant and at the same time transferred a capital sum from a productive class to one that would use it for the purposes of consumption (V. ii. c. 12).

In addition, Smith defended the granting of temporary monopolies to groups of merchants who were prepared to undertake the great risks involved in establishing a new branch of trade, and like privileges to the inventors of new machines or the authors of new books (V. i. e. 30). In special circumstances, and for the sake of the community, Smith was pre-

---

[14] In his *Defence of Usury* (1787), Jeremy Bentham objected to Smith's defence of regulation of the rate of interest on the ground that it was inconsistent with his (Smith's) general position.

pared to support bounties on the exportation of corn (IV. v. b. 39), and a moderate tax on the exportation of wool (IV. viii. 29). He advised governments that where they were faced with taxes imposed by others retaliation could be in order, especially if it had the effect of procuring 'the repeal of the high duties or prohibitions complained of. The recovery of a great foreign market will generally more than compensate the transitory inconveniency of paying dearer during a short time for some sorts of goods' (IV. ii. 39). Smith also noted:

it may sometimes be a matter of deliberation, how far, or in what manner it is proper to restore the free importation of foreign goods, after it has been for some time interrupted . . . when particular manufactures, by means of high duties or prohibitions upon all foreign goods which can come into competition with them, have been so far extended as to employ a great multitude of hands. Humanity may in this case require that the freedom of trade should be restored only by slow gradations, and with a good deal of reserve and circumspection (IV. ii. 40).

There is perhaps enough here to justify Jacob Viner's contention that Smith 'saw a wide and elastic range of activity for government',[15] and it may well be true that the changed role of government in modern times owes as much to change in the conditions faced as it does to alteration in the criteria involved.

IV

The Cultural Functions of Government

For Smith, the broad historical record which treated of the origin and nature of the exchange economy was essentially a record of improvement; improvement in terms of the elimination of bonds of dependence, of political institutions and experience, as well as in terms of the dramatic increase in the level of real income which had become attainable in the context of the fourth economic stage. The policies which we have so far reviewed were really designed to further this progression, as distinct from creating it, by ensuring the most favourable environment within which the constant desire to better our condition could work with best effect. The preoccupation is

[15] Viner, op cit. 154.

with economic growth, although it must also be remembered that the historical perspective invites a wider interpretation of benefit; a point confirmed by a number of dicta which are scattered about Smith's writings. Progress in the terms so far considered is after all associated with developments in the arts and sciences as well as language, and also linked to such specific developments as the improvement in manners which follow on the elimination of dependency (LJ(B), 204, ed. Cannan, 155); probity (LJ(B), 328, ed. Cannan, 255); and even the treatment of prisoners (LJ(B), 346, ed. Cannan, 271).

But even in the framework of the lectures, Smith draws attention to the point that civilization is not an unqualified good,[16] in adverting to the loss of martial spirit which is said to be associated with refinement, and a cause of the dissolution of most previous civilizations (LJ(B), 331, ed. Cannan, 257). In the modern state, it seemed that 'The minds of men are contracted and rendered incapable of elevation, education is despised or at least neglected, and heroic spirit is almost utterly extinguished. To remedy these defects would be an object worthy of serious attention' (LJ(B), 333, ed. Cannan, 259).

Two major issues arise:

(1) It will be recalled that for Smith moral judgement depends on our capacity for acts of imaginative sympathy, and that such acts can therefore only take place within the context of some social group (TMS III. i. 3).[17] However, Smith also observed that the mechanism of the impartial spectator might well break down in the context of the modern economy, due in part to the size of some of the manufacturing units and of the cities which housed them.

Smith observed that in the actual circumstances of modern society, the poor man could find himself in a situation where the 'mirror' of society (TMS III. i. 3) was ineffective. As Smith noted, the 'man of rank and fortune is by his station the distinguished member of a great society, who attend to every part of his conduct, and who thereby oblige him to

[16] The phrase is Joseph Cropsey's, from 'Adam Smith and Political Philosophy', *Essays on Adam Smith,* 151. See also Donald Winch, *Adam Smith's Politics* (1978), chapter 4.

[17] See above, chapter 3.

attend to every part of it himself. .... He dare not do any thing which would disgrace or discredit him in it, and he is obliged to a very strict observation of that species of morals, whether liberal or austere, which the general consent of this society prescribes to persons of his rank and fortune.'[18] But, Smith went on, the 'man of low condition', while 'his conduct may be attended to' so long as he is a member of a country village, 'as soon as he comes into a great city, he is sunk in obscurity and darkness. His conduct is observed and attended to by nobody, and he is therefore very likely to neglect it himself, and to abandon himself to every sort of low profligacy and vice' (WN V. i. g. 12). In the *Theory of Moral Sentiments* itself, it is observed that 'the man who associates chiefly with the profligate and the dissolute ... must soon lose, at least, all his original abhorrence of profligacy and dissolution of manners'; a problem unlikely to be offset by membership of the family, since the prevailing mode of earning subsistence makes it easy for them to 'separate and disperse, as interest or inclination may direct' (TMS VI. ii. 1. 17, 13).

In the modern context, Smith suggests that the individual thus placed would naturally seek some kind of compensation, often finding it not merely in religion but in religious *sects*: that is, small social groups within which he can acquire 'a degree of consideration which he never had before' (WN V. i. g. 12). Smith noted that the morals of such sects were often disagreeably 'rigorous and unsocial', recommending two policies to offset this.

The first of these is learning, on the ground that science is 'the great antidote to the poison of enthusiasm and superstition', although it is interesting to observe that what Smith had in mind was an informed 'middling' rank of men whose influence would secure the poorer from their effects. In this context, Smith suggested that government should act ⸜

not by giving salaries to teachers in order to make them negligent and idle, but by instituting some sort of probation, even in the higher and more difficult sciences, to be undergone by every person before he was permitted to exercise any liberal profession, or before he could be received as a candidate for any honourable office of trust or profit. If

---

[18] Above, 63.

the state imposed upon this order of men the necessity of learning, it would have no occasion to give itself any trouble about providing them with proper teachers (V. i. g. 14).

The second remedy was through the encouragement given to those who might expose or dissipate the folly of sectarian bitterness by encouraging an interest in painting, music, dancing, drama — and satire (V. i. g. 15).

The state, by encouraging, that is by giving entire liberty to all those who for their own interest would attempt, without scandal or indecency, to amuse and divert the people by painting, poetry, musick, dancing; by all sorts of dramatic representations and exhibitions, would easily dissipate, in the greater part of them, that melancholy and gloomy humour which is almost always the nurse of popular superstition and enthusiasm. Publick diversions have always been the objects of dread and hatred, to all the fanatical promoters of those popular frenzies (V. i. g. 15).[19]

Smith also drew attention to the political significance of religious groups in suggesting that ideally the state should encourage a number of sects in the interest of stability (a kind of competitive equilibrium). In such a situation, Smith suggested, the sovereign

would have no occasion to give himself any concern about them, further than to keep the peace among them, in the same manner as among the rest of his subjects; that is, to hinder them from persecuting, abusing, or oppressing one another. But it is quite otherwise in countries where there is an established or governing religion. The sovereign can in this case never be secure, unless he has the means of influencing in a considerable degree the greater part of the teachers of that religion (V. i. g. 16).

The historical sketch which follows, dealing with the influence of the Church of Rome, its (temporal) decline, and the origins of the Reformation, complements that Book III of the *Wealth of Nations* and amply confirms Hobbes's anxieties concerning the role of the 'ghostly' power.

(2) If the problems of solitude and isolation consequent on the growth of cities explain Smith's first group of points, a related trend in the shape of the division of labour helps to account for the second. It will be recalled that in discussing

---

[19] To this extent Smith regarded types of labour previously defined as unproductive (II. iii) to be indirectly productive of benefit. See above, 172.

the division of labour Smith had emphasized that the undertaker or entrepreneur would naturally endeavour 'both to
make among his workmen the most proper distribution of
employment, and to furnish them with the best machines
which he can either invent or afford to purchase' (WN II.
Intro. §4). While the objective is gain to the employer, there
is inevitably a gain to society at large in the shape of improved
productivity; partly through time saved and the greater
opportunities which arise for the use of machines, but largely
because 'reducing every man's business to some one simple
operation, and by making this operation the sole employment
of his life, necessarily increases very much the dexterity of the
workman' (WN I. i. 6). But, on the other hand, Smith noted
later that this important source of economic benefit (which
is emphasized to an extraordinary degree in the *Wealth of
Nations*) could also involve important social costs. Or, as
Smith put it in one of the most famous passages from the
Wealth of Nations:

In the progress of the division of labour, the employment of the far
greater part of those who live by labour, that is, of the great body of
the people, comes to be confined to a few very simple operations;
frequently to one or two. But the understandings of the greater part of
men are necessarily formed by their ordinary employments. The man
whose whole life is spent in performing a few simple operations, of
which the effects too are, perhaps, always the same, or very nearly
the same, has no occasion to exert his understanding, or to exercise his
invention in finding out expedients for removing difficulties which
never occur. He naturally loses, therefore, the habit of such exertion,
and generally becomes as stupid and ignorant as it is possible for a
human creature to become. The torpor of his mind renders him, not
only incapable of relishing or bearing a part in any rational conversation,
but of conceiving any generous, noble, or tender sentiment, and consequently of forming any just judgment concerning many even of the
ordinary duties of private life. Of the great and extensive interests of his
country, he is altogether incapable of judging . . . (V. i. f. 50).

Smith went on to point out that despite the greater command
over material resources, the modern worker could be relatively
worse off than the poor savage, since in such primitive
societies the varied occupations of all men, economic, political, and military, preserve their minds from that 'drowsy
stupidity, which, in a civilized society, seems to benumb the

understanding of almost all the inferior ranks of people'
(V. i. f. 51).

On the other hand there is a greater variety of occupations
in a modern society taken as a whole, thus placing those who
have the opportunity to exercise their understanding well in
advance of even the greatest men found in the savage nation.
Smith concluded:

Unless those few, however, happen to be placed in some very particular
situations, their great abilities, though honourable to themselves, may
contribute very little to the good government or happiness of their
society. Notwithstanding the great abilities of those few, all the nobler
parts of the human character may be, in a great measure, obliterated
and extinguished in the great body of the people (V. i. f. 51).

It is the fact that the 'labouring poor, that is the great body
of the people' must necessarily fall into the state outlined
that makes it necessary for government to intervene.

Smith's justification for intervention is, as before, market
failure, in that the labouring poor, unlike those of rank and
fortune, lack the leisure, means, or (by virtue of their occupation) the inclination to provide education for their children
(V. i. f. 53). In view of the nature of the problem, Smith's
programme seems rather limited, based as it is on the premiss
that 'the common people cannot, in any civilized society, be
so well instructed as people of some rank and fortune' (V. i.
f. 54). However, he did argue that they could all be taught
'the most essential parts of education . . . to read, write, and
account' together with the 'elementary parts of geometry and
mechanicks' (V. i. f. 54, 55). Characteristically, Smith added
that

The publick can facilitate this acquisition by establishing in every parish
or district a little school, where children may be taught for a reward so
moderate, that even a common labourer may afford it; the master being
partly, but not wholly paid by the publick; because if he was wholly, or
even principally paid by it, he would soon learn to neglect his business
(V. i. f. 55).

It is interesting to observe in this context that Smith was
prepared to go so far as to infringe the natural liberty of the
subject, at least where the latter is narrowly defined, in
remarking that

The publick can *impose* upon almost the whole body of the people the necessity of acquiring those most essential parts of education, by obliging every man to undergo an examination or probation in them before he can obtain the freedom in any corporation, or be allowed to set up any trade either in a village or town corporate (V. i. f. 57; italics supplied).

Distinct from the above, although connected with it, is Smith's concern with the decline of martial spirit which is the consequence of the nature of the fourth, or commercial stage. This is partly because the practice of military exercises tends to fall into disuse as feudal obligations are eroded; partly because, in the case of the labouring poor 'The uniformity of his stationary life naturally corrupts the courage of his mind, and makes him regard with abhorrence the irregular, uncertain, and adventurous life of a soldier. It corrupts even the activity of his body . . .' (V. i. f. 50). Smith regarded this as a matter of great moment, since the coward 'wants one of the most essential parts of the character of a man':

He is as much mutilated and deformed in his mind, as another is in his body, who is either deprived of some of its most essential members, or has lost the use of them. He is evidently the more wretched and miserable of the two; because happiness and misery, which reside altogether in the mind, must necessarily depend more upon the healthful or unhealthful, the mutilated or entire state of the mind, than upon that of the body (V. i. f. 60).

Smith returned to this theme, perhaps significantly, in his last piece of writing (Part VI of the *Theory of Moral Sentiments*) where he commented favourably on the qualities of mind and character of the true soldier: his courage, fortitude, and magnanimity (TMS VI. ii. 3. 4; VI. iii. 7).

In the *Wealth of Nations* Smith seems to have had in mind the provision of some kind of military education, and although the scheme is not developed in any detail it is clearly defended on the ground of public utility. It is suggested for example that the enhanced martial spirit of the people might make it possible to have a smaller standing army than would otherwise be required, facilitate defence against foreign invasion, and offset the political danger which a standing army can sometimes represent. Smith also defended military education in its own right; that is, as a contribution to the well-being of the individual, irrespective of the contribution to national defence.

He concluded that 'Even though the martial spirit of the people were of no use towards the defence of the society, yet to prevent that sort of mental mutilation, deformity and wretchedness, which cowardice necessarily involves in it, from spreading themselves through the great body of the people would still deserve the most serious attention of government' (WN V. i. f. 60). Smith went on to liken the control of cowardice to the prevention of 'a leprosy or any other loathsome and offensive disease' — thus moving Jacob Viner to add public health to Smith's already lengthy list of governmental functions.[20]

V

The Functions of Government and Constraint

When one speaks of Adam Smith and the functions of the state it is necessary to avoid giving a false impression of the kind which can arise simply from the enumeration of those functions of which he did approve. Smith was after all very far from adopting the perspective of his great contemporary, Sir James Steuart, who, in his economic work, constantly supposed 'a statesman at the head of government, systematically conducting every part of it, so as to prevent the vicissitudes of manners, and innovations, by their natural and immediate effects or consequences, from hurting any interest within the commonwealth'.[21] Yet as we have seen, Smith did emphasize that governments had important responsibilities especially with regard to justice, defence, and public works. He was quite prepared to grant to the state important functions in calling for the reform of existing institutions and policies, and to make a number of highly detailed suggestions

[20] Viner, op.cit. 150. There is now a considerable literature on the so-called 'alienation' issue, although two of the earliest writers, Nathan Rosenberg and E.G. West, remain among the most instructive. The references are conveniently collected by the latter in 'Adam Smith and Alienation', in *Essays on Adam Smith*. Robert Lamb in particular has emphasized the link with the *Theory of Moral Sentiments* in 'Adam Smith's Concept of Alienation', *Oxford Economic Papers*, 25 (1973). Cf. D.N. Winch, op.cit. 82, and generally chapter 5, 'Martial Spirit and Mental Mutilation'.

[21] *Principles of Political Oeconomy* (1767, ed. A.S. Skinner, 1966), 122. A.O. Hirschman *contrasts* the positions adopted by Smith and Steuart in *The Passions and the Interests* (1977).

in specific economic areas such as banking, taxation, and the rate of interest. Indeed the criteria employed to justify intervention in specific cases may be of much more interest than the enumeration of the cases themselves, arguing as he did that those exertions of the natural liberty of a few individuals which might damage the interest of society at large 'are, and ought to be, restrained by the laws of all governments' (WN II. ii. 94). It is interesting to recall that Smith should have given such emphasis to the need to deliver the people from those institutions which, while once relevant, now constitute impediments to natural liberty: institutions such as corporation laws, or the laws of primogeniture and entail. This important area of policy suggests in effect that while the fourth economic stage is the product of historical forces over which men and governments have no control, still some action may be needed to facilitate the emergence of the system of natural liberty properly so called. To put the point in another way, the fourth economic stage may be regarded as necessary but not of itself sufficient to generate an 'obvious and simple system of natural liberty', which only establishes itself in fact once all systems of restraint have been 'completely taken away' (WN IV. ix. 51).

The attention which Smith gave to what is now loosely known as the 'alienation problem' is also worth emphasizing, not just in relation to the division of labour as such but also in connection with the specific issue of isolation which affects the individual in the great city or manufactory. As we have seen, it was this concern which led Smith to recommend the *imposition* of educational requirements and even to grant to the state what could be described as a 'cultural purpose'. This aspect of Smith's work has prompted parallels with such diverse figures as Marx and T.H. Green, together with an older tradition of 'civic humanism'.[22] While this side of Smith's work is probably best understood against the background of his ethical and historical analyses, both are relevant for our final problem, namely the discussion of the constraints

---

[22] See for example J.G.A. Pocock, *Politics, Language and Time* (1972).

to which governments are subject when fulfilling their obligations as defined above.

Some of these constraints are quite obvious and arise from the nature of the economic laws which Smith set out to elucidate and on the basis of which he made his general policy recommendations. In economic terms, Smith simply confirmed a point which was also central to Steuart's *Principles* and to the latter's wide-ranging discussion of economic policy, namely, that the 'statesman' 'is neither master to establish what oeconomy he pleases, or, in the exercise of his sublime authority, to overturn at will the established laws of it, let him be the most despotic monarch upon earth'.[23]

Government, while bound by the laws of political economy, is by the same token faced with the necessity of understanding them and of being capable of implementing policies which are appropriate to particular cases. This obviously places a considerable burden of responsibility on governments, and requires an advanced level of knowledge to handle even the restricted list of economic functions which Smith suggested. Moreover, Smith noted that knowledge, especially as applied to particular cases, was always likely to be imperfect: a point which is especially important in the discussion of taxation and debt — areas where the government is peculiarly liable to offend the people and to be constrained by the necessity of preserving some 'degree of confidence in the justice of government' (WN V. iii. 7).

But perhaps the most striking and interesting constraints arise when it is recalled that for Smith the fourth economic stage could be seen to be associated with a particular form of social and political structure which determines the outline of government and the context within which it must function. It may be recalled in this connection that Smith associated the fourth economic stage with the advent of freedom in the 'present sense of the term'; that is, with the elimination of the relation of direct dependence which had been a characteristic of the feudal/agrarian period. Politically, the significant and associated development appeared to be the diffusion of power consequent on the emergence of new forms of wealth

---

[23] *Principles of Political Oeconomy*, 16.

which, at least in the peculiar circumstances of England, had
been reflected in the increased significance of the Commons
and the emergence of a situation where liberty was secured
'by an assembly of the representatives of the people, who
claim the sole right of imposing taxes' (WN IV. vii. b. 51). Now
Smith was far from equating political and personal liberty,[24]
nor did he suggest that absolutism was incompatible with the
fourth economic stage. But what he did seem to recognize was
that 'free governments', especially of the kind which had been
confirmed by the Revolution Settlement, now operated within
a relatively sensitive political and economic environment. A
number of points might be offered by way of illustration.

First, it is interesting to note how often Smith referred
to the constraints presented by the 'confirmed habits and
prejudices' of the people, and of the necessity of adjusting
legislation to what 'the interests, prejudices, and temper of
the times would admit of' (WN IV. v. b. 40, 53; V. i. g. 8).
Smith returned to this point in TMS VI. ii. 2. 16, where it is
stated that when the statesman

cannot conquer the rooted prejudices of the people by reason and
persuasion, he will not attempt to subdue them by force . . . He will ac-
commodate, as well as he can, his public arrangements to the confirmed
habits and prejudices of the people; and will remedy as well as he can,
the inconveniencies which may flow from the want of those regulations
which the people are averse to submit to. When he cannot establish the
right, he will not disdain to ameliorate the wrong; but like Solon, when
he cannot establish the best system of laws, he will endeavour to establish the best that the people can bear.

Secondly, Smith gave a good deal of attention to man's
innate conservatism; a conservatism which under some circumstances can also contribute to the stability of governments.
Here the link is with the analysis of the *Theory of Moral
Sentiments* and the emphasis given to habits of deference; a
disposition on which the 'distinction of ranks and the order
of society' is ultimately founded. He concluded: 'That kings
are the servants of the people, to be obeyed, resisted, deposed,
or punished, as the public conveniency may require, is the

[24] This point is clearly made by Duncan Forbes, 'Sceptical Whiggism, Commerce,
and Liberty', in *Essays on Adam Smith*, 179–201.

doctrine of reason and philosophy; but it is not the doctrine of Nature. Nature would teach us to submit to them for their own sake . . . ' (TMS I. iii. 2. 3). In a passage added, perhaps significantly in 1790, Smith went on to note that man's natural love of his own country normally produced 'a certain respect and reverence' for the established government and 'an earnest desire to render the condition of our fellow-citizens as safe, respectable, and happy as we can' (TMS VI. ii. 2. 11).

In peaceable and quiet times, those two principles generally coincide and lead to the same conduct. . . . But in times of public discontent, faction, and disorder, those two different principles may draw different ways . . . In such cases, however, it often requires, perhaps, the highest effort of political wisdom to determine when a real patriot ought to support and endeavour to re-establish the authority of the old system, and when he ought to give way to the more daring, but often dangerous spirit of innovation (TMS VI, ii. 2. 12).

While Smith himself believed that at 'the Revolution the Stewart family were set aside, for excellent reasons' (LJ(B), 82, ed. Cannan, 58), his own attitude may be summed up in the statement that 'No government is quite perfect, but it is better to submitt to some inconveniences than make attempts against it' (LJ(B), 95, ed. Cannan, 69).

Thirdly, Smith makes the point that while all governments are subject to the above constraints in some degree, 'free' governments are likely to be particularly sensitive to public opinion. He made this point quite explicitly in the Memorandum on the American War written in 1778, where he commented on the limited options· open to a government which even 'in times of the most profound peace, of the highest public prosperity, when the people had scarce even the pretext of a single grievance to complain of, has not always been able to make itself respected by them' (§13, Corr., p. 383). A similar point was made in the *Wealth of Nations* itself when commenting on the general benefits of education, namely that an educated people 'are always more decent and orderly' than an ignorant one:

They are more disposed to examine, and more capable of seeing through, the interested complaints of faction and sedition, and they are, upon that account, less apt to be misled into any wanton or unnecessary opposition to the measures of government. In free countries, where the

safety of government depends very much upon the favourable judgment which the people may form of its conduct, it must surely be of the highest importance that they should not be disposed to judge rashly or capriciously concerning it (WN V. i. f. 61).

Fourthly, Smith drew attention to the fact that government itself was a complex instrument. In this connection Smith seems to have felt, for example, that the management of Parliament through the distribution of offices was 'a necessary feature of the British mixed government' (Cf. WN IV. vii. c. 69);[25] a point which is in turn linked to the fact that the pursuit of office was itself a 'dazzling object of ambition': a competitive game with as its object the attainment of 'the great prizes which sometimes come from the wheel of the great state lottery of British politicks' (WN IV. vii. c. 75). Smith added, in a passage which reflects the psychological assumptions of the *Theory of Moral Sentiments* (I. iii. 2, 'Of the Origin of Ambition'), that

Men desire to have some share in the management of publick affairs chiefly on account of the importance which it gives them. Upon the power which the greater part of the leading men, the natural aristocracy of every country, have of preserving or defending their respective importance, depends the stability and duration of every system of free government (WN IV. vii. c. 74).

In the *Theory of Moral Sentiments* too Smith noted that many groups whose activities impinge on the working of government are chiefly devoted to the maintenance of their own power, making the general point that

Every independent state is divided into many different orders and societies, each of which has its own particular powers, privileges, and immunities. Every individual is naturally more attached to his own particular order or society, than to any other. His own interest, his own vanity, the interest and vanity of many of his friends and companions, are commonly a good deal connected with it. He is ambitious to extend its privileges and immunities. He is zealous to defend them against the encroachments of every other order or society' (TMS VI. ii. 2. 7).

Politics, like economics, thus appears to be a competitive activity. To this extent Smith would have been surprised to find Professor Tullock referring to a *newly* established

[25] Forbes, op.cit. 183.

'economics of politics' which assumes that 'all the individuals in government aim at raising their own utility'.[26]

In fact this point leads on to another which was greatly emphasized by Smith, namely that the same economic forces which had served to elevate the House of Commons to a superior degree of influence had also served to make it an important focal point for sectional interests — a development which could seriously affect the legislation which was passed and thus affect that extensive view of the common good which ought ideally to direct the activities of Parliament.[27]

It is recognized in the *Wealth of Nations* that the landed, moneyed, manufacturing, and mercantile groups all constitute special interests which could impinge on the working of government. Smith referred frequently to their 'clamourous importunity', and in speaking of the growth of monopoly pointed out that government policy 'has so much increased the number of some particular tribes of them, that, like an overgrown standing army, they have become formidable to the government, and upon many occasions intimidate the legislature' (WN IV. ii. 43). In this connection it was suggested that the nature of the colonial relationship with America had been the product of the 'sneaking arts of underling tradesmen', and he concluded that: 'Of the greater part of the regulations concerning the colony trade, the merchants who carry it on, it must be observed, have been the principal advisers. We must not wonder, therefore, if, in the greater part of them, their interest has been more considered than either that of the colonies or that of the mother country' (WN IV. vii. b. 49). Indeed Smith went further in suggesting that the legislative power possessed by employers generally could seriously disadvantage other classes in the society.[28] As he put it, 'Whenever the legislature attempts to regulate the differences

---

[26] Gordon Tullock, *The Vote Motive* (1976), 2.

[27] This point has led E.G. West to emphasize the problem of 'government failure' in addition to that of 'market failure', in 'Adam Smith's Economics of Politics', *History of Political Economy*, 8 (1976). In the process of developing this argument Professor West appears as the critic of George Stigler's 'Smith's Travels on the Ship of State', in *Essays on Adam Smith*.

[28] The issue of power and its uses has been particularly examined by Warren Samuels, 'Adam Smith and the Economy as a System of Power', *Revue of Social Economy*, 31 (1973).

between masters and their workmen, its counsellors are always the masters. When the regulation, therefore, is in favour of the workmen, it is always just and equitable; but it is sometimes otherwise when in favour of the masters' (WN I. x. c. 61; cf. I. viii. 12, 13). Smith thus insisted that any legislative proposals emanating from this class

ought always to be listened to with great precaution, and ought never to be adopted till after having been long and carefully examined, not only with the most scrupulous, but with the most suspicious attention. It comes from an order of men, whose interest is never exactly the same with that of the publick, who have generally an interest to deceive and even to oppress the publick, and who accordingly have, upon many occasions, both deceived and oppressed it (WN I. xi. p. 10).

For all these reasons, Smith recognized that in fact the nature of government was such as to make it unlikely that the 'obvious and simple system of natural liberty' (WN IV. ix. 51) would ever be realized in its entirety. In one place he pointed out that 'To expect, indeed, that the freedom of trade should ever be entirely restored in Great Britain, is as absurd as to expect that an Oceana or Utopia should ever be established in it' (IV. ii. 43), and indeed criticized the French economist Quesnay for having seemed to suggest that a country could 'thrive and prosper only under a certain precise regimen, the exact regimen of perfect liberty and perfect justice' (IV. ix. 28). On the contrary, Smith insisted, 'If a nation could not prosper without the enjoyment of perfect liberty and perfect justice, there is not in the world a nation which could ever have prospered' (ibid.). Smith was thoroughly aware of the real complexity of the world as it is; of the problems of knowledge, communication, influence, and of the innate conservatism of both peoples and governments. But at the same time he was also aware of certain underlying trends; trends which seemed to suggest a continuing diffusion of political power and a gradual development of both personal and political liberty. In the economic sphere Smith was also aware of the fact that the constant effort of every man to better his condition (a point which received a great deal of attention in the *Theory of Moral Sentiments*) would sustain the process of growth, despite the presence of 'obstructions'. Smith in fact offered a telling summary of his position in a

notable passage which occurs in the discussion of the regulations governing the corn trade:

That security which the laws in Great Britain give to every man that he shall enjoy the fruits of his own labour, is alone sufficient to make any country flourish, notwithstanding these and twenty other absurd regulations of commerce; and this security was perfected by the revolution, much about the same time that the bounty was established. The natural effort of every individual to better his own condition, when suffered to exert itself with freedom and security, is so powerful a principle, that it is alone, and without any assistance, not only capable of carrying on the society to wealth and prosperity, but of surmounting a hundred impertinent obstructions with which the folly of human laws too often incumbers its operations; though the effect of these obstructions is always more or less either to encroach upon its freedom, or to diminish its security. In Great Britain industry is perfectly secure; and though it is far from being perfectly free, it is as free or freer than in any other part of Europe (WN IV. v. b. 43).

We thus come full circle; returning by a circuitous route to that perspective on government with which Smith as an economist is usually associated and which remains fundamentally valid. As Jacob Viner pointed out in a lecture delivered on the 150th anniversary of the *Wealth of Nations*, there remains in Smith's work, despite numerous qualifications, a 'general presumption against government interference',[29] thus echoing a point which had figured prominently at the Political Economy Club's Centenary Dinner of 1876. Here Robert Lowe singled out free trade as the most important consequence of Smith's teaching, while William Newmarch predicted that 'there will be what may be called a large negative development of Political Economy tending to produce an important and beneficial effect; and that is, such a development of Political Economy as will reduce the functions of government within a smaller and smaller compass'.[30]

Yet as we have seen this perspective on Smith requires modification, especially with regard to his ethical and sociohistorical analysis. For the student of Smith, this wider perspective raises a number of interesting problems, not the

[29] Op.cit. 141.
[30] These points are reported in R.D.C. Black, 'Smith's Contribution in Historical Perspective', in *The Market and the State*, ed. A.S. Skinner and T. Wilson (1976), 50-1.

least of which is the question of consistency between the parts of the system in the form ascribed to it by Cumming.[31] But these problems arise in many ways, not the least of them being that while the political analysis makes it plain that self-regarding actions may affect this sphere of activity as well as the economic, it does not provide a model which matches that offered in the latter field. Taken complexly, as Smith would say, the wider perspective also raises a question as to whether or not he was as optimistic with regard to the fate of mankind as the economic analysis, when taken in isolation, often seems to imply.

It is this complexity which now seems likely to sustain the interest of *economists* to some extent disillusioned by the restricted scope of a subject of which Adam Smith is often regarded as the founder. As Collison Black pointed out in a lecture delivered in Glasgow as part of the celebration of the 200th anniversary of the *Wealth of Nations*:

Many economists today are disenchanted about the prospects and results of economic growth, and many are likewise dubious or defensive about the long-vaunted idea of economics as a science, positive and value free. It is little wonder that such authors can find fresh interest in a system of thought which placed economic problems firmly in the context of ethics and jurisprudence and which was informed throughout by a concept of justice.[32]

It is merely necessary to remember that Smith's concept of justice had less to do with equality than it had to do with fair play in a competitive situation, whether economic (which is likened to a species of warfare at WN V. i. e. 30), social, or political.[33]

---

[31] R.D. Cumming, *Human Nature and History* (1969), 174–8, 213–16.
[32] Black, op.cit. 62.
[33] Cf. L. Billet, 'The Just Economy: The Moral Basis of the *Wealth of Nations*', *Review of Social Economy*, 34 (1976).

APPENDIX A

Extract from the 1762–3 Lecture Notes
Tuesday, 5 April 1763

Having given an account of the nature of opulence and the things in which the riches of a state might consist, I proceeded to shew that this was greatly promoted by the division of labour, which took its rise from the disposition to truck, etc., as well as the means by which it produced that effect.— We may observe on this head that as the division of labour is occasioned immediately by the market one has for his commodities, by which he is enabled to exchange one thing for every thing, so is this division greater or less according to the market. If there was no market everyone would be obliged to exercise every trade in the proportion in which he stood in need of it. If the market be small he can't produce much of any commodity. If there are but ten persons who will purchase it he must not produce as much as will supply 100, otherwise he would reap no benefit by it; far less will he be induced to bring about the great increase which follows on the farther improvement of this division. The being of a market first occasioned the division of labour, and the greatness of it is what puts it in one's power to divide it much. A wright in the country is a cart-wright, a house-carpenter, a square-wright or cabinet-maker, and a carver in wood, each of which in a town makes a separate business. A merchant in Glasgow or Aberdeen who deals in linnen will have in his warehouse Irish, Scots, and Hamburg linnens, but at London there are separate dealers in each of these. The greatness of the market enables one to lay out his whole stock not only on one commodity but on one species of a commodity and one assortment of it. This also lessens his correspondence and gives him less trouble; besides that as he deals in a large quantity he will get them cheaper and consequently can get the higher profit. Hence as commerce becomes more and more extensive the division of labour becomes more and more perfect. From this also we may see the necessity of a safe and

easy conveyance betwixt the different places from whence the commodities are carried. If there is no conveyance of this sort the labour of the person will not be extended beyond the parish in which he lives. If the roads are infested by robbers the commodities will bear a higher price on account of the risque. If the roads are bad in winter the commerce is then greatly retarded, if not altogether stopped. A horse in a bad road in winter will take four times the time he took before to carry his loading of equall quantity, that is, will carry one-quarter of the goods he formerly did, whereas when they are good, winter and summer makes no odds. And hence we see that the turnpikes of England have within these thirty or forty years increased the opulence of the inland parts. This may show us also the vast benefit of water carriage thro the country. Four or five men will navigate a vessel betwixt Scotland and England, Norway, etc., which may contain perhaps 200 tons. The whole expense of the carriage is the tear and wear of the ship and the wages of these men backwards and forwards, that is, if we suppose she returns empty; but if she returns loaded this will be born in half by the second cargo. If we should suppose that this should be carried by land the expense is far greater. If a wagon carries five tons, it will be requisite to have forty wagons for 200 tons. Each of these have six or eight horses with two men. The expense here will be much greater. The tear and wear is much the same, but the wages is much higher, besides that the ship does it in a much shorter time. Land carriage therefore obstructs the supply of goods and the greatness of the market. Hence also we may see the great benefit of commerce, not as it brings in money into the country, which is but a fanciful advantage, but as it promotes industry, manufactures, and opulence and plenty made by it at home (vi. 63–6).

Since the texts of both fragments are now published in LJ(A), the corrections which Smith made in the originals are here omitted in the interest of readability.

Fragment "A"

who, for an equal quantity of work, would have taken more time and consequently have required more wages, which must have been charged upon the goods. The philosopher, on the other hand, is of use to the porter; not only by being sometimes an occasional customer, like any other man who is not a porter, but in many other respects. If the speculations of the philosopher have been turned towards the improvement of the mechanic arts, the benefit of them may evidently descend to the meanest of the people. Whoever burns coals has them at a better bargain by means of the inventer of the fire-engine. Whoever eats bread receives a much greater advantage of the same kind from the inventers & improvers of wind & water mills. Even the speculations of those who neither invent nor improve any thing are not altogether useless. They serve, at least, to keep alive & deliver down to posterity the inventions & improvements which have been made before them. They explain the grounds & reasons upon which those discoveries were founded & do not suffer the quantity of useful science to diminish.

As it is the power of exchanging which gives occasion to the division of labour, so the extent of this division will always be in proportion to the extent of that power. Every species of industry will be carried on in a more or less perfect manner, that is will be more or less accurately subdivided, into the different branches according to which it is capable of being split, in proportion to the extent of the market, which is evidently the same thing with the power of exchanging. When the market is very small it is altogether impossible that there can be that separation of one employment from another which naturally takes place when it is more extensive. In a country village, for example, it is altogether impossible that there

should be such a trade as that of a porter. All the burdens which, in such a situation, there can be any occasion to carry from one house to another would not give full employment to a man for a week in the year. Such a business can scarce be perfectly separated from all others in a pretty large market town. For the same reason, in all the small villages which are at a great distance from any market town, each family must bake their own bread & brew their own beer, to their own great expence & inconveniency, by the interrruption which is thereby given to their respective employments, and by being obliged on this account to maintain a greater number of servants than would otherwise be necessary. In mountainous and desart countries such as the greater part of the Highlands of Scotland, we cannot expect to find in the same manner, even a smith, a carpenter, or a mason within less than twenty or thirty miles of another smith carpenter or mason. The scattered families who live at ten or fifteen miles distance from the nearest of any of those three artisans, must learn to perform themselves a great number of little pieces of work for which, in more populous countries, they would readily have recourse to one or other of them, whom they now can afford to send for only upon very extraordinary occasions. In a savage tribe of North Americans, who are generally hunters, the greatest number who can subsist easily together seldom exceeds one hundred, or one hundred & fifty persons.[1] Each village is at so great a distance from every other, & it is so very difficult & dangerous to travel the country, that there is scarce any intercourse between the different villages even of the same nation except what war & mutual defence give occasion to. In such a country it is impossible that any one employment should be entirely separated from every other. One man may excel all his companions, in some particular piece of dexterity, but it is impossible that he can be wholly employed in it, for want of a market to take off & exchange for other commodities the greater part of the goods which he would, in this case, necessarily produce. Hence the poverty

[1] In WN V. i. a. 2, Smith refers to the hunting stage of the North American Indians as 'the lowest and rudest state of society', and adds that 'An army of hunters can seldom exceed two or three hundred men. The precarious subsistence which the chace affords could seldom allow a greater number . . . ' (V. i. a. 5).

which must necessarily take place in such a society. In a tribe of Tartars, or wild Arabs, who are generally shepherds, a greater number can live conveniently in one place. They do not depend upon the precarious accidents of the chace for subsistence, but upon the milk and flesh of their herds & flocks, who graze in the fields adjoining to the village.[2] The Hottentots near the Cape of Good-hope are the most barbarous nation of shepherds that is known in the world.[3] One of their villages or Kraals, however, is said generally to consist of upwards of five hundred persons. A Hord of Tartars frequently consists of five, six or even ten times that number. As among such nations, therefore, tho' they have scarce any foreign commerce, the home market is somewhat more extensive, we may expect to find something like the beginning of the division of labour. Even in each village of Hottentots, therefore, according to Mr. Kolben,[4] there are such trades as those of a smith, a taylor & even a phisician, & the persons who exercise them, tho' they are not entirely, are principally supported by those respective employments, by which too they are greatly distinguished from the rest of their fellow citizens. Among the Tartars & Arabs we find the faint commencements of a still greater variety of employments. The Hottentots, therefore, may be regarded as a richer nation than the north Americans, & the Tartars & Arabs as richer than the Hottentots. The compleat division of labour, however, is posteriour to the invention even of agriculture. By means of agriculture the same quantity of ground not only produces corn but is made capable of supporting a much greater number of cattle than before. The home market, in consequence, becomes much more extensive. The smith, the mason, the carpenter, the weaver & the taylor soon find it for their interest not to trouble themselves with cultivating the ground,

---

[2] In WN V. i. a. 3, Smith describes 'nations of shepherds' (typified by the Tartars and Arabs) as 'a more advanced state of society'. The main use of the division into socio-historical stages in the *Wealth of Nations* is in the discussion of the expense of defence and justice in Book V.

[3] Cf. WN IV. vii. c. 100.

[4] Peter Kolben (or Kolb), *The Present State of the Cape of Good Hope, or a particular account of the several nations of the Hottentots* (German edn., 1719; English edn., 1731).

but to exchange with the farmer the produces of their several employments for the corn & cattle which they have occasion for. The farmer too very soon comes to find it equally for his interest not to interrupt his own business, with making cloaths for his family, with building or repairing his own house, with mending or making the different instruments of his trade, or the different parts of his houshold furniture, but to call in the assistance of other workmen for each of those purposes whom he rewards with corn & with cattle.

Fragment "B"

or ten men, & sailing from the port of Leith, will frequently in three days, generally in six days, carry two hundred tuns of goods to the same market. Eight or ten men, therefore, by the help of water carriage, can transport, in a much shorter time, a greater quantity of goods from Edinburgh to London than sixty six narrow wheeled waggons drawn by three hundred & ninety six horses & attended by a hundred & thirty two men: or than forty broad wheeled waggons drawn by three hundred & twenty horses & attended by eighty men. Upon two hundred tuns of goods, therefore, which are carried by the cheapest land carriage from Edinburgh to London there must be charged the maintenance of eighty men for three weeks, both the maintenance &, what, tho' less than the maintenance, is however of very great value, the tear & wear of three hundred & twenty horses as well as of forty waggons. Whereas upon two hundred tuns of goods carried between the same markets by water carriages, there is to be charged only the maintenance of eight or ten men for about a fortnight & the tear & wear of a ship of two hundred tuns burden. If there was no other communication, therefore, between Edinburgh & London but by land, as no goods could be transported from the one place to the other except such whose price was very high in proportion to their weight, there would not be the hundredth part of the commerce which is at present carried on between them, nor, in consequence, the hundredth part of the encouragement which they at present mutually give to each other's industry. There could be very little commerce of any kind between the distant parts of the world. How few goods are so precious as to bear the expence of land carriage between London & Canton in China, which at present carry on so extensive a commerce with one another & give consequently so much mutual encouragement to each other's industry? The first improvements, therefore, in arts & industry are always made in those places where the conveniency of water carriage affords the most extensive

market to the produce of every sort of labour. In our north American colonies the plantations have constantly followed either the sea coast, or the banks of the navigable rivers & have scarce any where extended themselves to any considerable distance from both. What James the sixth of Scotland said of the county of Fife, of which the inland parts were at that time very ill while the sea coast was extremely well cultivated, that it was like a coarse woollen coat edged with gold lace, might still be said of the greater part of our North American colonies. The countries in the world which appear to have been first civilised are those which ly round the coast of the Mediterranean Sea. That sea, by far the greatest inlet that is known in the world, having no tides nor consequently any waves except such as are caused by the wind only, was by the smoothness of its surface as well as by the multitude of its islands & the proximity of its opposite coasts extremely favourable to the infant navigation of the world, when from the want of the compass, men were afraid to quit the coast & from the imperfection of the art of shipbuilding to abandon themselves to the boisterous waves of the ocean. Egypt, of all the countries upon the coast of the Mediterranean, seems to have been the first in which either agriculture or manufactures were cultivated or improved to any considerable degree. Upper Egypt scarce extends itself any where above five or six miles from the Nile; & in lower Egypt that great river breaks itself into a great many different canals which with the assistance of a little art afforded, as in Holland at present, a communication by water carriage not only between all the great towns but between all the considerable villages & between almost all the farm houses in the country. The greatness & easiness of their inland navigation & commerce, therefore, seem to have been evidently the causes of the early improvement of Egypt. Agriculture and manufactures too seem to have been of very great antiquity in some of the maritime provinces of China & in the province of Bengal in the East Indies. All these are countries very much of the same nature with Egypt, cut by innumerable canals which afford them an immense inland navigation.

APPENDIX D

Extract from the "Early Draft"[1]

A porter is of use to a philosopher, not only by sometimes carrying a burden for him, but by facilitating almost every trade and manufacture whose productions the philosopher can have occasion for. Whatever we buy from any shop or ware-house comes cheaper to us by means of those poor despised labourers, who in all great towns have set themselves aside for the particular occupation of carrying goods from one place to another, of packing and unpacking them, and who in consequence have acquired extraordinary strength, dexterity, and readiness in this sort of business. Every thing would be dearer if before it was exposed to sale it had been carried, packt, and unpackt by hands less able and less dexterous,[2] who for an equal quantity of work, would have taken more time, and must[3] consequently have required more wages, which must have been charged upon the goods. The philosopher on the other hand is of use to the porter, not only by being sometimes an occasional customer, as well as[4] any other man, who is not a porter, but in many other respects. If the speculations of the philosopher have been turned towards the improvement of the mechanic arts, the benefit of them may evidently descend to the meanest of the people. Whoever burns coals, has them at a better bargain by means of the inventor of the fire engine. Whoever eats bread receives a much greater advantage of the same kind from the inventors and improvers of wind and water mills. Even the speculations of those who neither invent nor improve any thing are not altogether useless. They serve at least to keep alive and deliver down to posterity the inventions and improvements which

[1] The extract reproduced here begins on the first page of folio 8 of the MS., and finishes about one-quarter of the way down the third page, at the end of the section on the division of labour.
[2] The counterpart of the first paragraph of FA begins here. The only substantive differences between the two passages are indicated in notes 3–6 below.
[3] FA omits 'must'.
FA has 'like' instead of 'as well as'.

had been made before them. They explain the grounds and reasons upon which those discoveries were founded, and do not allow[5] the quantity of usefull knowledge[6] to diminish.[7] In opulent and commercial societies, besides, to think or to reason comes to be, like every other employment, a particular business, which is carried on by a very few people, who furnish the public with all the thought and reason possessed by the vast multitudes that labour. Let any ordinary person make a fair review of all the knowledge which he possesses concerning any subject that does not fall within the limits of his particular occupation, and he will find that almost every thing he knows has been acquired at second hand, from books, from the literary instructions which he may have received in his youth, or from the occasional conversations which he may have had with men of learning. A very small part of it only, he will find, has been the produce of his own observations or reflections. All the rest has been purchased, in the same manner as his shoes or his stockings, from those whose business it is to make up and prepare for the market that particular species of goods. It is in this manner that he has acquired all his general ideas concerning the great subjects of religion, morals, and government, concerning his own happiness or that of his country. His whole system concerning each of those important objects, will almost always be found to have been originally the produce of the industry of other people, from whom either he himself or those who have had the care of his education, have procured it in the same manner as any other commodity, by barter and exchange for some part of the produce of their own labour.

[5] FA has 'suffer' instead of 'allow'.
[6] FA has 'science' instead of 'knowledge'.
[7] The counterpart of the first paragraph of FA ends here.

Table of Corresponding Passages
of *The Wealth of Nations.*

The first column gives part and paragraph numbers from the Glasgow edition. The second and third columns give the corresponding pages in the (5th) Cannan edition (Methuen, 1930) and in the Modern Library version (New York, 1937).

I.i	1930	1937	I.iv	1930	1937
1	5	3	5	26	24
2	5–6	3–4	6	26	24
3	6–7	4–5	7	26–27	24–25
4	7–9	5–7	8	27–28	25–26
5	9	7	9	28	26
6	9–10	7–8	10	28–29	26–28
7	10	8–9	11	29–30	28
8	10–11	9–10	12	30	28
9	12	10	13	30	28
10	12–13	11	14	30	28
11	13–14	11–12	15	30	28
			16	30	28
I.ii			17	30	29
			18	30–31	29
1	15	13			
2	15–16	13–14	I.v		
3	17	15			
4	17–18	15–16	1	32	30
5	· 18	16	2	32–33	30–31
			3	33	31
I.iii			4	33	31
			5	33–34	31–32
1	19	17	6	34	32
2	19–20	17–18	7	34–35	32–33
3	20–21	18–19	8	35	33
4	21	19	9	35	33
5	21–22	19–20	10	35–36	33–34
6	22	20	11	36	34
7	22	20	12	36	34
8	22–23	20–21	13	36–37	34–35
			14	37	35
I.iv			15	37–38	35–36
			16	38	36
1	24	22	17	38–39	36–37
2	24–25	22–23	18	39	37
3	25	23	19	39	37
4	25–26	23–24			

I.v	1930	1937
20	39–40	37–38
21	40	38
22	40	38
23	40–41	38–39
24	41	39
25	41	39
26	41	39–40
27	42	40
28	42–43	40–41
29	43	41
30	43	42
31	43–44	42
32	44	42
33	44	42–43
34	45	43
35	45	43–44
36	45–46	44
37	46	44
38	46	44–45
39	47	45
40	47–48	45–46
41	48	46
42	48	46

I.vi	1930	1937
1	49	47
2	49	47
3	49	47
4	49–50	47–48
5	50	48
6	50–51	48–49
7	51	49
8	51	49
9	52	50
10	52	50
11	52	50
12	53	51
13	53	51
14	53	51
15	53	51–52
16	54	52
17	54	52
18	54–55	52–53
19	55	53

I.vi	1930	1937
20	55	53
21	55	53
22	55	53
23	55	53–54
24	56	54

I.vii	1930	1937
1	57	55
2	57	55
3	57	55
4	57	55
5	57–58	55–56
6	58	56
7	58	56
8	58	56
9	58–59	56
10	59	57
11	59	57
12	59	57
13	59	57
14	60	57–58
15	60	58
16	60	58
17	60–61	58–59
18	61	59
19	61	59
20	62	59
21	62	60
22	62	60
23	62	60
24	62–63	60–61
25	63	61
26	63	61
27	63	61
28	63–64	61
29	64	62
30	64	62
31	64	62
32	64	62
33	65	62–63
34	65	63
35	65	63
36	65	63
37	65	63

I.viii	1930	1937	I.viii	1930	1937
1	66	64	45	84	82–83
2	66	64	46	85	83
3	66	64	47	85	83
4	66–67	64–65	48	85	83–84
5	67	65	49	86	84
6	67	65	50	86	84
7	67	65	51	86–87	84–85
8	67	65	52	87	85
9	67–68	65–66	53	87	85
10	68	66	54	87	85–86
11	68	66	55	87–88	86
12	68	66	56	88	86
13	68–69	66–67	57	88	86
14	69	67			
15	69–70	67–68	I.ix		
16	70	68			
17	70	68	1	89	87
18	70–71	69	2	89	87
19	71	69	3	89	87
20	71	69	4	90	88
21	71	69	5	90–91	88–89
22	71–72	69–70	6	91	89
23	72–73	70–71	7	91	89–90
24	73–74	71–72	8	92	90
25	74	73	9	92–93	90–91
26	74–75	73	10	93–94	91–92
27	75	73–74	11	94–95	92–93
28	75	74	12	95	93–94
29	76	74	13	95–96	94
30	76	74	14	96	94–95
31	76–77	74–75	15	96–97	95
32	77	75	16	97	95–96
33	77–78	75–76	17	97	96
34	78–79	76–78	18	97–98	96
35	79–80	78	19	98	96
36	80	78–79	20	98	96–97
37	80–81	79	21	98	97
38	81	79	22	98–99	97
39	81	79	23	99	97
40	81–82	80	24	99–100	97–98
41	82–83	80–81			
42	83	81	I.x.a (Of Wages and Profit in the		
43	83	81	different Employments of La-		
44	83–84	81–82	bour and Stock)		
			1	101	99

I.x.a	1930	1937	I.x.b	1930	1937
2	101	99	38	115	113–14
3	101	99	39	116	114
			40	116	114
I.x.b (Inequalities arising from the			41	116	114
Nature of the Employments			42	116	114–15
themselves)			43	116	115
			44	117	115
1	102	100	45	117	115
2	102	100	46	117–18	115–16
3	102–03	100–01	47	118	116
4	103	101	48	118	116
5	103	101	49	118	116–17
6	103	101	50	119	117
7	103	101	51	119	117
8	103–04	101–102	52	119–20	117–18
9	104	102			
10	104	103	I.x.c (Inequalities occasioned by		
11	105	103	the Policy of Europe)		
12	105	103			
13	105	103–04	1	120	118
14	105–06	104	2	120	118
15	106	104	3	120	118–19
16	106	105	4	120	119
17	107	105	5	120–21	119
18	107	105	6	121	119
19	107	105	7	121–22	120
20	107	105	8	122	120
21	107	106	9	122–23	120–21
22	107–08	106	10	123	121
23	108	106–07	11	123	121
24	108	107	12	123	121–22
25	108–09	107	13	123–24	122
26	109	107	14	124	122
27	109–10	108	15	124	122–23
28	110	108–09	16	124–25	123
29	110–11	109	17	125–26	123–24
30	111	109	18	126	124
31	111–12	109–10	19	126–27	124–25
32	112	110	20	127	125
33	112–13	110–11	21	127	125–26
34	113	111	22	127–28	126
35	113	112	23	128	126–27
36	114	112	24	128–29	127
37	114–15	112–13	25	129	127–28
			26	129–30	128

I.x.c	1930	1937
27	130	128
28	130	128–29
29	130	129
30	130–31	129
31	131	129
32	131	129
33	131	129
34	131–33	129–31
35	133	131
36	133	131
37	133	131–32
38	133–34	132
39	134–35	132–34
40	135–36	134
41	136	134
42	136	134
43	136–37	134–35
44	137	135
45	137	135
46	137	135–36
47	137–38	136
48	138	136
49	138	136–37
50	138	137
51	138–39	137
52	139	137
53	139	137–38
54	139–40	138
55	140	138–39
56	141	139–40
57	141	140
58	141–42	140
59	142	141
60	142–43	141
61	143–44	141–42
62	144	142–43
63	144	143

I.xi.a (Of the Rent of Land)	1930	1937
1	145	144
2	145–46	144–45
3	146	145
4	146	145
5	146	145

I.xi.a	1930	1937
6	146	145
7	146	145
8	147	145–46
9	147	146

I.xi.b (Part I)	1930	1937
1	147	146
2	147	146
3	147–48	146–47
4	148	147
5	148–49	147–48
6	149	148
7	149	148
8	149–50	148–49
9	150	149
10	150	149
11	150	149
12	150–51	149–50
13	151	150
14	151	150–51
15	152	151
16	152	151
17	152	151
18	152	151
19	152–53	151–52
20	153	152
21	153	152
22	153	152
23	153	152
24	153	152
25	153–54	152–53
26	154	153–54
27	155–56	154–55
28	156	155
29	156	155
30	156	155
31	156–57	155–56
32	157–58	156–57
33	158–59	157–58
34	159	159
35	159–60	159
36	160	159
37	160	159–60
38	160	160

I.xi.b	1930	1937
39	161	160
40	161	160
41	161–62	160–61
42	162	161

I.xi.c (Part II)

	1930	1937
1	162	161
2	162	161
3	162	161–62
4	163	162
5	163–64	162–63
6	164	163
7	164–65	163–64
8	165	164
9	165	164–65
10	165	165
11	165	165
12	166	165
13	166	165
14	166	165
15	166	165
16	166–67	165–66
17	167	166
18	167–68	166–67
19	168	167
20	168	167
21	168	167–68
22	168–69	168
23	169	168
24	169	168
25	169–70	168–69
26	170–71	169–70
27	171	170
28	171–72	170–71
29	172	171
30	172	171–72
31	172–73	172
32	173	172–73
33	173–74	173
34	174	173
35	174	173–74
36	174–75	174

I.xi.d (Part III)

	1930	1937
1	175–76	174–75

I.xi.d	1930	1937
2	176	175
3	176	175
4	176	176
5	176	176
6	177	176
7	177	176

I.xi.e (Digression on Silver. First Period)

	1930	1937
1	177	176
2	177–78	176–77
3	178	177–78
4	178–79	178
5	179	178
6	179	178–79
7	179	179
8	179	179
9	180	179
10	180	179
11	180	179–80
12	180–81	180
13	181	180
14	181–82	180–81
15	182	181
16	182	181
17	182–83	181–82
18	183	182
19	183	182–83
20	183	183
21	183–84	183
22	184	183–84
23	184–85	184–85
24	185–86	185
25	186–87	185–86
26	187	186
27	187	186
28	187	186–87
29	187–88	187
30	188	187–88
31	188	188
32	188	188
33	188–89	188
34	189	188–89
35	190	189–90
36	190	190

I.xi.e	1930	1937
37	190	190
38	190–91	190
39	191	190–91

I.xi.f (Second Period)

	1930	1937
1	191	191
2	191	191
3	191–92	191
4	192	191–92
5	192	192

I.xi.g (Third Period)

	1930	1937
1	192	192
2	192–93	192
3	193	192–93
4	193–94	193
5	194	194
6	194–96	194–96
7	196	196
8	196	196
9	196	196
10	196–97	196–97
11	197	197
12	197	197
13	197	197
14	197	197
15	197–98	197–98
16	198	198
17	198–99	198–99
18	199–200	199–200
19	200	200
20	200	200–01
21	201	201
22	201	201
23	201–02	202
24	202	202
25	202	202
26	202–04	202–04
27	204–05	204–05
28	205–07	205–07
29	207	207
30	207	207–08
31	207	208

I.xi.g	1930	1937
32	208	208
33	208–09	208–09
34	209	209
35	209	209–10
36	209–10	210
37	210	210

I.xi.h (Variation in . . . the respective values of Gold and Silver)

	1930	1937
1	210–11	211
2	211	211
3	211	211–212
4	211	212
5	211–12	212–13
6	212–13	213–14
7	213	214
8	214	214–15
9	214	215
10	214–15	215
11	215	215–16
12	215	216
13	215	216

I.xi.i (Grounds of the Suspicion that the Value of Silver still continues to decrease)

	1930	1937
1	216	216
2	216	216–17
3	216	217

I.xi.j (Different Effects of the Progress of Improvement upon . . . different Sorts of rude Produce)

	1930	1937
1	216–17	217

I.xi.k (First sort)

	1930	1937
1	217–18	218–19

I.xi.l (Second Sort)

	1930	1937
1	219	219–20
2	219–20	220
3	220–22	220–22

I.xi.l	1930	1937	I.xi.n	1930	1937
4	222–23	222–23	10	241	241–42
5	223	224	11	242	242
6	223	224			
7	223	224	I.xi.o (Effects of the Progress of
8	223–24	224–25	Improvement upon . . . manu-
9	224–25	225–26	factures)
10	225	226			
11	225–27	226–27	1	242	242–43
12	227	227–28	2	242	243
13	227	228	3	242	243
			4	242–43	243
I.xi.m (Third Sort)			5	243	243–44
			6	243	244
1	228	228	7	243–44	244
2	228	228–29	8	244	244
3	228	229	9	244	245
4	228	229	10	245	245
5	228	229	11	245	245
6	228–29	229–30	12	245–46	246
7	229–30	230	13	246	246
8	230	230–31	14	246	246–47
9	230–31	231	15	246	247
10	231–32	231–32			
11	232–33	232–33	I.xi.p (Conclusion of the Chapter)
12	233–34	233–34			
13	234	234	1	247	247
14	234	234–35	2	247	247
15	234–35	235	3	247	247–48
16	235	235	4	247	248
17	235	235–36	5	247	248
18	235	236	6	248	248
19	235–36	236	7	248	248
20	236	236	8	248	248–49
21	236–37	236–37	9	248–49	249
			10	249–50	249–50
I.xi.n (Conclusion of the Digression)					
			II		
1	237–38	237–39			
2	238	239	1	258	259
3	238–39	239	2	258–59	259
4	239	239–40	3	259	260
5	239–40	240	4	259	260
6	240	240	5	259	260
7	240	240	6	259–60	260–61
8	240	240–41			
9	240	241			

II.i	1930	1937	II.ii	1930	1937
1	261	262	12	272	273
2	261	262	13	272	273
3	261	262	14	272–73	273–74
4	261–62	262–63	15	273	274
5	262	263	16	273	274
6	262	263	17	273	274
7	262	263	18	273–74	274–75
8	262	263	19	274	275
9	262	263	20	274	275
10	262–63	263–64	21	274	275
11	263	264	22	274-75	275–76
12	263–64	264–65	23	275	276
13	264	265	24	275	276
14	264	265	25	275	276
15	264	265	26	275	276
16	264	265	27	276	277
17	264–65	265–66	28	276	277
18	265	266	29	276	277
19	265	266	30	276–77	277–78
20	265	266	31	277	278
21	265	266	32	277	278
22	265	266	33	277–78	278–79
23	265	266	34	278	279
24	265–66	266–67	35	278	279
25	266	267	36	278	279
26	266	267	37	278–79	279–80
27	266	267	38	279	280
28	266–67	267–68	39	279	280
29	267	268	40	279–80	280–81
30	267	268	41	280	281
31	267–68	268–69	42	280–81	281–82
			43	281	282
II.ii			44	281–82	282–83
			45	282	283
1	269	270	46	282–83	283–84
2	269	270	47	283	284
3	269	270	48	283–84	284–85
4	269–70	270–71	49	284	285
5	270	271	50	284	285
6	270	271	51	284–85	285
7	270–71	271–72	52	285	285–86
8	271	272	53	285	286
9	271	272	54	285	286
10	272	273	55	286	286–87
11	272	273			

II.ii	1930	1937	II.ii	1930	1937
56	286–87	287–88	101	310	311
57	287	288	102	310	311–12
58	287	288	103	310–11	312
59	287	288	104	311	312
60	288	288–289	105	311–12	312–13
61	288	289	106	312	313
62	288–89	289–90			
63	289–90	290–91	II.iii		
64	290–91	291–92			
65	291–92	292–93	1	313–14	314–15
66	292	293	2	314	315
67	292–93	293–94	3	314	315
68	293	294	4	315	315–16
69	293–94	294–95	5	315	316
70	294–95	295–96	6	315	316
71	295	296	7	315–16	316–17
72	295–96	296–97	8	316	317
73	296–98	297–99	9	316–17	317–18
74	298–99	299–300	10	317	318
75	299	300	11	317–18	318–19
76	299	300	12	318–19	319–20
77	299–300	300–01	13	319–20	320–21
78	300–01	301–02	14	320	321
79	301	302	15	320	321
80	301	302–03	16	320	321
81	302	303	17	320	321
82	302	303	18	320–21	321–22
83	302	303–04	19	321	322
84	303	304	20	321	322
85	303	304	21	321	322–23
86	303–04	304–05	22	322	323
87	304	305–06	23	322	323
88	305	306	24	322–323	323–24
89	305–06	306–07	25	323	324
90	306	307	26	323	324
91	306	307	27	323	324
92	306	307	28	323–24	324–25
93	306–07	307–08	29	324	325
94	307	308	30	324–25	325–26
95	307	308	31	325	326
96	307–08	308–09	32	325–26	326–27
97	308	309	33	326	327
98	308–09	309–10	34	326	327
99	309	310	35	326–27	327–28
100	309–10	310–11	36	327–28	328–29

II.iii	1930	1937	II.v	1930	1937
37	328	329	17	345	346
38	328–29	329–30	18	345	346
39	329–30	330–31	19	346	346–47
40	330	331	20	346	347
41	330	331–32	21	346–47	347–48
42	331	332	22	347	348
			23	347	348
II.iv			24	347–48	348–49
			25	348	349
1	332	333	26	348	349
2	332–33	333	27	348	349
3	333	334	28	349	350
4	333	334	29	349–50	350–51
5	333–34	334–35	30	350–51	351–52
6	334	335	31	351–52	352–53
7	334–35	335–36	32	352	353
8	335	336	33	352	353
9	335–36	336–37	34	352–53	353–54
10	336	337	35	353	354
11	336–37	337–38	36	353	354
12	337–38	338–39	37	354	355
13	338	339			
14	338	339	**III.i**		
15	338–39	339–40			
16	339	340	1	355–56	356–57
17	339	340	2	356	357
			3	356–57	357–58
II.v			4	357–58	358–59
			5	358	359
1	340	341	6	358	359
2	340	341	7	358–59	359–60
3	340	341	8	359	360
4	340	341	9	359	360
5	340–41	341			
6	341	342	**III.ii**		
7	341–42	342–43			
8	342	343	1	360	361
9	342	343	2	360	361
10	342–43	343–44	3	360–61	361–62
11	343	344	4	361	362
12	343–44	344–45	5	361–62	362–63
13	344	345	6	362	363
14	344	345	7	362–63	363–64
15	344	345	8	363–64	364–65
16	344–45	345–46	9	364	365
			10	364–65	365–66

III.ii	1930	1937	III.iv	1930	1937
11	365	366	9	386	388
12	365–66	366–67	10	386–87	388–89
13	366–67	367–68	11	387	389
14	367–68	368–69	12	387–88	389–90
15	368	369	13	388	390
16	368	369	14	388	390
17	368	369–70	15	389	390–91
18	368–69	370	16	389	391
19	369	370	17	389–90	391–92
20	369–70	370–71	18	390	392
21	370	371–72	19	390–91	392–93
			20	391–92	393–94
III.iii			21	392–93	394–95
			22	393	395
1	371	373	23	393	395
2	371–72	373–74	24	393–94	395–96
3	372–73	374–75			
4	373	375	**IV**		
5	373	375			
6	373–74	375–76	1	395	397
7	374	376	2	395	397
8	374–75	376–77			
9	375–76	377–78	**IV.i**		
10	376	378			
11	376	378–79	1	396	398
12	376–77	379	2	396-97	398–99
13	377–78	379–80	3	397	399
14	378	380	4	397	399
15	378	380	5	398	400
16	378	380–81	6	398	400
17	378–79	381	7	398	400
18	379	381	8	398–99	400–02
19	379–80	381–82	9	400	402
20	380–81	382–83	10	400–01	402–03
			11	401–02	403–04
III.iv			12	402	404
			13	402–03	404–05
1	382	384	14	403	405
2	382	384	15	403	405–06
3	382–83	384–85	16	404	406
4	383	385	17	404	406
5	383–84	385–86	18	404–05	406–07
6	384	386	19	405–07	407–09
7	384–85	386–87	20	407	409
8	385–86	387–88	21	407	409

IV.i	1930	1937
22	407	409
23	407–08	409–10
24	408	410
25	408	410
26	408–09	410–11
27	409	411
28	409–10	411–12
29	410–11	412–13
30	411–12	413–15
31	413	415
32	413–14	415–16
33	414–15	416–17
34	415–16	417–18
35	416	418
36	416	418
37	416	418
38	416	418
39	416	418
40	416	418–19
41	417	419
42	417	419
43	417	419
44	417	419

IV.ii	1930	1937
1	418	420
2	418–9	420–21
3	419	421
4	419	421
5	419	421
6	419–20	421–22
7	420	422–23
8	421	423
9	421	423
10	421	423
11	421–22	423–24
12	422	424
13	422–23	425
14	423	425
15	423–24	425–26
16	424	426
17	424–25	426–27
18	425	427
19	425	427–28
20	425–26	428
21	426–27	428–29
22	427	429
23	427	429
24	427	429–30
25	427	430
26	428	430
27	428	430
28	428	430
29	428–29	430–31
30	429	431
31	429–30	431–32
32	430	432
33	430	432–33
34	430	433
35	431	433
36	431	433
37	431	433–34
38	431–32	434
39	432–33	435
40	433	435–36
41	433–34	436
42	434–35	436–37
43	435–36	437–38
44	436	438–39
45	436	439

IV.iii.a (Part I)		
1	437–38	440–41
2	438–39	441–42
3	439	442
4	439	442
5	439–40	442–43
6	440	443
7	440–41	443–44
8	441	444
9	441–42	444
10	442	445
11	442–43	445–46

IV.iii.b (Digression concerning Banks of Deposit)		
1	443	446
2	443–44	446–47

IV.iii.b	1930	1937	IV.iv	1930	1937
3	444	447	8	3	468
4	444–45	447	9	3–4	468–69
5	445	447–48	10	4–5	469–70
6	445–46	448–49	11	5	470
7	446–47	449–50	12	5	470
8	447	450	13	6	470–71
9	447–48	450	14	6	471
10	448	451	15	6	471
11	448–49	451	16	6	471
12	449	451–52			
13	449	452	IV.v.a (Of Bounties)		
14	449–50	452–53			
15	450–51	453–54	1	7	472
16	451	454	2	7–8	472
17	451–52	454–55	3	8	473
			4	8	473
IV.iii.c (Part II)			5	8–9	473–74
			6	9	474
1	452–53	455	7	9	474
2	453	456	8	10–11	475–76
3	453	456	9	11	476
4	453	456	10	11	476
5	454	456–57	11	11	476
6	454	457	12	11	476–77
7	454–56	457–59	13	11–12	477
8	456–57	459–60	14	12	477
9	457–58	460	15	12	477
10	458	461	16	12	477–78
11	458–59	461–62	17	12–13	478
12	459–60	462–63	18	13	478
13	460	463	19	13–15	478–80
14	461	463–64	20	15	480–81
15	461	464	21	15–16	481
16	461	464	22	16	481
17	461–62	464–65	23	16–17	481–82
			24	17–18	482–83
IV.iv			25	18–19	483–84
			26	19	484
1	1	466	27	19	484
2	1–2	466	28	20	485
3	2	466–67	29	20	485
4	2	467	30	20	485
5	2	467	31	20–21	485–86
6	2–3	467	32	21	486
7	3	467–68	33	21–22	486–87

IV.v.a	1930	1937
34	22	487–88
35	22–23	488
36	23	488–89
37	24	489
38	24	489
39	24	489–90
40	24	490

IV.v.b (Digression concerning the Corn Trade)

	1930	1937
1	25	490
2	25	490
3	25–26	490–91
4	26–27	491–92
5	27	492–93
6	27–28	493
7	28	493
8	28–29	493–94
9	29	494
10	29	494
11	29–30	494–95
12	30	495
13	30–31	495–96
14	31	496
15	31–32	496–97
16	32	497
17	32–33	497–98
18	33	498
19	33	498
20	33	498–99
21	33–34	499
22	34	499
23	34	499
24	34	499-500
25	34–35	500
26	35	500–01
27	36	501
28	36	501
29	36	501
30	36	501
31	36	501
32	36–37	501–02
33	37–38	502–03
34	39	504

I.v.b	1930	1937
35	39	504
36	39	504–05
37	40	505
38	40–41	505–06
39	41–42	506–07
40	42	507
41	42	507
42	42	507–08
43	42–43	508
44	43	508
45	43	508–09
46	44	509
47	44	509
48	44	509–10
49	44–45	510
50	45	510
51	45	510
52	45	510
53	45	510

IV.vi	1930	1937
1	46	511
2	46–47	511–12
3	47	512
4	47	512
5	47–48	512–13
6	48	513
7	48	513
8	48	513–14
9	49	514
10	49	514
11	49	514
12	50	515
13	50	515
14	50–51	515–16
15	51	516
16	51	516
17	51	516
18	51–52	516–17
19	52–53	517–18
20	53	518
21	53–54	518–19
22	54	519
23	54–55	519–20

IV.vi	1930	1937	IV.vii.b (Part II)	1930	1937
24	55	520	9	71	536
25	55	520	10	71	536–37
26	55	520	11	71–72	537
27	55	520	12	72	537–38
28	55–56	520–21	13	72–73	538
29	56	521	14	73	538
30	56–57	521	15	73	538
31	57	521–22	16	73	538
32	57	522	17	73	538–39
			18	73–74	539
IV.vii.a (Part I)			19	74–75	539–40
			20	75–76	540–41
1	58	523	21	76	541–42
2	58	523	22	76–77	542
3	59–60	523–25	23	77–78	542–43
4	60	525	24	78	543
5	60	525	25	78	543–44
6	60–61	525–26	26	78	544
7	61	526	27	79	544
8	61–62	526–27	28	79	544
9	62	527	29	79	544
10	62	527	30	79	544–45
11	62	527	31	79–80	545
12	62	527	32	80	545
13	62–63	527–28	33	80	545
14	63	528	34	80	545–46
15	63	528	35	80–81	546
16	63–64	528–29	36	81–82	546–47
17	64	529	37	82	547
18	64–65	529–30	38	82	547
19	65	530	39	82	547
20	65–66	530–31	40	82	547–48
21	66	531	41	82–83	548
22	66	531	42	83	548
			43	83	548–49
IV.vii.b (Part II)			44	83–84	549
			45	84	549
1	66	531–32	46	84	549
2	67	532	47	84	549–50
3	67–68	532–33	48	84–85	550
4	68	533	49	85–86	550–51
5	68	533–34	50	86	551
6	68–69	534	51	86–87	551–52
7	69–70	534–35	52	87	552–53
8	70–71	535–36	53	87–88	553

IV.vii.b	1930	1937	IV.vii.c	1930	1937
54	88	553–54	32	100–01	566
55	89	554	33	101	566
56	89	554–55	34	101	566
57	89	555	35	101	566–67
58	89	555	36	102	567
59	90	555	37	102	567
60	90	555	38	102–03	567–68
61	90	555	39	103	568
62	90	555–56	40	103–04	568–70
63	91	556	41	105	570
64	91	556	42	105	570
			43	105–06	570–71

IV.vii.c (Part III)

	1930	1937	IV.vii.c	1930	1937
			44	106–07	571–72
			45	107–08	572–73
1	91	557	46	108	573
2	91	557	47	108	573
3	91–92	557	48	108–09	574
4	92	557	49	109	574
5	92	557	50	109	574–75
6	92	557	51	109–10	575
7	92–93	557–58	52	110	575
8	93	558	53	110	575–76
9	93–94	558–59	54	110–11	576
10	94	559	55	111	576
11	94	559	56	111	576–77
12	94	559–60	57	111	577
13	94	560	58	112	577
14	95	560	59	112	577–78
15	95	560–61	60	112	578
16	95	561	61	112–14	578–79
17	95–96	561	62	114	579
18	96	561–62	63	114–15	579–80
19	96–97	562	64	115–16	580–81
20	97	562	65	116	581
21	97	562	66	116–17	581–82
22	97–98	562–63	67	117–18	582–83
23	98–99	563–64	68	118	583
24	99	564	69	118	583–84
25	99	564–65	70	118–19	584
26	100	565	71	119	584–85
27	100	565	72	119–20	585
28	100	565	73	120–21	585–86
29	100	565–66	74	121	586–87
30	100	566	75	121–22	587–88
31	100	566	76	122–23	588

IV.vii.c	1930	1937	IV.viii	1930	1937
77	123–24	588–89	11	145	611
78	124	589	12	145	611
79	124	589–90	13	145	611
80	125	590–91	14	145–46	611–12
81	125–26	591	15	146	612
82	126	591–92	16	146	612
83	126–27	592	17	146	612
84	127	592	18	146–47	612–13
85	127	592–93	19	147	613
86	127–28	593	20	147–48	613–14
87	128–29	593–94	21	148	614
88	129	594–95	22	148–49	614–15
89	129	595	23	149	615
90	129–30	595	24	149–50	615–16
91	130	595–96	25	150	616
92	130	596	26	150–51	616–17
93	130	596	27	151–52	617–18
94	130–31	596	28	152	618
95	131	596	29	152	618
96	131	596–97	30	152	618
97	131–32	597	31	152	618–19
98	132	597–98	32	153	619
99	132–33	598–99	33	153	619
100	133–34	599–600	34	153–54	619–20
101	134–36	600–01	35	154	620
102	136	601–02	36	154	620–21
103	136–37	602–03	37	155	621
104	137	603	38	155	621
105	138–39	603–04	39	155	621
106	139–40	604–05	40	155–56	622
107	140	605–06	41	156–57	622–23
108	140	606	42	157	623
			43	157–58	623–24
IV.viii			44	158	624
			45	158	624
1	141	607	46	158	624
2	142	607–08	47	158	625
3	142	608	48	159	625
4	142–43	608–09	49	159	625
5	143	609	50	159	625
6	143	609	51	159	625
7	143–44	609–10	52	159–60	625–26
8	144	610	53	160	626
9	144	610	54	160	626
10	144	610			

IV.ix	1930	1937	IV.ix	1930	1937
1	161	627	45	180–81	646–47
2	161	627	46	181	647
3	161–62	627–28	47	181–83	647–49
4	162	628	48	183–84	649–50
5	162–63	628	49	184	650
6	163	629	50	184	650–51
7	163–64	629–30	51	184–85	651
8	164	630	52	185	651–52
9	164	630			
10	164–65	630–31	V.i.a (Part I)		
11	165	631			
12	165–66	631–32	1	186	653
13	166–67	632–33	2	186	653
14	167	633	3	186–87	653–54
15	167–68	633–34	4	187	654
16	168	634	5	187–88	654–55
17	168	634	6	188	655
18	168	634	7	188–89	655–56
19	168	634	8	189	656
20	168–69	634–35	9	189–90	656–57
21	169	635	10	190	657
22	169	635	11	190–91	657–58
23	169–70	635–36	12	191	658
24	170	636	13	191	658
25	170	636–37	14	191–92	658–59
26	171	637	15	192	659
27	171–72	637–38	16	192	659
28	172	638	17	192–93	659–60
29	172	638–39	18	193	660
30	172–73	639	19	193	660
31	173	639	20	193	660
32	173–74	639–40	21	193–94	660–61
33	174	640	22	194	661
34	174	640–41	23	194	661
35	174–75	641	24	194–95	661–62
36	175	641	25	195	662
37	175–76	641–42	26	195	662
38	176–77	642–43	27	195–96	662–63
39	177	644	28	196	663
40	177–78	644	29	196	663
41	178–79	644–45	30	196	663
42	179	645	31	196–97	663–64
43	179	645–46	32	197	664
44	179	646	33	197	664
			34	197	664

V.i.a	1930	1937
35	197–98	664–65
36	198–99	665–66
37	199	666
38	199–200	666–67
39	200	667
40	200	667
41	200–01	667–68
42	201	668
43	201–02	668–69
44	202	669

V.i.b (Part II)

	1930	1937
1	202	669
2	202–03	669–70
3	203	670
4	203	670
5	204	671
6	204	671
7	204–05	671–72
8	205	672–73
9	206	673
10	206	673
11	206	673–74
12	207	674
13	207–08	674–75
14	208	675
15	208–09	675–76
16	209–10	676–77
17	210	677
18	210	677
19	210	677
20	210–11	677–78
21	212	679
22	212–13	679–80
23	213	680
24	213–14	680–81
25	214	681

V.i.c (Part III)

	1930	1937
1	214	681
2	214–15	681–82

V.i.d (Article 1st)	1930	1937
1	215	682
2	215	682
3	215	682
4	216	683
5	216	683
6	216	683
7	216–17	683–84
8	217	684
9	217–18	684–85
10	218	685
11	218	685
12	218–19	685–86
13	219	686
14	219	686
15	219	686–87
16	220	687
17	220–22	687–89
18	222	689
19	222	689

V.i.e

	1930	1937
1	223	690
2	223	690–91
3	224	691
4	224	691
5	224	691
6	224–25	691–92
7	225	692
8	225	692
9	225–26	692–93
10	226–28	693–95
11	228–29	695–96
12	229	696
13	229–30	696–97
14	230–32	697–99
15	232	699
16	232	699
17	232	699
18	232–33	699–700
19	233	700
20	233–34	700–01
21	234–35	701–02
22	235–36	703
23	236	703

V.i.e	1930	1937
24	236–37	704
25	237	704–05
26	237–44	705–11
27	244	711
28	244	711–12
29	244–45	712
30	245–46	712–13
31	246	713
32	246	713
33	246	713–14
34	247	714
35	247	714
36	247	714–15
37	247	715
38	248	715
39	248	715
40	248	715–16

V.i.f (Article 2d)

	1930	1937
1	249	716
2	249	716
3	249	716
4	249–50	717
5	250	717
6	250	717
7	250	717–18
8	250–51	718
9	251	718–19
10	251	719
11	252	719
12	252	719
13	252	719–20
14	252–53	720
15	253	720–21
16	253–54	721
17	254	721
18	254	721
19	254	722
20	254–55	722
21	255–56	722–23
22	256	723
23	256	723
24	256	723–24
25	256–57	724

V.i.f	1930	1937
26	257	724–25
27	258	725
28	258	725–26
29	258	726
30	259	726–27
31	259	726–27
32	259	727
33	259–60	727
34	260	727
35	260	727–28
36	260–61	728
37	261	728
38	261	728
39	261	728–29
40	261–62	729–30
41	262–63	730
42	263	730
43	263–64	730–31
44	264–65	731–32
45	265–66	732–33
46	266	733
47	266–67	734
48	267	734
49	267	734
50	267–68	734–35
51	268–69	735–36
52	269	736–37
53	269	737
54	270	737
55	270	737–38
56	270	738
57	270	738
58	271	738
59	271	738–39
60	271–72	739
61	272–73	739–40

V.i.g (Article 3d)

	1930	1937
1	273–74	740–41
2	274–75	741–42
3	275	742
4	275	742–43
5	275–76	743
6	276	743

V.i.g	1930	1937	V.i.i	1930	1937
7	276–77	743–44	2	300	767
8	277–78	744–45	3	300	767
9	278–79	746	4	300	767–68
10	279	746–47	5	300–01	768
11	279–80	747	6	301	768
12	280	747–48			
13	280	748	**V.ii**		
14	281	748			
15	281	748	1	302	769
16	281–82	748–49			
17	282–83	749–50	**V.ii.a (Part I)**		
18	283	750			
19	283–84	750–51	1	302	769
20	284–85	751–52	2	302	769
21	285	752	3	302	769
22	285–87	752–54	4	302–03	769–70
23	287	754	5	303	770–71
24	287–88	754–55	6	304	771
25	288	755–56	7	304	771
26	289	756	8	304	771
27	289–90	756–57	9	304–05	772
28	290	757	10	305	772
29	290	757	11	305	772–73
30	290–91	757–58	12	306	773
31	291	758	13	306	773
32	291	758–59	14	306	773
33	291–92	759	15	306–07	773–74
34	292–93	759–60	16	307–08	774–75
35	293	760	17	308	775
36	293–94	760–61	18	308–09	775–76
37	294–95	761–62	19	309	776
38	295	762	20	309	776
39	295–96	762–64	21	309	776–77
40	296–97	764			
41	297–98	764–66	**V.ii.b (Part II)**		
42	299	766			
			1	310	777
V.i.h (Part IV)			2	310	777
			3	310	777
1	299	766	4	310–11	778
2	299	766	5	311	778
3	299	766–67	6	311–12	778–79
			7	312	779
V.i.i (Conclusion)					
1	300	767			

V.ii.c (Article 1st)	1930	1937
1	312	779–80
2	313	780
3	313	780–81
4	313–14	781
5	314	781
6	314	781–82
7	314–15	782
8	315	782
9	315	782
10	315	782
11	315	782–83
12	315–16	783
13	316	783
14	316	783
15	316–17	783–84
16	317	784
17	317	784
18	317–18	784–85
19	318	785
20	318	785–86
21	318–19	786
22	319	786
23	319	786
24	319	786–87
25	320	787
26	320	787
27	320–21	787–88

V.ii.d (Taxes which are proportioned . . . to the Produce of Land)		
1	321	788
2	321	788–89
3	322	789
4	322	789
5	322–23	789–90
6	323	790
7	323	790
8	323–24	790–91
9	324	791

V.ii.e (Taxes upon the Rent of Houses)		
1	324	791

V.ii.e	1930	1937
2	324–25	791–92
3	325	792
4	325	792
5	325–26	792–93
6	326–27	793–94
7	327	794
8	327–28	794–95
9	328	795
10	328	795–96
11	329	796
12	329	796
13	329	796–97
14	330	797
15	330	797
16	330	797
17	330	797
18	330–31	797–98
19	331	798
20	331	798

V.ii.f (Article 2d)		
1	331	798
2	331–32	789–99
3	332–33	799–800
4	333	800
5	333	800
6	333	800
7	333–34	800–01
8	334	801
9	334	801
10	334–35	801–02
11	335	802
12	335–36	802–03
13	336	803
14	336	803

V.ii.g (Taxes upon the Profit of particular Employments)		
1	336	803–04
2	336–37	804
3	337	804
4	337–38	804–05
5	338	805

V.ii.g	1930	1937
6	338–39	805–06
7	339–40	806–07
8	340	807
9	340–41	807–08
10	341	808
11	341	808
12	341–42	809
13	342	809

V.ii.h (Appendix to Articles 1st & 2d)

	1930	1937
1	342	809
2	343	810
3	343	810
4	343–44	810–11
5	344	811
6	344	811
7	344–45	811–12
8	345	812
9	345	812
10	345	812–13
11	345–46	813
12	346	813
13	346–47	813–14
14	347	814
15	347	814
16	347	814
17	348	815

V.ii.i (Article 3d)

	1930	1937
1	348–49	815–16
2	349	816–17
3	350	817
4	350	817
5	350	817
6	350	817–18
7	351	818

V.ii.j (Article 4th)

	1930	1937
1	351	818–19
2	351–52	819
3	352	819
4	352	819

V.ii.j	1930	1937
5	352	819–20
6	352–53	820
7	353	820–21
8	353	821
9	354	821

V.ii.k (Taxes upon Consumable Commodities)

	1930	1937
1	354	821
2	354	821
3	354–55	821–22
4	355	822
5	355	822–23
6	355–56	823
7	356	823–24
8	356–57	824
9	357	824–25
10	357	825
11	358	825
12	358	825–26
13	359	826
14	359–60	826–27
15	360	827
16	360	827
17	360	827–28
18	360–62	828–29
19	362	829
20	362	829–30
21	362	830
22	363	830
23	363–64	830–31
24	364–65	831–32
25	365	832
26	365	832
27	365	832–33
28	365–66	833
29	366	833
30	366–67	833–34
31	367	834
32	367	834
33	367	835
34	367	835
35	367–68	835
36	368	835

V.ii.k	1930	1937	V.iii	1930	1937
37	368	835–36	1	392–93	859–60
38	368–69	836	2	393–94	860
39	369–70	836–37	3	394	861
40	370	837	4	394–95	861–62
41	370	837	5	395	862
42	370	837–38	6	395	862
43	370–71	838	7	395–96	862–63
44	371–72	839	8	396	863
45	372	839–40	9	396	863
46	372	840	10	396–97	863
47	372–73	840	11	397	863–64
48	374	840–41	12	397–98	864–65
49	374	841–42	13	398	865
50	374–75	842	14	398	865
51	375	842	15	398	865
52	375	843	16	398–99	865
53	376	843	17	399	865–66
54	376–77	843–44	18	399	866
55	377	844–45	19	399	866
56	377–78	845	20	399	866
57	378	845–46	21	399	866
58	378–79	846–47	22	399	866
59	379	847	23	400	866–67
60	379–80	847	24	400	867
61	380	847	25	400	867
62	380–81	847–48	26	400–01	867–68
63	381	848–49	27	401	868
64	381–82	849	28	401	868
65	382–83	849–50	29	401	868
66	383	850	30	402	868–69
67	383–84	850–51	31	402–03	869–70
68	384	851	32	403	870
69	384	851–52	33	403	870
70	384–85	852	34	403–04	870–71
71	385	853	35	404	871
72	385–86	853	36	404–05	871–72
73	386	853–54	37	405	872
74	387	854	38	405–06	872–73
75	387–88	854–55	39	406	873
76	388	855	40	406	873
77	388–89	855–56	41	407	873–74
78	389–90	856–57	42	407	874
79	390	857	43	407	874
80	390–91	857–58	44	407	874

V.iii	1930	1937	V.iii	1930	1937
45	407–08	874–75	69	419	887
46	408–09	875–76	70	420	887
47	409–10	877	71	420	887
48	410–11	877–78	72	420–21	887–88
49	411	878	73	421	888
50	411	873–79	74	421–22	888–89
51	412	879	75	422	889
52	412	879	76	422–24	889–91
53	412	879	77	424–25	891–92
54	412–13	879–80	78	425	892
55	413	880	79	425	892–93
56	413	880–81	80	426	893
57	414	881	81	426	893–94
58	414–15	881–82	82	427	894
59	415	882	83	427	894
60	415–16	882–83	84	427	894–95
61	416–17	883–84	85	427–28	895
62	417	884	86	428	895
63	417–18	884–85	87	428–29	896
64	418	885	88	429–30	896–97
65	418	885	89	430	897
66	418–19	885–86	90	430–31	897–98
67	419	886	91	431	898
68	419	886–87	92	431–33	898–900

Index

REFERENCES TO SMITH'S WORKS